Eminent Charlotteans

ALSO BY SCOTT SYFERT
AND BY MCFARLAND

*The First American Declaration of Independence?:
The Disputed History of the Mecklenburg
Declaration of May 20, 1775* (2014)

Eminent Charlotteans

*Twelve Historical Profiles
from North Carolina's Queen City*

SCOTT SYFERT

McFarland & Company, Inc., Publishers
Jefferson, North Carolina

LIBRARY OF CONGRESS CATALOGUING-IN-PUBLICATION DATA

Names: Syfert, Scott, author.
Title: Eminent Charlotteans : twelve historical profiles from North Carolina's Queen City / Scott Syfert.
Description: Jefferson, North Carolina : McFarland & Company, Inc., Publishers, 2018 | Includes bibliographical references and index.
Identifiers: LCCN 2018003199 | ISBN 9781476666495 (softcover : acid free paper) ∞
Subjects: LCSH: Charlotte (N.C.)—Biography. | Charlotte (N.C.)—History.
Classification: LCC F264.C4 S94 2018 | DDC 975.6/76—dc23
LC record available at https://lccn.loc.gov/2018003199

BRITISH LIBRARY CATALOGUING DATA ARE AVAILABLE

ISBN (print) 978-1-4766-6649-5
ISBN (ebook) 978-1-4766-3061-8

© 2018 Scott Syfert. All rights reserved

No part of this book may be reproduced or transmitted in any form or by any means, electronic or mechanical, including photocopying or recording, or by any information storage and retrieval system, without permission in writing from the publisher.

Front cover: *Nopkahee*, King of the Catawba Indians, famously known as King Haigler, as imagined by Carolina artist Dan Nance (courtesy Dan Nance)

Printed in the United States of America

McFarland & Company, Inc., Publishers
   Box 611, Jefferson, North Carolina 28640
   www.mcfarlandpub.com

To Gail, Harrison & Madison,
lovers of history, and especially of Harpers Ferry

Table of Contents

Preface and Acknowledgments 1
Introduction 7

1. King Haigler and the Catawba Indians 9
2. Crackers: Thomas "Kanawha" Spratt and the Scots-Irish 25
3. No Surrender: The Rev. Alexander Craighead and the Presbyterians 41
4. The Founding Father: Thomas Polk 52
5. Charlotte's Paul Revere: Captain James Jack and the Mecklenburg Declaration of independence 66
6. Freedom for Slaves: Ishmael Titus and the African Americans in the American Revolution 80
7. The Roman: Joseph Graham 93
8. The Forgotten Charlotteans: African American Slaves 113
9. The Silent Barber: Thaddeus Lincoln Tate 120
10. The Cavalryman: Lt. William Ewen Shipp 135
11. Dr. Annie: North Carolina's First Woman Physician 154
12. H. Douglas Crotts and the Greatest Generation 167

Chapter Notes 187
Bibliography 199
Index 203

"These essays on Great Men of our age have been written by me at intervals during the last eight years. Although each is self-contained, they throw, from various angles, a light upon the main course of the events through which we have lived. I hope they will be found to illustrate some of its less well-known aspects. Taken together they should present not only the actors but the scene. In their sequence they may perhaps be the stepping-stones of historical narrative."

—Winston Churchill, *Great Contemporaries*

Preface
and Acknowledgments

> eminent
> ADJECTIVE
> (of a person) famous and respected within a particular sphere: "one of the world's most eminent statisticians."
> —*Oxford English Dictionary*

In 1918, British writer Lytton Strachey published a book called *Eminent Victorians*, in which he wrote critical yet witty accounts of leading British figures, including Florence Nightingale, General Charles Gordon and others. I bought the book in the dreary, wet and cold winter of 1990 from a used book store on Charing Cross Road, just up from the Leicester Square tube station, when I was a student in London. (We students at first mis-pronounced it "*LIE*-chester," to the amusement of the Brits, until we wised up.) There were loads of used book stores along Charing Cross at that time, and in your free time, and with little money as a foreign exchange student, you spent hours in them, trying to immerse yourself, to *breathe in*, English culture, through its literature. And, of course, books were more difficult to come by then. You had to go to *them*; you had to go find them, which was often an adventure in and of itself. You had to earn it.

Eminent Victorians was one book I read as I tried to understand London, this strange but also familiar city, but there were others: Manchester's biography of Winston Churchill; Martin Gilbert's bio as well; C.V. Wedgwood's trilogy on the English Civil Wars (and *A Coffin for King Charles*); Lord Macaulay's *History*; and so forth. I recall leaving these dusty bookstores in the mid-afternoon dark and cold of mid–February, tightening my scarf, and walking back towards my flat.

I also read *Great Contemporaries*, by Churchill, sometime that year. Churchill's work (which I constantly mis-remembered as *Eminent Contemporaries*), was published in 1937. I still own a first edition in royal blue leather.

The book contained a series of brilliant literary sketches of leading political figures (including Joseph Chamberlain, George Bernard Shaw, Hindenburg, and King George V) whom Churchill had known or worked with during the period prior to the Second World War. They are essays, really, not proper history, but boy, are they fun to read.

Churchill's prose and eye for detail is astonishing, and his descriptions became the last word on many of these famous men (and they were all men). For example, of General Douglas Haig, the British general who commanded Allied forces during the years of slaughter on the Western Front in the First World War, Churchill said this:

> He presents to me in those red years the same mental picture as a great surgeon before the days of anæsthetics, versed in every detail of such science as was known to him: sure of himself, steady of poise, knife in hand, intent upon the operation; entirely removed in his professional capacity from the agony of the patient, the anguish of relations, or the doctrines of rival schools, the devices of quacks, or the first-fruits of new learning. He would operate without excitement or he would depart without being affronted; and if the patient died, he would not reproach himself.[1]

It is a passage invariably quoted by historians in any discussions of Haig. And of the German ex-Kaiser, Wilhelm II, Churchill wrote: "An immense responsibility rests upon the German people for their subservience to the barbaric idea of autocracy. This is the gravamen against them in history—that, in spite of all their brains and courage, they worship Power, and let themselves be led by the nose."[2]

For many years later, and for whatever reason, possibly because I bought them at the same store on Charing Cross, Strachey's *Eminent Victorians* and Churchill's *Great Contemporaries* remained conjoined in my mind. The plot took another twist in 1994 when the British historian Andrew Roberts, with whom I have been privileged to become acquainted in the last several years, published a book called *Eminent Churchillians*. As Roberts noted, the title was "a nod to Lytton Strachey's revisionist masterpiece 'Eminent Victorians.'" Again that theme: *eminent*.

In some part of my brain, I had always nurtured a thought (a feeling?) that my hometown of Charlotte needed a work similar to Strachey's or Churchill's. That is, a go-to summary of the key figures of its eminent citizens. Most of our local history is and remains buried, torn down, forgotten, and unkept.

So, quite bizarrely, I arrived at the title of this book—*Eminent Charlotteans*—well before I knew what the book was about or even had any interest in writing it.

The immediate need for such a book became clear to me on the morning of May 20, 2010. On that day, under a warm, sunny Carolina sky, a bronze equestrian statue of Captain James Jack was unveiled along the Little Sugar

Creek Greenway near Central Piedmont Community College, not far from uptown Charlotte. A local volunteer community board called the "Trail of History," on which I served, helped fund and construct the statue of Captain Jack.

The statue (called the "Spirit of Mecklenburg") by artist Chas Fagan, an internationally-recognized painter and sculptor who lived in Charlotte, not far from me, marked a remarkable resurgence in the historical memory of Captain Jack. Once proudly known, in North Carolina at any rate, as "the South's Paul Revere," he personified a curious historical episode known as the "Mecklenburg Declaration of Independence." This story, and Jack's story, had been largely forgotten by the turn of the 21st century. Yet on that day in May 2010, thousands of people arrived for the unveiling, many waving historical flags or wearing Revolutionary War attire in honor of this little-known patriot.

I wanted to learn more about Captain Jack: *who was he; what did he look like; what was his story?* But I quickly learned that unearthing any definitive facts about Captain Jack was difficult. Sure, there were various historical accounts, many written well after his death, or dry, genealogical studies. But nowhere could anyone point me to the *one source* that told Jack's story.

And as I looked more closely into Charlotte's history, I found there were dozens of stories like Captain Jack's: stories like Joseph Graham and his fight at the Battle of Charlotte; or Ishmael Titus, the African American patriot who fought at the battles of Kings Mountain and Guilford Courthouse; or Thaddeus Tate, an African American barber who was known by everyone in town in the 1920s; or William Shipp, who hunted Geronimo in the American West and is the subject of the tallest historical memorial in Charlotte. Some of these individuals are commemorated in statues along the Trail of History (King Haigler; Thomas Spratt; and Thad Tate), while others are not.

Each one had a story, a great story—but who knew them? And where could they be found? Like the story of the Mecklenburg Declaration (or "MecDec," as we call it), some of these stories existed only in local lore or by word of mouth. Fixing that problem was the genesis of this book.

A number of individuals have helped in ways large and small, and without whom an undertaking such as this is never possible. Charlie Succop acted as my research assistant and did a large amount of the uncelebrated but critical "digging." Collins Bailey has kept me organized for years, which was a massive challenge in and of itself. The staff at the Carolina Room of the Charlotte-Mecklenburg Public Library is, as always, invaluable in research, editorial and other assistance (specifically, Tom Cole, Jane Johnson and Shelia Bumgarner—thanks). Thanks to Kay Peninger formerly of the Charlotte Museum of History for her suggestions and good ideas. Nothing "historical" happens in Charlotte without the input and assistance of Jim and Ann Williams; thanks for all the editorial assistance and suggestions, which were critically important. Thanks, Hugh Dussek of CPCC.

Wenonah G. Haire, DMD, gave me ideas and thoughts on King Haigler.

The story of Ishmael Titus was told to me by Marti Mongiello. Marti and his wife Stormy own an excellent bed and breakfast in Grover, S.C., called the "Inn of the Patriots" and in their spare time operate a museum on the American Revolutionary War called the American Revolutionary War Living History Center (or ARWLHC). Marti commissioned a painting of Ishmael Titus and has a passion for his story. I asked Marti what drew him to Titus' story. "The primary reason I am doing these paintings with the ARWLHC," he told me, "is because there are several local heroes who fought in the Revolution that have never been seen or heard of. I became dismayed upon finding out that they had never been drawn or painted and no one knew what dozens of them looked like, let alone their deeds in life to create America. I made it my goal to illuminate them." Thanks to Marti and Stormy for all they do and their passion for our local history. Other information on Titus, specifically on White Oaks and Williamstown, was provided by Mike Miller, David Primmer and Juliana Haubrich (the latter of the Milne Public Library in Williamstown).

Serena (Wei Shen) Chu, a high school student in Greenville, N.C., submitted and received approval for a N.C. State Historical Marker for Dr. Annie Alexander, which was unveiled on December 20, 2016, in uptown Charlotte, on North Tryon Street. Serena gave me good insights into Dr. Annie. The world's Dr. Annie expert, in addition to Serena, is Shelia Bumgarner at the Charlotte-Mecklenburg Public Library. Thanks for her assistance and comments as well.

Earl Gulledge, a graduate of Harding High School in Charlotte, was a student of H. "Doug" Crotts in 1961. In preparation for his fiftieth high school reunion, Earl began doing research on his teachers and was astonished to discover that Crotts had been an infantryman and tank spotter at the battle of Tarawa, one of the most savage engagements in the Pacific in the Second World War. He told me the story of Crotts and shared his research, which is how that chapter came to be. It also led me to the excellent book by Oscar "Ed" Gilbert and Romain Cansiere, *Tanks in Hell*, about the tanks at Tarawa, from which I have drawn much of the moment-to-moment accounts of Crotts and the tank *Colorado* during the battle. Mr. Gilbert and Monsieur Cansiere were generous in responding to my requests for additional information. Ed's book, *Marine Tank Battles of the Pacific*, was also of great use and is excellent. In the course of my correspondence with Ed, we discovered we had two mutual friends: Dan Nance, whose work is shown in here, and Marti Mongiello, the man who helped keep the story of Titus alive. (Grace appears in small, seemingly unconnected events.)

Thanks to Dan Nance and Chas Fagan for allowing me to use their splendid art work, and to Charles Jonas for his enthusiasm and friendship. Bob Morgan is not only an advocate for Charlotte, but for Charlotte's history, and gave me great suggestions. John and Bev Lassiter inspired me over jazz and wine. And finally Dr. Tony Zeiss remains a constant source of inspiration and friendship, and his energy, optimism and passion is an example to us all.

Finally, thanks to my parents, who gave me the passion for history; my wife Gail, who remains my greatest supporter and friend; and my children, Harrison and Madison, who served as my historical guinea pigs and (sometimes unwilling) travel companions.

Introduction

This book highlights notable and important—*eminent*—figures in the history of Mecklenburg County.

Deciding which individuals to select was quite difficult, and some may quibble with my choices, either of selection or omission. Without question there are many, many others who could have been chosen, but for various reasons were not. So let me say from the outset, any errors of selection were mine and mine alone.

Let me also admit up front that my choices of which individuals to select were idiosyncratic to me, and while I have strived for balance, in historical periods, race and gender, and so forth, I have largely chosen stories on the sole criteria *that I thought they were interesting and believed others would find them so as well.* Not a very scientific criteria, arguably, but so be it.

That being said, here were three other conceptual thoughts I had in making these selections of eminent Charlotteans.

First, I made little effort to give proportionality to historical periods. The settlement and Revolutionary War period (1750–1800) is arguably overrepresented. The stories of King Haigler, Thomas Spratt, Captain Jack and Joseph Graham are, to varying degrees, set against the backdrop of the American Revolution in the Carolinas. This period, in my view, is simply more interesting than other, later eras of Mecklenburg County. And how could it not be? The stories of contact between the Europeans and the indigenous Catawba Indians; the Scots-Irish emigration; the outbreak of revolution and resulting civil war in the backcountry; the British occupation of Mecklenburg County and "hornet's nest" are pretty hard stories to beat. (In fact, some have made the case that nothing much of interest has happened in our area since Lord Cornwallis came through town in September 1780. That is something of an overstatement, of course, but by the same token it is reasonable and fair to conclude that the Revolutionary period, and its key actors, punches above its weight.)

Second, I have tried to stay somewhat faithful to the choices made by the Trail of History in its selection of bronze statues of Mecklenburg notables. I have done this for a few reasons. First, those individuals have gone through extensive vetting by the local historical community and so without question are worthy of commemoration. Second, many of these folks (Thad Tate comes to mind, but this can be said of others) are not well known outside of a small circle of historically-focused individuals. Part of the purpose of the Trail of History is to make them more widely known in our community. To the degree this book echoes that effort, I have used their list as a framework.

Third, and finally, I have deliberately stayed away from contemporary history or living individuals, under the theory that no good deed goes unpunished. (The most recent figure in this book, Doug Crotts, died in 2011.) There are of course many eminent Charlotteans who are living. In no order whatsoever, the names of Harvey Gantt, Bruton Smith, Hugh McColl, Pat McCrory, Andreas Bechtler and others come to mind. These and others (such as the late Billy Graham) certainly deserve recognition. But straying into contemporary events and recent politics seemed like a thankless and no-win proposition, and would in any event diminish the recognition of the lesser-known historical personalities described here.

1
King Haigler and the Catawba Indians

> "I look upon the English and ourselves as many good things put into one pockett as Brothers that have issued from one Womb."
> —King Haigler, May 28, 1756

In the summer of 1749, South Carolina Royal Governor James Glen sent a report to his superiors in London, the Lords Commissioners of Trade and Plantations. Glen had been tasked to survey, as best he could, the boundary line between the two adjacent Provinces of North and South Carolina, in hopes of "preventing dispute[s]" between the settlers and the Indians who lived in the area. The backcountry border, he wrote, was the home of "an Indian Nation called the Catawba," who lived "in amity with this Government."

The Indians were not the problem, Glen concluded. The source of the unrest was the settlers. Many of them were squatters, living illegally and refusing to pay leasehold fees (or "quit rents") to the government. Most were Scots-Irish immigrants, unwilling to cooperate with Glen and the South Carolina officials. Perhaps that was not surprising, as they were also (again, illegally) encroaching upon Catawba land, selling the Indians rum and firearms, and generally making a dangerous nuisance of themselves. In fact, in contrast to the local Indians, the settlers were so lawless and disobedient that Glen was having difficulty surveying at all. His orders, he wrote, were "so express and plain that one would imagine there could be no dispute" in carrying them out. Yet the backwoods were filled with "lawless People [who] never want a Pretext not to do what they have no mind to."

"I am sorry to say that numbers of such who are settled in those parts without legal Titles evade paying any Quit Rents to the Crown and shew little regard to either Government," he reported. In fact, "when they are questioned by the Officers of this Province [of South Carolina] they pretend they belong to North Carolina whose Officers I suppose they rather silence than satisfie by a like answer."[1]

The "Crown," of course, to which Glen referred, was King George II of Great Britain, or to give him his full title, as Glen would have done, *Our Sovereign, Lord George the Second, by the Grace of God, of Great Britain, France, and Ireland King Defender of the Faith*, etc. That year, 1749, was the twenty-second year of his reign over the Empire, which included the far-away Carolina wilderness.

But King George II was not the only king in the wild border country between the Carolinas. About that time, a new headman of the Catawba Indians would be chosen, named *Nopkehee*. It was said that he took the title "King" (which was uncommon among the Catawba, and for that matter among the Carolina Indians generally) to place himself on the same level as King George II. According to other reports, such as one made by North Carolina Royal Governor Dobbs in 1755, he sometimes "calls himself [the] Prince of Wales."[2] What cheek, the British must have thought. He would later be known as King Haigler.

Nopkehee

His date of birth is not known, although Nopkehee was probably born sometime around 1700. It is possible and interesting to speculate that Haigler was briefly educated in Virginia in a European school. In April 1717, eleven Catawba children were sent to Fort Christanna to be educated by the white settlers. This was not an act of charity. In reality, they were little more than hostages sent to guarantee the Catawba nation's pledge to withdraw from the Yamasee War. Haigler may have been one of the eleven students.[3] Certainly if true, this would explain his facility with the English language, which many of his contemporaries commented upon.

The Catawba called him *Nopkehee*, but the English called him *Haigler*, which was Anglicized variously as *Haiglar* or *Hagler*. He had other tribal names, such as *Arataswa* or *Oroloswa*, and perhaps more. Names were fluid in Indian culture and were given based on one's age, experience and role in the tribe. According to John Lawson, who travelled amongst the Catawba around 1701, "the *Indians* give a Name to their Children, which is not the same as the Father or Mother, but what they fancy. This Name they keep, (if Boys) till they arrive to the Age of a Warriour, which is sixteen of seventeen Years; then they take a Name to themselves, sometimes, *Eagle, Panther, Alligator,* or some such wild Creature."[4]

Haigler became leader of the Catawba sometime in the early months of 1750, in unpleasant and difficult circumstances. The previous autumn, the leaders of the Catawba (and many other tribes) were summoned to a meeting with colonial officials in Charleston to settle outstanding grievances between the Creek and Cherokee. Virtually all of the Catawba headmen were to attend, including their leader, Young Warrior (*Yanabe Yalangway*). Haigler was on a hunting expedition and did not attend.

Indians had a great fear of European towns, and particularly of Charleston, with its fetid air and rank water, which often caused them to become ill.

"Another Inconvenience attending the Indian Meeting in Charles Town," wrote Governor Glen in a report to the Board of Trade in December 1749, "is the Sickness contracted there by them from the great change of Air, but chiefly of the Water. The latter never fails after a Short stay to produce a remarkable Alteration in their Health; to which a freer Diet also Contributes; which renders them very impatient to be gone again. Fevers and Fluxes attack them soon after, and frequently carry off some in their return homeward."[5] The Indians associated the white settlements with Death and were anxious to avoid entering them. Prior to the meeting, various tribal leaders sent Glen "pressing Letters earnestly praying that I would meet at Fort Moore ... at about one hundred and Fifty Miles distance from Charles Town," but Glen refused.

The governor did, however, attempt to alleviate the Indians' concerns, arranging "convenient houses for them at a Mile or two's distance from Town, where they have the benefite of fresh Air and wholesome Water and plenty of Food of the best kind." Despite this, the Indian leaders "came with the greatest reluctance and unwillingness, [and] Stayed with great uneasiness." They were right to be uneasy.

Within days, Governor Glen reported:

> Many of them very Soon fell Sick, and tho they were Attended by the best Physicians here, yet they began to drop off.... The Catabaws who were als[o] present at this Meeting Suffered more than the rest, they were wa[y]laied in their way home by their Enemies, who Attacked them even in our Settlements, and killed nine of them, but the Sickness which they Carried with them from hence, proved their greatest Enemie, and Carried of[f] their King, whom every person that knew, must Acknowledge to be the finest Indian that ever was Seen, and as he was a very great Warriour, and a remarkable friend to the English.

In addition to the Catawba chief named Young Leader, the "whole [Catawba] Headmen died, towit Captain Taylor, Captain Harris, Captain Jamie, Captain Peter etc. to the number of fifteen and upwards." Virtually all of the headmen fell as a result of the trip to Charleston, a loss Glen described as "irreparable." So devastating was the situation, he wrote, that "I am Afraid it must End in the Total destruction of that poor Nation, they having now few or none left to be Leaders."

Glen's pessimism was firmly grounded. The Catawba Nation, after all, as was true of all the indigenous Carolina tribes, had been in a calamitous demographical decline for fifty years. Wave after wave of illness (smallpox being the most lethal) had reduced Indian tribes to fractions of their former size within just a few generations. "By the time the tide of white settlement reached [the Catawba]," in 1750, writes one historian, "they had decreased to about 250–300 warriors," and a total population of "probably no more than 1,000 persons, including the remnants of the Cheraw and other small Siouan tribes of eastern Carolina."[6] (One undated report of about this same period reported the "Catawba Nation under King Hagler are of Warriors 240."[7])

There was no reason to think this decline would be arrested. And with the entire warrior leadership class dead, surely Glen would be proven correct, and the Nation would end in "total destruction." As a result, a betting man in 1750 would no doubt have wagered that the Catawba would be extinct within a decade. It was in these harrowing circumstances that Nopkehee became their leader.

People of the River

Their name in their own language is "Yap Ye Iswa" (pronounced "pay-yay-iswong"), which translates loosely to "people of the river."[8] They had settled along the banks of the large, slow-moving and muddy Catawba river at some time in the unknowable past. Lawson, who visited the area around 1701, found thousands of Catawba living in several towns along the river or smaller feeder creeks, such as Sugar Creek. According to "their own traditions," wrote a European who travelled amongst them, they had "come to their present lands by the way of the west, from a far distant country, and where there was no variegation of colour in human beings."[9]

Although known as the Catawba (or sometimes the "Nation"), they were in fact a confederation of numerous smaller tribes (primarily the Sugaree, Shuteree, Esaw and Waxhaw), who had merged together over many years in order to survive. One observed in 1717 that "there were many Nations [that lived] under that [Catawba] name."[10]

The Catawba themselves spoke a dialect of Sioux (as opposed to the Cherokee, who spoke Iroquois). In 1743, James Adair observed that the Nation "consisted of almost 400 warriors, of above twenty different dialects. I shall mention a few of the national names of those, who make up this mixed language;—the *Kátahba*, is the standard, or court-dialect—the *Wateree*, who make up a large town; [and also the] *Eenó, Charàh*, now *Chowan, Canggaree, Nachee, Yamasee, Coosah*, &c."[11]

The bottomlands where they lived were excellent for hunting and fishing; the climate was mild; and the river afforded food and protection. Rivers were important to all the Indian cultures in the Carolinas. The Cherokee, for example, said one visitor, were "strongly attached to rivers,—all retaining the opinion of the ancients, that rivers are necessary to constitute a paradise," and the same was no doubt true of the Catawba. The river, said Adair, was "beneficial to them, on account of purifying themselves, and also for the services of common life,—such as fishing, fowling, and killing of deer, which come in the warm season, to eat the saltish moss and grass, which grow on the rocks, and under the surface of the waters."[12] The men caught fish with spears, dams or lines. Freshwater was plentiful year round.

In addition, the clayish land, heavily timbered, was easy to farm. Women planted beans, corn, squash and wild greens, and gathered mushrooms, nuts and berries. The men hunted deer, usually by driving them with controlled brush fires into enclosed areas, such as swamps or juts of land. According to Lawson, "they go and fire the Woods for many Miles, and drive the Deer and other Game into small Necks of Land and Isthmus's, where they kill and destroy what they please."[13] In addition to deer, they hunted and ate bears, rabbits, beavers, muskrat and possum. "All small Game, as Turkeys, Ducks, and small Vermine, they commonly kill with Bow and Arrow, thinking it not worth throwing Powder and Shot after them."[14]

"I have been often in their Hunting-Quarters," remembered Lawson, "where a roasted or barbakued Turkey, eaten with Bears Fat, is held a good Dish; and indeed, I approve of it very well."[15]

They would not, however, eat certain animals on ethical or spiritual grounds. "They reckon all birds of prey, and birds of night, to be unclean, and unlawful to be eaten," noted Adair. Similarly, they would not consume animals that were "either carnivorous, or live on nasty food; as hogs, wolves, panthers, foxes, cats, mice, [and] rats."[16] (Bears were an exception, however.)

The Catawba were known for making intricate clay pottery, described by one as "large pitchers to carry water; bowls, dishes, platters, basons, and a prodigious number of other vessels." They glazed them "over a large fire of smoky pitch pine, which makes them smooth, black and firm. Their lands abound with proper clay, for that use."[17] In addition to using them, they sold and traded them with other tribes as well as with white settlers.

Like most other Carolina tribes, the Catawba lived in a handful of small, scattered towns, each usually containing ten or so huts or wigwams. If their huts resembled those in Lawson's report, they were "cabins built of Bark, which are made round like an Oven." He wrote that the Indians "make the Fire in the middle of the House, and have a Hole at the Top of the Roof right above the Fire, to let out the Smoke. These Dwellings are as hot as Stoves, where the *Indians* sleep and sweat all Night." The wigwams had benches around the walls, and "on these they lay Beast-Skins, and Mats made of Rushes, whereon they sleep and loll. In one of these, several Families commonly live, though all related to one another."[18]

An Indian trader named John Evans prepared a map in 1756 in which he marked the towns of Nassaw, Weyapee and Noostee along the east bank of the Catawba River, and Sucah, Weyane and Charraw along Sugar Creek, near present day Fort Mill. The largest (probably Weyane) was also known as "King's Town." They were meager settlements. In December 1757 Governor Glen explained to the Board of Trade that "the Map of the Catawbaws is not worth sending, there being only seven Towns lying all within two or three miles of one another."[19]

There are no pictures or descriptions of Haigler himself, although we can extrapolate from other writers of the period what he might have looked like. According to the eye-witness Lawson:

> The *Indians* of North-*Carolina* are a well-shap'd clean-made People, of different Staturies, as the *Europeans* are, yet chiefly inclin'd to be tall. They are a very streight People, and never bend forwards, or stoop in the Shoulders, unless much overpower'd by old Age.... Their Eyes are black, or of a dark Hazle; The White is marbled with red Streaks, which is ever common to these People, unless when sprung from a white Father or Mother. Their Colour is of a tawny, which would not be so dark, did they not dawb themselves with Bears Oil, and a Colour like burnt Cork.[20]

The warriors "wore shirts, made of drest deer-skins, for their summer visiting dress," Adair reported, "but their winter-hunting clothes were long and shaggy, made of the skins of panthers, bucks, bears, beavers, and otters.... The men wear, for ornament, and the conveniences of hunting, thin deer-skin boots, well smoked, that reach so high up their thighs, as with their jackets to secure them from the brambles and braky thickets."[21]

When they went to war, they wore turkey feathers in their hair, colored their faces a deep vermillion, and painted circles around their eyes, one black and one white. When "thus painted," as Lawson put it, "they make the most frightful Figures that can be imitated by men, and seem more like Devils than Human Creatures."[22]

As a "King," and especially when he had to interact with English or colonial officials, Haigler would wear special outfits of distinction, a common practice among headmen. One European visitor in 1730 reported that King Blunt of the Tuscarora had a "suit of *English* Broadcloth on, and a pair of Women's Stockings, of a blue Colour, with Clocks [silk patterns on stockings], a tolerable good Shirt, Cravat, Shoes, Hat, &c." while King Durant, of the Yeopim, "had on an old Blue Livery," and a waistcoat with silver lace, as well as "Shirt, Stockings, Shoes, &c. made after the *English* manner."[23] The Chowan King (Highter) would wear "a Soldiers red Coat, Wastecoat, and Breeches." Importantly, however, Brickell pointed out, these outfits were for European ceremonial occasions *only*, and "after their return to their Towns, that they never wear these Cloaths till they make the State Visit amongst the *Christians*."[24]

A "Devil of Disorder"

If the Catawba life along the river sounds as if it were an idyllic paradise, upon closer examination it was anything but. By Haigler's time the Nation was slowly dying and had been so for many decades. The principal culprit was various diseases that the white settlers brought with them, diseases for which the Indians had no natural immunity.

The main killer was smallpox, a highly contagious airborne virus. The disease was named for its most common symptoms: small, pus-filled blisters which erupted on a victim's face and body, and then burst, leaving horrible scars. Victims experienced aches, vomiting, fever, rashes and blindness. As early as 1700, Lawson had written with alarm that "the Small-Pox has been fatal to them; they do not often escape, when they are seiz'd with that Distemper, which is a contrary Fever to what they ever knew ... it destroy'd whole Towns, without leaving one *Indian* alive in the Village."[25]

The disease, usually carried from the coast or settlements by traders, would suddenly and mercilessly strike every decade or so, devastating whole villages. Because they had no idea what caused or spread the virus, the Indians were unable to contain or alleviate its spread. "At first it made slow advances, and as it was a foreign, and to them a strange disease, they were so deficient in proper skill, that they alternately applied a regimen of hot and cold things, to those who were infected," as one witness put it.[26]

It appeared to be curse from hell; a "Devil of a Disorder," the Cherokee called it.[27] Shamans and religious healers ascribed the illness "to the divine anger" and blamed the victims for angering the spirits.[28] The shaman's treatments were useless and often as bad as the disease itself.

> Immediately, they ordered the reputed sinners to lie out of doors, day and night, with their breast frequently open to the night dews, to cool the fever; they were likewise afraid, that the diseased would otherwise pollute the house, and by that means, procure all their deaths. Instead of applying warm remedies, they at last in every visit poured cold water on their naked breasts, sung their religious mystical song, *Yo Yo,* &c. with a doleful tune, and shaked a calabash with the pebble-stones, over the sick, using a great many frantic gestures, by way of incantation.
>
> When they found their theological regimen had not the desired effect, but that the infection gained upon them, they held a second consultation, and deemed it the best method to sweat their patients, and plunge them into the river ... [many] immediately expired; upon which, all the magi and prophetic tribe broke their old consecrated physic-pots, and threw away all the other pretended holy things they had for physical use, imagining they had lost their divine power by being polluted; and shared the common fate of their country.
>
> A great many killed themselves ... some shot themselves, others cut their throats, some stabbed themselves with knives, and others with sharp-pointed canes; many threw themselves with sullen madness into the fire, and there slowly expired, as if they had been utterly divested of the native power of feeling pain.[29]

One 1760 report from Charleston noted, "the Small Pox has lately raged with great Violence among the Catawba Indians, and that it has carried off near one Half of that Nation, by throwing themselves into the River as soon as they found themselves ill."[30] The next year Governor Dobbs wrote that the Nation "consisted within these few years of about 300 fighting men but last year [1760] the small pox ravaged in their Towns which made them desert them and leave their sick behind them to perish; by an account from their King Haglar to me they are reduced to 60 fighting and about as many old men and boys and a suitable number of Women."[31]

All Indian tribes suffered massively. One witness in a Cherokee village in the autumn of 1766 recalled the devastation. "When I got up this Morning I cou'd hear nothing but the Cries of Women and Children for the loss of their Relations; in the Evenings there are nothing to be seen but smoak and houses on fire, the dwellings of the deceased; I never remember to see any Sickness like the present."[32]

So great was the loss of life that by 1761, Dobbs told London, "The only Tribes or remains of Tribes of Indians residing in this Province [of North Carolina] are the Tuskerora[,] Sapona[,] Meherin and Maramuskito Indians." The Tuskerora, he reported, "have about 100 fighting men the Saponas and Meherrin Indians about 20 each and the Maramuskitos about 7 or 8."[33] The future was so bleak for the tribes, he concluded, that "[i]t would seem that a curse were resting upon them and oppressing them."

The recurrent waves of disease "made such a Destruction amongst them," Lawson wrote, that "there is not the sixth Savage living within two hundred Miles of all our Settlements, as there were fifty Years ago. These poor Creatures have so many Enemies to destroy them, that it's a wonder one of them is left alive near us."[34]

Sadly, the other "enemy to destroy them" were the Catawba themselves, which they did through widespread alcohol abuse. The Indians generally, Lawson had noted, were "much addicted to Drunkenness, a Vice they never were acquainted with, till the Christians came amongst them."[35] Like Smallpox, alcohol was a European infection, and one it seemed the Catawba had no power to resist.

"They never are contented with a little, but when once begun, they must make themselves quite drunk…. In these drunken Frolicks, (which are always carried on in the Night) they sometimes murder one another, fall into the Fire, fall down Precipices, and break their Necks."[36] The principal vice was rum, brought up from Augusta by unscrupulous white traders.

The "Rum Traders place themselves near the Towns, in the way of the Hunters returning home with their deer Skins," one official complained. "The poor Indians in a manner fascinated, are unable to resist the Bait; and when Drunk are easily cheated. After parting with the fruit of three or four Months

Toil, they find themselves at home, without the means of buying the necessary Clothing for themselves or their Families."[37] Colonial officials sought to regulate trade with Indians to curb these abuses, but in the far flung frontier, they had little influence. "The People inhabiting the Frontiers of this Province Carry on a Trade with the Indians by bartering Rum for Horses," complained John Stuart to the Earl of Hillsborough in 1769. This was "the Source of many disorders, [the Indians'] Young Men being thereby encouraged to Steal Horses from the neighbouring Provinces."[38]

Booze led to fights, murders, property theft and personal injury. Settlers complained of drunken Indians trespassing on their farms and stealing their property. On the other hand, the whites would "cheat the Indians most abominably both in Weight and Measure; as well as otherwise abuse them," according to one report.[39] So bad was the problem that by a Royal Proclamation of 1763 "no Trader shall by himself, Substitute or Servant, carry more than fifteen Gallons of Rum, at any one time, into any Nation of *Indians*."[40]

Disease, alcohol, Indian war and encroaching settlers. These were the myriad problems which beset Haigler and his people. If the Nation were to survive, he would have to find a solution to each of these threats.

The Tuscarora Example

At the time, it seemed entirely plausible that the Nation would *not*, in fact, survive. Exhibit A of this argument was the Tuscarora tribe. Once it was the largest and most feared in the Carolinas. But by Haigler's time, it had been almost eradicated. One writer in 1752 concluded:

> The condition of the Indians in N. C. is rather a deplorable one. The tribe of Chowans is reduced to a few families. Their land has been taken away from them. The Tuscaroras ... are a remnant of that tribe that waged war with N. C.; & then took refuge with the 5 Nations, & became incorporated with them. Those that have remained here are treated with great contempt, & will probably soon be entirely exterminated.[41]

The Tuscarora were a cautionary example to other tribal leaders. They had lived along the flat coastal plain along the eastern North Carolina shore. As such, they were essentially on the front line of the surging invasion of European settlers from the coastal villages on the Atlantic Ocean. Relations between the Tuscarora and Europeans deteriorated around the beginning of the eighteenth century with murders, enslavement and kidnapping commonly committed both by and against the tribe. "The Tuscarora, by all odds the dominant Indian power in North Carolina, had watched the settlers with distrust, seething over each movement into a new area. When the tide of European civilization flowed into the Pamlico-Neuse region, they saw the handwriting on the wall and decided they must make a stand or gradually be overrun."[42]

The final straw was likely the founding of the city of New Bern on Tuscarora hunting land.

On September 22, 1711, without warning, the Tuscarora launched a preemptive war of extermination, attacking plantations and villages along the coast and murdering hundreds—men, women and children alike—in vile and barbarous ways. Survivors fled.

The South Carolina government responded by sending an expedition of militia under Colonel John Barnwell against the Tuscarora. Barnwell negotiated a conditional surrender from the tribe, but his expedition was considered a failure by the Colonial Assembly, who were looking for a more permanent solution to their Tuscarora problem than Barnwell had provided them.

A second expedition was organized by Colonel James Moore. Moore recruited tribes deemed friendly to the settlers (or, put differently, hostile to the Tuscarora), foremost of which was the Catawba. The denouement of this so-called Second Tuscarora War was the destruction and massacre of the Tuscarora at a place called Neoheroka by Carolina militia and their Catawba, Cherokee and Yamasee allies.

The Tuscarora stronghold of Neoheroka was an irregularly shaped log and earth fort located on the Contentnea creek, less than sixty miles from the salt water of the Pamlico River. The fort was over an acre and a half in size, sheltered behind a palisade wall.[43] Lawrence Lee, author of *Indian Wars in North Carolina*, describes the setting:

> Along this wall, at strategically located points, were bastions and blockhouses. Within the enclosure were houses and caves. An enclosed passageway, or "waterway," led to the nearby branch of Contentnea Creek. When Colonel Moore arrived before this impressive fortification, he began careful preparations to destroy it. Three batteries were constructed nearby and from the Yamasee Battery facing the fort, a zig-zag trench was dug to within a few yards of the front wall. This trench provided protective cover for men to approach and build a blockhouse and battery near the fort. Both of these structures were higher than the walls of the fort so that the enemy within might be subject to direct fire. A tunnel also extended from the trench to the front wall so that it might be undermined with explosives.[44]

After a siege lasting several weeks, the fort was reduced to a smoldering ruin, littered with the bodies of men, women and children. Colonel Moore lost five to seven killed and eighty-two wounded, but this was nothing compared to the massacre of the Tuscarora. According to some estimates, over 500 Tuscarora were killed, with the Catawba and other Indians slaughtering and scalping many of the wounded.

After the siege of Neoheroka, only a few scattered, smaller Tuscarora villages remained. The remnants of the tribe fled from North Carolina, eventually finding their way to the upstate of New York, where they aligned with the Five Nations (which then became known as the *Six* Nations). Unlike Barnwell's half-hearted measures, *this* was the result the colonists were looking for as payback for the September 1711 attack.

The Tuscarora's fall was the Catawba's gain. It cemented their alliance with the British and crushed an age-old enemy. It was not the end of the internecine bloodletting, however. Revenge was central to Indian warfare, and they kept long ledgers of past wrongs. As Lawson put it, "The *Indians* ground their Wars on Enmity, not on Interest, as the Europeans generally do; for the Loss of the meanest Person in the Nation, they will go to War and lay all at Stake." They were "very revengeful," he said, and "never forget an Injury done, till they have receiv'd Satisfaction."[45]

Such was the case with the Tuscarora. The Catawba had won the battle, but the longer war would grind on and on between the northern and southern tribes. As one writer describes it:

> Although the Tuscarora had fled, they knew the warpath from the Five Nations to the Catawba Nation. From 1715 [onward] ... the Catawba paid dearly for their participation in the two Tuscarora wars. These wars intensified the murder of Catawba tribal members of all ages and both sexes. Revenge did not require the death of only men. A woman caught drawing water from a spring or a child who wandered from the camp fulfilled the demand for blood. From the Six Nations in New York to the Catawba Nation, no one was safe.[46]

Haigler's objective was to end this interminable war. In June 1751, as almost his first order of business, he, five headmen and a translator boarded HMS *Scorpion* in Charleston harbor and set sail for New York for a meeting with the Six Nations. The Catawba party arrived in Albany on June 30. By one account, Haigler and his men "had to be guarded from harm from Iroquois who did not want to see a peace made."[47]

The Mohawks, another of the tribes comprising the Six Nations, demanded a ritual humiliation of Haigler and the Catawba. It was a mortification which must have wounded him, but in the greater interests of peace, he accepted. "The Catawba approached the Mohawk in full regalia, singing and dancing, feathers pointed towards the ground," a symbol of deference.[48] While the dancing continued, Haigler offered a peace pipe, which he and the Mohawk chief shared, cementing the fragile peace. "When the Six Nations presented the Catawba with a wampum belt, the peace was final."[49] As a gesture of the truce, the next year the king of the Iroquois visited the Catawba nation, without incident. Apart from vigilante and some militant attacks, murders and raids abated along the western frontiers.

Internal peace secured, Haigler's other task was to maintain peace with the European settlers who were moving into the Catawba hunting grounds in large numbers. These borderlands, lying between North and South Carolina, were largely unmapped and unsurveyed. They were not, however, entirely uninhabited as a slow trickle of settlers, largely Scots-Irish but also some Germans, filtered into what became Mecklenburg County and farther south. The settlers were of different religions, ethnicities and cultures. In addition to the Scots-Irish families, others roamed the desolate shrub-brush and forests: run-away slaves, thieves, religious dissidents, and mercenary hunters, as well as eagle-eyed English land speculators.

The area was legally owned by a variety of absentee British landlords, so, technically, the settlers were trespassing. They were described by one official as "people of desperate fortune, and without any property or possession" other than the lands "which they hold by force."[50]

Fighting and provocations between the settlers and the Catawba in the area were ongoing. "[M]any Complaints" were reported arising from "jealousies and Fears ... between the said Catawba Indians and the Inhabitants."[51]

Robbery by hungry Indians of food from settlers' homes was a common occurrence. Horses were repeatedly stolen. Governor Dobbs, in a letter dated July 18, 1756, was sorry to hear "that there has been Several abuses and robberies committed by Strolling Parties of Indians" against settlers.[52] Bishop Spangenberg observed that quite often the Indians "conduct themselves in such a way that the whites are afraid of them. If they enter a house & the man is not at home they become insolent & the poor woman must do as they command. Sometimes they come in such large Companies that even the man is sorely put to it if compelled to deal with them."[53]

The problems were exacerbated by the nefarious selling of alcohol to the Indians. "You Yourselves are to Blame very much," Haigler told the colonial officials at one meeting. "You Rot Your grain in Tubs, out of which you take and make Strong Spirits[.] You sell it to our young men and give it them, many times." As a result, the Indians "get very Drunk with it [and] this is the Very Cause that they oftentimes Commit those Crimes that is offensive to You and us."

Haigler attempted to ameliorate the growing animosity that existed between the settlers and Indians. "I have very often charged our young Fellows not to mol[e]st nor rob the white People," he told officials in 1752. "What they have done I could not prevent, but if they commit any more Acts of Violence, [I] shall immediately acquaint you." The problem, as he pointed out, was that "the white People were settled too near us."[54]

Governor Dobbs gave "Strict Orders" to Haigler that his "hunters and warriors [were] not to rob Kill or abuse the English Planters their Bretheren and [not to] Destroy their Horses[,] cows[,] Swine or Corn." If Haigler could not control his warriors, Dobbs warned, the English "would be Obliged to repell force with force."[55] Despite Haigler's efforts, relations continued to deteriorate to the point that the governor of South Carolina feared the settlers "will draw on an Indian War."[56]

This was not an idle threat, nor one that Haigler could ignore. The Catawba were by all measures a diminished force. The English colonists, by contrast, were growing by the day. They had guns, horses and men. It was an entirely uneven fight and growing more so. All-out war such as the Tuscarora had launched in 1711, was impossible. Haigler's only option, the only course that might save his people, was reconciliation.

"that Chain of Friendship which has so long remained between us"

As he had with the Iroquois in New York, Haigler turned his feathers downward and pled for peace. In August 1754, in the simmering Carolina heat, he and his warrior leaders met with British commissioners to settle outstanding complaints against his tribe. His goal was to build trust and a lasting relationship so that genocidal wars, such as the Tuscarora had lost, would not be repeated against the Catawba.

"I am Exceeding glad to meet you here this day," Haigler began, "and to have the opportunity of having a talk one with an Other in a Brotherly and Loveing manner, and to Brighten, and Strengthen, that Chain of Friendship which has so long remained between us and the people of those three Provinces."[57] But despite the niceties, the Catawba has a number of charges to answer for.

A settler named William Morrison had been badly mistreated when some of Haigler's warriors appeared unannounced at Morrison's mill and proceeded to dump water into the meal trough. When Morrison attempted to stop them, the Indians "made many attempts to striek him with their guns over his head." It was a minor but emblematic episode in part due to the gaping chasms of culture expectations. The Indians, Haigler explained, only intended "to put a handful or Two of the meal into it to make a kind of a Drink which is their way and Custom."

He explained that it was fortunate that his warriors had not killed Morrison, for if they had, "we would surely have killed [the offender] for they would not let him Live above the ground, but would put him under the ground, as Lately we have Done to one of our Young Fellows who got Drunk and in his Liquor met with a little girl on his way below the Waxhaw Settlement and kill'd her."

Capital punishment was the sole punishment for almost all crimes against whites, and drunkenness was no excuse.

More settlers "laid sundry things to the Indians Charge," such as complaints about the Catawba "taking Bread[,] meat[,] meal and Cloaths" from them. When the Europeans attempted to resist, the Indians attempted "to stab men and women" who were resisting.

To these charges Haigler answered, "Brothers as You are Wariors Yourselves, You well know that we oftentimes goe to War against our Enemies and Many Times we are Either making our Escape from our Enemies or in pursuit of them, which prevents us from hunting for meat to Eat when we are in Danger, least our Enemy should Discover us."

In these cases, he said:

> We are forced to go to Your houses when Hungry, and no sooner we do appear but your Dogs bark and as soon as You Discover Our Comeing You Imediately hide Your Bread Meal and Meat or any Other thing that is fit to Eat about your houses, and we being sensible that this is the Case, it is True we se[a]rch, and if we finde any Eatables in the house we Take some, and Especially from those who behave so Churlish and ungreatfull to us, as they are very well assured, of our great need many times for the Reasons we now give.

He pleaded that it was his "Earnest Desire that Love and Friendship" which the Nation enjoyed with the settlers "should Ever Continue." He promised that upon his return to their village "I will Call all our nation Together and charge the young men and Wariors Not to Misbehave on any Consideration whatever to the white people." With that, recorded the official minutes, "they shook Hands all round."[58]

Amity between the Catawba and settlers was restored, for a spell. But still tensions persisted. In a second meeting in May 1756, Haigler with "15 of his principal Warriors and about 30 of his young Men painted and armed in the manner that they are when going to War" met with Peter Henley, the North Carolina chief justice.[59]

"Mine is a small Nation," Haigler began, "yet they are brave men, and will be fast friends to their Brothers the White people as long as the sun endures." The whites complained about harassment by the Indians, but the settlers were oftentimes just as guilty.

When Indians would approach settlers' houses asking for food, "some of the White People are very bad and quarrelsome and whip my people about the head, beat and abuse them." Again he raised the settlers' practice of making and selling liquor, which was a root cause of much of the problems.

> I desire a stop may be put to the selling strong Liquors by the White people to my people especially near the Indian Nation. If the White people make strong drink let them sell it to one another or drink it in their own Families. This will avoid a great deal of mischief which otherwise will happen from my people getting drunk and quarrelling with the White people.
>
> Should any of my people do any mischief to the White people I have no strong prisons like you to confine them for it, Our only way is to put them under ground and all these men (pointing to his Warriors again) will be ready to do that to those who shall deserve it.

His goal was to maintain concord between them. As he memorably put it, "I look upon the English and ourselves as many good things put into one pockett as Brothers that have issued from one Womb."

Fixing the Land

Despite the niceties, however, the issue of land festered.

"I have had Complaints sent to me that Haglar King of the Catawba has threatened and dispossessed several of the Planters who had got out Patents [for land] within 30 miles of the Catawba's Town," Dobbs complained to London.[60] Dobbs recommended that the Crown create "a Circle of 30 miles round their Towns within which radius no white man should settle."[61]

The desire to "fix the lands" culminated in the Treaty of Pine Tree Hill in 1760. Haigler was forced to concede much of the extra lands which Dodd complained of, moving his people from the Pine Tree Hill area to the Old Waxhaw Fields. He had little choice. Settlers continued to stake claims on Catawba lands, and with their diminishing numbers the Catawba could neither resist them nor even maintain a reasonable argument to the colonial authorities that they needed so much of it (unless one subscribed to the absurd belief that the land rightfully belonged to its original owners).

Clay bust of Haigler by Chas Fagan, which was used as a model for the bronze statue of Haigler on Charlotte's Trail of History. "I look upon the English and ourselves as many good things put into one pockett as Brothers that have issued from one Womb," said King Haigler (courtesy Chas Fagan).

Many settlers, land agents and government officials were unhappy with any concessions to the Catawba. Just two years later, in the winter of 1762, the Governor's Council was told that the "number of Warriors have been reduced in [the last] few years by Haglars Confession from 300 to 50 and all their males dont exceed 100 old and young included so they are now scarce a Nation but a small village."[62]

That being the case, Dobbs argued with a sinister undertone, "the Tuskarorars who had and still have 300 Warriors were content to enjoy a Township of 40,000 Acres." Why did the Catawba need so much land? Why did they deserve it?

Murder and Conspiracies

In late August 1763, Haigler was ambushed and murdered somewhere in the South Carolina backcountry. Seven Shawnee braves were reported to have been the attackers. By one account he was shot six times, scalped, and his bloody body left dead in the pines. The timing of this murder—or was it assassination?—has since raised numerous conspiracy theories.

First, the motives are strange, for one of Haigler's singular achievements had been the peace treaty with the Six Nations. Since then, a steady if fragile truce had existed between the long-standing enemies. Murdering the king of the Catawba was a singularly provocative act of aggression.[63] Would it make sense to kill him and thus trigger a new round of internecine Indian war?

The timing is also coincidental, given that a further conference was scheduled to begin in Augusta, Georgia, just a few months later between the Catawba and colonial officials for the purpose of fixing the final boundaries of the Catawba's lands. Haigler had been the leading negotiator for years on these issues. Per one historian, "it is a fact that both Carolinas had an easier time negotiating with the Catawba without the brilliance of King Haigler present."[64] Whatever the motivations or politics, the Catawba lands were, in the end, fixed at 15 miles square, roughly half of what Haigler thought they were owed.

Was Haigler murdered by South Carolina officials to weaken the Catawba's negotiating position? Or did colonial officials instigate an assassination, perhaps using the Shawnee as a pawn, by exploiting their unrequited desire for revenge? Or was he another victim in the tit-for-tat Indian raids that had gone on for generations? As one writer darkly muses, "[w]e will never know exactly what happened on August 30, 1763."[65]

While that is true, we *do* know that despite Haigler's death, and against all odds, the Catawba Nation endured. Indeed, his descendants live on the same land to this very day.

According to tribal legend, sixteen warriors guarded Haigler's tomb for the required grieving period. It is also said that white traders enticed the guards with liquor, got them drunk, then robbed Haigler's tomb. The tribe was forced to secretly rebury Haigler's body.

Whether the story is true or not, the murder of Haigler, and the robbery and desecration of his tomb, remains a powerful metaphor for his life spent in struggle, against all odds.

2
Crackers: Thomas "Kanawha" Spratt and the Scots-Irish

"His blood was spil'd in freedom's cause, Rather than submit to British laws."
—Gravestone of Thomas Spratt

Throughout the Carolina Piedmont are scattered antique cemeteries from the Colonial era. Many of them (sometimes called "old burying grounds") lie near Presbyterian churches established before the Revolutionary War. There were seven (possibly eight) principal such churches in Mecklenburg County, sometimes called the "Seven Sisters" or the *Pleiades*. All seven were organized around the same period (1750–1770), when the first large influx of Scotch-Irish Presbyterians began settling in great numbers in Mecklenburg. (The 1767 List of Taxables described the county succinctly as "mostly Presbyterians."[1])

These seven churches—Sugar Creek (c. 1750); Steele Creek (1760); Hopewell (1762); Poplar Tent (1764); Centre (1765); Providence (1767); and Clear Creek (later called *Philadelphia*)(1770)–still exist, although not in their original guises.[2] The cemeteries, however, are exactly as they were left, haunting and unique reminders of the centuries-old past. They are nearly all that remains of Revolutionary era Mecklenburg County. Unlike larger, richer, colonial cities such as Philadelphia, Charleston or Boston, which could afford stone and brick houses and grand public buildings, the backwoods was a frontier area, and buildings were, with very few exceptions, wood-framed or log daubed with mud or clay. The buildings are long gone, but the hand-carved, quite beautiful and detailed gravestones of the old Presbyterian cemeteries survive. They are the public architecture, the cathedrals, of the pre–Revolutionary backcountry world.

Some, like the ancient Clear Creek burying ground set back in the woods along a residential road in Mint Hill, or the Phifer family cemetery near Concord, are no longer associated with a nearby church, or any existing farm or lands. The family cemetery of Thomas Spratt (or "Sprot"), along a grassy farm lane in Fort Mill, South Carolina, falls into this category as well. A handful of listing stone tablets behind an ugly stone and concrete wall tells the story of the remarkable Spratt family and two of its members in particular: Thomas "Kanawha" Spratt and Peter Harris, a Scots-Irish frontiersmen and his adopted Indian son.

The Scots-Irish

In the middle of the eighteenth century, around 1750, a wave of immigration from Maryland and Pennsylvania slowly but inexorably poured south into the Carolina Piedmont like paint from a spilled can. The color of this human tide would have been the sky-blue of the Scottish Saltire, or perhaps Irish green, or maybe a mixture of the two. In any event, it was certainly not English red. These people were the Scots-Irish, so called because of their mixed heritage as emigrants, first to Ireland from Scotland, and thence from Ireland to America.

They left Ireland for a variety of reasons. First, they were a dissident religious minority (Presbyterians) amongst a hostile population (Anglicans) governed by a foreign power (England). The Presbyterians endured a long and bloody history under English rule. In the American colonies, they heard that they would be free. "The Presbyterian ministers have taken their share of pains to seduce their poor ignorant hearers," wrote one Irish official in 1729, "by bellowing from their pulpits against the Landlords and the Clergy … at the same time telling them that God has appointed a country for them to depart thence, where they will be freed from the bondage of Egypt and go to the land of Canaan."[3]

In addition to religious freedom (expressly promised in the Great Charter of the Lords Proprietors of 1663; a promise, incidentally, the Scots-Irish never forgot) was the promise of a better life. That promise was easily kept. Ireland was a desperate place, subject to famine, punitive taxation, oppressive landlords, lawlessness and general poverty. One Irishman of the period complained of "the hardship England is putting upon us … the saddest robbing in the country that ever was known and not only robbing but murdering, killing almost everywhere, where they rob. This is all occasioned by the scarceness of money."[4]

The Irish exodus to the American Colonies was on a biblical scale, and the immigrants saw it as such, giving Old Testament names to their places in the woods and building "meeting houses" where churches were forbidden. Between 1771 and 1775, 17,500 Irish men and women left for the American colonies, and by 1800, over a quarter million had gone.[5] The Londonderry *Journal* in April 1775 reported in alarm that "the North of Ireland has in the last five or six years been drained of one-fourth of its trading class, and the like proportion of the manufacturing people."⁶ So many Irish were arriving, wrote James Logan, Provincial Secretary of Pennsylvania in 1729, that "it looks as if Ireland is to send all its inhabitants hither." Indeed, so powerful was the incoming tides of humanity, he said, that "[t]he common fear is if they continue to come, they will make themselves proprietors of the province."⁷

The Scots-Irish were particularly drawn to the Carolinas, where they did indeed "make themselves proprietors." The English, for their part, were happy to have them settle in the backcountry (that is, the wilderness away from the coast and the main settlements) in order to form a buffer between them and the Indians. The thinly settled areas south of Virginia were particularly appealing to them. In 1755, Royal Governor Dobbs found seventy-five families living on his land near Mecklenburg. There were, he reported:

> 5 or 6 to 10 children in each family, each going barefooted in their shifts in the warm weather, no woman wearing more than a shift and one thin petticoat; They are a Colony from Ireland removed from Pennsylvania, of what we call Scotch Irish Presbyterians who with others in the neighbouring Tracts had settled together in order to have a teacher of their own opinion and choice.⁸

As Dobbs pointed out, the English called them Scotch (or Scots) Irish. They were also known as *Irish, Ulstermen* or *Presbyterians*, but the English simply called them *trouble*. They fit in nowhere. They were Presbyterians in an Anglican Empire; Scots amidst the English; Republicans in a sea of Monarchists.

It takes some work to get a clear picture of the earliest settlers in Mecklenburg. Family stories, gathered a hundred years later, glorify these "patriots and heroes." Accounts from the British army excoriate them for failing to support the king and join the British cause. Descriptions from loyalists or Anglican ministers made them out as little more than brute savages. They lived in primitive, filthy and, to the Anglicans, unholy conditions. The truth of course is somewhere in the middle.

Their later admirers described them in glowing terms as *rugged, courageous, devoted to liberty, proud*, and so forth. This was a polite way of describing qualities that others would describe as *savage; reckless; ornery;* or *aggressive*. A modern English writer, Ian Saberton, editor of Cornwallis' papers, sums it up as well as anyone has, describing the backcountry Scots-Irish as "aggressive, courageous, emotional, fiercely intolerant, hard-drinking, and in many cases inclined to indolence ... [they] surpassed all other sects in bigotry and fierce denominationalism, going to lengths which are almost unbelievable. Men of God, their ministers brought politics into the pulpit, exhorted rebellion, and in some cases ... took up arms themselves."⁹

They generally arrived in America poor and dirty, with nothing but a noticeable haughtiness and a latent (and sometimes expressed) resentment of the English. They were considered poor servants due to their bad attitude. They trespassed on lands they didn't own, and when they were confronted by—wait for it—English landlords, they resisted, sometimes with force. In one episode in Mecklenburg County in 1762, the Sheriff and his posse were called to restore order among Scotch-Irish squatters. The rioters "damned the King and his peace, and beat and wounded several of those whom the Sheriff had called to his Assistance."[10] In short, it was quite clear, concluded the English officer Banastre Tarleton, echoing many witnesses, "that the Irish were the most adverse of all other settlers to the British government in America."[11]

The English found them to be uncouth, uncivilized and unwashed. They are "certainly the worst Vermin on Earth," according to one Anglican minister named Charles Woodmason, who lived and traveled in the Carolinas in the mid-1760s.[12] "Ignorant, mean, worthless, beggarly Irish Presbyterians," he ranted in his diary, "the Scum of the Earth, and Refuse of Mankind."[13]

Many English, like the acerbic Woodmason, found the Scots-Irish's rustic manner of life alarming and uncultured, and frankly we would probably agree if we were transported back in time to be among them. In Woodmason's description of their daily life, their rustic log cabins were "quite open and expos'd" and with "Little or no Bedding, or anything to cover them." They wore, he said, only "a Shirt and Trousers[,] Shift and Petticoat.... No Shoes or Stockings," while their "children run half naked. The Indians are better Cloathed and Lodged."[14] They were barefoot most of the year, made their own clothes, washed little, drank quite a bit, cursed openly, and liked to fight, which they did quite viciously, all attributes they carried with them from the Old Country.

"Living in log cabins or primitive shelters on the edge of western civilization, very many Back Country settlers no longer conformed to accepted standards of behavior," Saberton snottily sums it up. "Criminality, immorality, and irreligion were rife, accentuated by the severe shortage of ministers of religion and the lack of education."[15] Or in the more caustic views of Woodmason, they lived a "low, lazy, sluttish, heathenish, hellish Life," he concluded, "and seem not desirous of changing it."[16] And if the Scots-Irish hated the English, well, the feeling was mutual.

Woodmason's views were strong, but not atypical. The British cavalry officer George Hanger, who fought against the backcountry settlers with Cornwallis in the Southern campaigns in 1780–1781, described them as cruel, treacherous and barbarous, with no religious scruples and no civilization. "In the back parts of Carolina," he wrote, "you may search after an angel with as much chance of finding one as a parson."[17]

"This distinguished race of men," Hanger snidely concluded, "are more savage than the Indians and possess *every* one of their vices but *not one* of their virtues."[18] Cornwallis himself was said to have remarked, in his quintessentially English way, that he "would not be godfather to any man's honesty in this province."[19]

The Scots-Irish were primitive, true, but this made them tough and ferocious enemies, as the British would learn to their detriment. According to Hanger: "I have known one of these fellows travel two hundred miles through the woods, never keeping any road or path, guided by the sun by day and the stars by night, to kill a particular person belonging to the opposite party. He would shoot him before his own door and ride away to boast of what he had done on his return."[20]

"I speak," he concluded, "of that *heathen race* known by the name of *crackers*."[21]

To Hanger and other Brits, a *cracker* was someone who was ignorant, poor, ruthless and violent. To the Scots-Irish frontiersmen, a *cracker* was proud, tough and independent. Whichever way you looked at it, the Carolina backcountry was their land, and Thomas "Kanawha" Spratt was a typical embodiment.

The Carolina Piedmont

His father, Thomas Spratt, Senior (1685–1757), was held by family tradition to be the first European settler to cross the Yadkin River in a wheeled cart, and thus amongst the very first settlers of the area that would become Mecklenburg County.[22] He personified the Scots-Irish story: born in Scotland, removed to Ireland as a youth, thence to America, where he made his way into the Carolina backcountry. James, Andrew and Samuel Spratt—probably his brothers—and their families also came down from Pennsylvania and settled in what was then Anson County. Spratt the elder purchased land on Twelve Mile Creek, near present-day Fort Mill, S.C., in 1753, in Catawba Indian country.

Others had come before the Spratts, of course. The first to arrive in Mecklenburg along the Wagon Trail, possibly as early as the first quarter of the seventeenth century (or earlier), were lone Indian traders. The area was opened to settlement in 1749, and by 1758 hundreds of land grants had been issued to arriving settlers.[23] By 1750, about the time the Spratts arrived, a small but steady trickle of European settlers were making their way into the Carolina Piedmont, on the western fringe of the American Colonies. "In the year 1746 I was up in the Country that is now Anson, Orange and Rowan Countys," wrote Colonial Governor Matthew Rowan, at which time "there was not then above one hundred fighting men." In 1753, however, just seven years later, Rowan reported "at least three thousand for the most part Irish Protestants and Germans and dayley increasing."[24]

Families like the Spratts had arrived first in Maryland, Delaware or Pennsylvania, where land was at a premium. From there the Scots-Irish exodus continued South, along the Great Wagon Road that ran from Philadelphia, through the Shenandoah Valley, and then terminated near the Indian lands in the disputed territories between the Carolinas.

The first settlers, like the Spratts, lived amongst the Indians, or even with them from time to time, learned their languages and way of life, including warfare. One mid-1750s observer saw "many hunters about here, who live like the Indians, they kill many deer selling their hides, & thus live without much work."[25] They traded beads, cloth, whisky, guns, powder, lead and other trade goods with the Indians in exchange for deerskins, beaver pelts, antlers and buffalo hides.

They called the area between the Yadkin (or "Deep" or "Peedee") River to the east and the Catawba to the west "the land between the rivers," or *Mesopotamia*—the ancient name for the Babylonian kingdom between the Tigris and Euphrates. It was a good area for settlement. There were rivers and creeks, providing water and power for mills, and game was abundant. In 1752, at about the time the Spratts entered the area, Moravian Bishop Spangenberg was scouting it for the same reason. "There are many springs & streams & even creeks, the water of which is as clear and sweet as anyone could possibly wish," he reported.

Clay bust of Thomas Spratt, better known as "Kanawha" or "Cainhoy," the first European settler in Mecklenburg. This model was used in the building of a sculpture of Spratt that resides on the Trail of History in Charlotte (courtesy Chas Fagan).

Bottoms & uplands are well stocked with wood. For stock this is an excellent country, as the reeds are still quite green.... There are many places which could be converted into good meadows & many more could be made because the water from the streams could be so conducted as to irrigate the land with but little labor.

The soil along the hill is a rich clay: in the bottom it is black soil. For the erection of mills there is abundant water & fall—stones are plentiful, & as we believe suitable for grindstones, but no limestone.[26]

The climate generally was mild, or certainly milder than farther north. That made it appealing to the poor, because they could live with lighter and fewer clothes and, more importantly, less food for their livestock during winter. For that reason alone, the bishop noted, "[n]umbers of Irish have therefore moved in," although he cautioned that "they will find themselves deceived because if they do not feed their stock in the winter they will find to their cost that they will perish."[27] (Spangenberg was wrong about this, as it happened; one of the great attractions of the area was that the cattle and hogs could run free in the woods for years at a time, only being rounded up twice a year for marking and branding.)

The area was remote, which made it both dangerous and appealing. There was virtually no government, few roads and almost no authority. The Scots-Irish found all that wonderful, for in the backcountry there were no (or very few) land agents, not to mention tax collectors, landlords or Anglican ministers. And of course there was land. Lots of land.

Not that life there was easy, by any stretch. The land had to be tilled by hand, fields cleared or fences built only with back-breaking labor. The nearest large cities were hundreds of miles away, over difficult and dangerous roads. "Here I must remark on some of the difficulties incidental to the colonizing of this country," wrote Spangenberg. "They will require salt & other necessaries which they can neither manufacture nor raise. Either they must go to Charleston, which is 300 miles distant. The distance is not the only objection—on the road they have mostly stinking water to drink; & are in danger on account of robbers."[28]

In short, it was a tough life, and it lent itself to a tough sort of people. Because the Piedmont backcountry was so remote and lawless, it was a natural magnet for runaway slaves or servants, dissidents, or just plain criminals. Again, Spangenberg said:

> The Inhabitants of North Carolina may be divided into two classes. Some are natives of the State, these can endure the climate pretty well, but are naturally indolent and sluggish. Others have come here from England, Scotland, & from the Northern Colonies some have settled here on account of poverty as they wished to own land & were too poor to buy in Pennsylvania or New Jersey[.]
> Others there are again who are refugees from justice or have fled from debt; or have left a wife & children elsewhere,—or possibly to escape the penalty of some other crime; under the impression that they could remain here unmolested & with impunity.
> Bands of horse thieves have been infesting portions of the State & pursuing their nefarious calling a long time. This is the reason North Carolina has such an unenviable reputation among the neighbouring provinces.[29]

The area was disputed by many folks, and for a variety of reasons. First, it was unclear who the area belonged to, and who the proper government was. South Carolina officials sought to expand the border north, and North

Carolina officials the opposite, but it wasn't clear to anyone where the border actually was. Settlers took advantage of the confusion, first "holding to the South" as it was called (that is, claiming to be residents of South Carolina to avoid authority or taxation when officials from North Carolina appeared) or vice versa, depending on which official was asking. For years, sheriffs who collected taxes in the area did not know which province to whom they should remit them.

Second, it wasn't clear who owned the land. Large swathes of it were (legally speaking) owned by absentee English landlords, but they had never set foot in the region nor intended to. Areas were unmapped and unsurveyed. Not surprisingly, this encouraged settlers to simply arrive and claim it as their own. A variety of disputes (and in some cases violent fights) routinely broke out between the settlers and English land agents (or other figures of authority), seeking payment of quit-rents from the trespassers. In 1762, a meeting of the North Carolina Governor's Council heard complaints that the high sheriff of Anson County had been "abused and Insulted by some of these settlers on Sugar and Reedy Creeks, in the Execution of the Duty of his office" and, after later attempting to execute warrants on the settlers, they "behave[d] in a riotous manner."[30]

Colonial officials blamed these and similar troubles on the people who lived there, the Scots-Irish. It was they who "in Order to possess themselves of the said Lands without paying any Consideration for the same and to avoid paying Taxes and Quit rents or other just demands against them in either Government [caused] all those disputes have arose."[31] A similar episode in 1765 in Mecklenburg became known as the "Sugar Creek War," and ended up with armed settlers beating land agents nearly to the death in the woods along Sugar Creek.

It was also Indian country. While relations were generally friendly, the chasm of expectations and cultural understandings—not least about what the settlers considered private property; ironic, of course, given that many were trespassing—caused constant and often violent confrontations. "Every man living alone is in this danger, here in the forest," as Spangenberg simply put it.[32] This was the hostile territory which the Spratt family set out to claim as their own.

Spratt Family Legends

The Spratt family prospered in the frontier region. The elder Spratt had a son—Thomas Spratt, Jr.—and seven daughters, one of whom (Susannah) married Thomas Polk, the founder of both Mecklenburg County and Charlotte. Thomas Jr., married "an immigrant girl" (as his grandson put it) named

Elizabeth Bigger in the frontier town of Charlotte, and they lived on his father's plantation, a mile or so from the Mecklenburg courthouse, on a small bluff in the woods. After his father's death, Thomas set out south to a new settlement on Cane Creek, just over the border into South Carolina. According to the (much later) recollections of his grandson, Thomas Dryden Spratt: "My grandfather set his stakes here, and remained on the spot where they camped for the night and there by that Spring wrested fields from the primeval forest, and there built his log house near the scorched spot where the camp fire had been kindled and there made his home."[33] The Catawba leased him a tract of virgin forest and meadows for a period of 99 years. The first white man, it was said, they leased land to.[34]

Thomas became better known by his nickname "Kanawha" (or "Cainhoy" which, one suspects, was a "crackerized" version of "Kanawha"). It is thought Spratt's nickname "Kanawha" was given to him by the Catawbas after the Battle of Point Pleasant, fought on the Kanawha River in West Virginia, on October 10, 1774, during an obscure historical episode known as Lord Dunmore's War (although whether he, or even the Catawbas, were actually present at that battle remains unclear).

If the story is true, it fulfills a long-standing narrative of Spratt's closeness to and friendship with local Catawba Indians. Per family tradition, the Spratts were on good relations with the local Catawba Indians, helping them lease their lands to newcomers, settling personal injury or property damage disputes even fighting in their wars.

Spratt was described by one who knew him late in life as "a tall, spare man, kindly spoken, and active for his years."[35] His grandson said he was "fully 6 feet or more in his socks" and possessed of "an iron constitution."[36] One of his earliest memories was of Spratt "riding me up the road by the graveyard, seated on his lap, and my looking up at his grey beard."[37]

In various recollections about Spratt, we get a glimpse of the rough and tumble, antique and primitive world of the first settlers in the Piedmont. Later writers describe life on the earlier Carolina frontier in glowing and romantic terms. In these accounts, it was a simple but pure sylvan life in the forests, with proud and noble Indians, church on Sunday, and so forth. The reality, at least as described by people living at the time, is somewhat different. "The manners of the North Carolinians in general are vile & corrupt the whole country is a stage of debauchery dissoluteness & corruption," wrote Woodmason in 1765. "[A]nd how can it be otherwise?" he asked. "The people are composed of the Outcasts of all the other Colonies who take refuge there."[38]

A modern historian, Dan Morrill, observes of Spratt's world:

> Drunkenness and fornication were widespread. Modern concepts of hygiene, derived largely from the advent of the germ theory of medicine, had no place in 18th century

life. The most common house form was the log cabin, sometimes with three walls. Typically, the only opening in the exterior wall was for an entry door. The floors were dirt. A permanent fire in a large fireplace at the end of the main room billowed smoke into the cramped living quarters, frequently turning the air into an acrid cloud. Privacy, even for the most intimate acts, was virtually unattainable.[39]

Backcountry life was primitive, to be sure, but not without its pleasures. They enjoyed hunting and fishing, as well as horse racing, gambling, shooting and something called "Long Bullets," where a 28 ounce iron ball roughly the size of a tennis ball was hurled down the road. The man who completed a set distance of several miles in the least number of throws won. There were constant complaints about horse racing and "frequent firing of Guns" and similar pursuits which had a "dangerous Tendency" towards personal injury and property damage.[40]

More often than not, social activity in the backcountry centered around the tavern. And booze. Lots of booze. Apple and peach brandy, cider and rye whiskey were the favorites. A tariff board in April 1775 for Mecklenburg County lists the most common offerings as whisky and brandy (5 shillings per gallon); West Indian rum (12 shillings per gallon); "good claret" and Madeira (6 shillings, 8 pence per bottle); and "strong beer imported" (2 shillings, 6 pence per bottle).[41] Most people brewed their own beer and ale or distilled rum or brandy. In taverns such as Patrick Jack's in Charlotte-Towne, "drunkenness, gaming, cheating, quarreling, and brawling were commonplace, particularly on days when court or other public business was transacted."[42] Spratt himself was said to go on "sprees" from time to time where he would hit the taverns for days on end.

As is well known, drinking leads to fighting. The Scots-Irish liked that as well. The county records of the period are full of stories of eyes gouged, swords drawn and people shot. Daniel Patterson, a historian of the Scots-Irish, points to a trial in Salisbury in 1767 for "felony maiming" (a legal term meaning assault with a tooth or a nail).[43] In another case in 1769 Joseph Avent attested that "his Right Ear was bit off by Henry Braswell."[44] Fighting of this sort had of course been common in Scotland and Ireland, but for various reasons, writes Patterson, "it had also grown in violence here, and more particularly in the southern backwoods."[45]

In this, Spratt was entirely representational. According to one story, Spratt "had a dispute with old Mr. Knox about the prior right to the tract of land called the 'mulberry fields' on the Catawba River." This "controversy terminated in a fight between the two, I have heard that they rolled over and over one another down a hill, from a spring on the premises, some fifty or more yards."[46]

His grandson recalled that Spratt was also "in the habit of treating pretty roughly and without much ceremony" certain of the lower-class settlers, who would squat (or "nest") on unoccupied land until forced to move on. In one episode, "[Spratt] was [away] from home and a wayfarer called in, and after treating the family rudely and disrespectfully and getting his breakfast, passed on over the [Catawba] river. Old ("Kanawha"), as he was called, coming home and hearing of the conduct of the man, mounted his horse, a famous one called Silver Heels, and pursued the traveler. He overtook him at the next house." Kanawha "immediately fell on him with a rawhide whip and after scoring him for some time, deliberately stripped down his breeches and branded him on the hip with the letters "T.S." using an instrument—a branding iron—which he kept for marking or branding his cattle."[47]

On another occasion, it was said, Kanawha beat the Catawba Indian Chief Old New River "with a pole all over the yard" for injuring a horse Spratt had loaned him.[48] Hearing these and other tales, the recollections of Major Hanger about crackers travelling two hundred miles to kill a man ring even more true. Small wonder it was these "hardy, illiterate and lawless backwoodsmen" of the Carolina Piedmont, writes Saberton, "whom the British came to fear more than most."[49]

The British were to find plenty of cause to fear Spratt and his neighbors in the summer and autumn of 1780, when Cornwallis' army moved up from Charleston through the Piedmont. Following the crushing defeat of the Americans at the Battle of Camden in August 1780, Cornwallis implemented a long desired plan to move his army into the Carolinas. Cornwallis' purpose was to inspire and rouse the loyalist militia, particularly in Tryon County to the west of Mecklenburg, raise troops and seize horses, and in general overawe the Americans in the "inveterate" (his words) counties of Mecklenburg and Rowan.

By late September, the British army was encamped on Camden Road (today's Highway 521) in the Waxhaws, only twenty or so miles from Charlotte. At the time, Brig. Gen. William Lee Davidson estimated the size of Cornwallis' army at 1,200 men, "nearly one half of his number Tories."[50]

American leader William R. Davie was encamped at Camp Providence, on what is now Providence Road, near the Presbyterian church of the same name, twenty-five miles above the British camp. The main force of Cornwallis' army was on the western side of the Waxhaw creek, while on the eastern, to the British right, a group of light infantry and South Carolina loyalists were camped near the plantation of Captain Walkup (pronounced *Wahab*).[51] Davie set out on an expedition to attack the loyalists, without seeking to engage the main British army. According to family legend, Spratt rode with Davie's men to what became known as the Battle of Wahab's Plantation.

Davie broke camp on the evening of September 20, 1780. He rode through the night with 116 men, as "Lighthorse" Harry Lee put it, "taking an extensive circuit, turned the left of Cornwallis and gained, unperceived, the camp of the loyalists."[52] At first light, he found between three and four hundred Tories breaking camp. Shielded by a cornfield, Davie's men approached and caught the loyalists by surprise, killing twelve and leaving forty others wounded in a matter of minutes. They retreated as quickly as they came, slipping back into the cornfield, but taking nearly a hundred Tory horses and as many captured rifles with them. The nearby British regulars of the 71st Regiment, awakened and alarmed by the gunfire, arrived shortly thereafter on the scene. Viewing the loyalist casualties on the ground, their commanding officer in a "diabolical fury," in the words of Lee—ordered Wahab's farmhouse burned to the ground.[53]

The only wounded amongst the Americans was Spratt (and by friendly fire, at least according to Davie). Per the recollections of his grandson, buckshot passed through the fleshy part of Spratt's right thigh, one of them grazing the bone.[54] Injured, Spratt had to be held onto his horse by two others as the Americans retreated back towards Charlotte.

At some point in the next few days following, the British arrived at Spratt's log house and began using it as a field hospital. "They were told that Mr. Spratt was ill; but they insisted on having the house for their own sick, and the owner was removed into the kitchen," according to family accounts. It was in Spratt's bed that "Major Frazer, of the British army died, while Cornwallis and Rawdon both stood by his bed, and averred, with lifted hands, that he was one of the best officers who had crossed the ocean." A Scotch physician was in attendance. After Frazer's death, he went into the kitchen to examine the injured Spratt. As the story goes, the Scottish surgeon said to Spratt:

> "What is the matter with you, maun?" he asked [Spratt].
> "I have a fever." The physician felt his pulse and exclaimed, "Why maun, you are wounded!"
> "And what if I am?" said the patient.
> "Ah, I am fearful you have been fighting against your lawful sovereign, King George."
> "I have been fighting for my country, and if I was well, I would do it again," replied Spratt.
> "Well, well, you are a brave solider, and I'll dress your wounds for you," said the Scotchman; and he did so, and attended on him as along as the British troops occupied the house.[55]

In another account of the same story:

> These unbidden guests took from Spratt a hundred head of cattle, hogs, &c. When the time came for marching, the army formed line before the door, and then formed a hollow square, with their drums muffled. These played a mournful air; till at length the army deployed, and took up the line of march with a lively tune and a quickstep. The cause of this ceremony was the punishment of one of their own soldiers, whose body

hung from the limb of a tree, he having been executed for an alleged attempt to desert, and join Davie's troops.[56]

In another version of the story, the British solider "was left hanging, and no person was left on the premises to cut him down and bury him, but a small negro boy."[57]

While the British camped at Spratt's farm,

> a considerable stir took place within their [British] lines, in consequence of the report of a gun up the Charlotte Road. The drums and bugles sounded an alarm; a guard was detailed, immediately, to go and report the cause of that gun's being fired. When the guard arrived at the outer lines of the camp ground, they found the sentinel dead, who had been posted between the Charlotte road and the cane-break.[58]

A local man, one of the (many) Alexanders in Mecklenburg (probably William "Black Bill" Alexander), hidden in the cane-break, had shot the guard through the heart as the soldier leaned against the tree. (A bullet mark on the tree "about the height of an ordinary man's breast" was still visible in 1848).[59]

In another episode: "Walker, who was just as violent a man as Alexander, shot a British sentinel in the mill house [owned by a Wilkes, four miles from Charlotte]. The sentry was standing near to and leaning his head against a window." Walker was one hundred and fifty or more yards away. "His ball took effect in the sentry's head, and I was told that the stain of the blood and brains was visible on the window shutter until 1820 or 1825, at which time the house underwent repairs and the bloody memento was removed."[60]

"Our Graves, will soon be our only habitations"

The engagement at Wahab's plantation, where Spratt was wounded, was one of a series of small partisan actions against the British in the area that made Mecklenburg legendary for its militancy. On October 21, 1780, Lt. Col. Francis Lord Rawdon wrote to Lt. Col Nisbet Balfour: "The inveteracy of the inhabitants of Mecklenburg County was so great that during the latter part of our stay there we were totally ignorant of the situation of any of our posts, all our expresses being waylaid and many of them murder'd on the road."[61] Similarly, two weeks after the Battle of Wahab's plantation, Cornwallis wrote to Balfour that "this County of Mecklenburg is the most rebellious and inveterate that I have met with in this country, not excepting any part of the Jerseys."[62] Spratt was only a bit player in this epic saga, like hundreds of other farmers or tradesmen.

Which brings us to the story of Peter Harris. Harris was a Catawba Indian whose parents died when he was just three years old, during one of the periodic Smallpox outbreaks that ravaged the tribe. It is said that he was adopted by Spratt and raised as one of his own sons.

One of Spratt's grandsons, Leonidas Spratt, later recalled, "my grandfather found him and raised him in the family."[63] When the Revolution broke out, Harris, like many of the Catawba, fought alongside Spratt and the other Carolina patriots. He fought at the Battle of Stono, where he was wounded in the foot, and also at the siege of Savannah. In July 1780, he joined General Sumter's Militia Brigade, along with some 35 or 40 other Catawba Indians, and served in that brigade for several months during 1780 and 1781.[64] The Catawba's support of the colonists was legendary. "I must here Mention the Catawba," wrote one veteran. "[W]e often Encamped on their land for days together [and] those friendly Indians drove to us Beef from their Own Stocks, and Several times brought Out their whole force and Encamped near us."[65]

Following the war, Harris was exploited by unscrupulous con artists. In a sad episode, he and two other Catawba were brought to London and exhibited as part of a travelling show.

According to Spratt's grandson, "some three white men, whose names I forget, took Peter and two other Catawbas to Europe for a show. After making some money out of them by taking them to London and Ireland and defrauding them as usual and leaving them." (A musical called "The Catawba Travellers" was shown in London at the Sadler's Wells theater in 1795.) On the return voyage to America, "the other two [Catawba] jumped in the sea and Peter alone came back to his old hunting grounds."[66]

Harris, like other Revolutionary War veterans, was eligible by an 1818 Act of Congress to apply for a federal pension of $8 a month. In his application in 1823, Harris set down, in a few short and powerful sentences, the story of his life, worth quoting in full. "I am one of the lingering embers of an almost extinguished race," he wrote.

> Our Graves, will soon be our only habitations. I am one of the few stalks, that still remain in the field, where the Tempest of the revolution passed, I fought against the British for your sake, the British have disappeared, and you are free, yet from me the British took nothing, nor have I gained anything by their defeat. I pursued the deer for my subsistence, the deer are disappearing, & I must starve. God ordained me for the forest, and my ambition is the shade, but the strength of my arm decays, and my feet fail in the chase, the hand which fought for your liberty is now open for your relief— In my Youth, I bled in battle, that you might be independent, let not my heart in my old age, bleed, for the want of your Commiseration.[67]

Kanawha Spratt died in 1807 and was buried in the small family cemetery on Brickyard Road, just south of the town limits of Fort Mill, South Carolina, near the Catawba lands. It is said that one day in 1823, Peter Harris arrived unannounced at the Spratt homestead. He was "going to die," he told the Spratt family, "and wished to be buried at the side of old Cainhoy." The family "promised to fulfil his wish. Peter then took his bed, and in about two weeks after died."[68] In a death bed confession, Harris said that his only regret in life was that he had killed a British soldier who laid aside his gun to get a drink of water at a spring. Harris said that it was the act of "a coward, rather than of a brave man, in which category he had always hoped his fellow-man would place him."[69]

Today the Spratt cemetery sits alone in field of overgrown summer weeds, behind a wall of rock and concrete. There are a few headstones visible, dating between 1803 and 1872. Some lie scattered and broken, or have been uprooted by trees. The graves of Kanawha Spratt and Harris, however, are still intact. Harris' headstone reads in part:

> The body of Peter Harris
> A Catawba Indian by his
> last request was buried
> here in 1823 Aged 70 years
> Left an orphan
> He was raised by Thomas
> Spratt Sen[r] Like all his
> tribe he was ever friendly
> to the Americans and for
> his service in our war of Independence received
> a pension from the State[70]

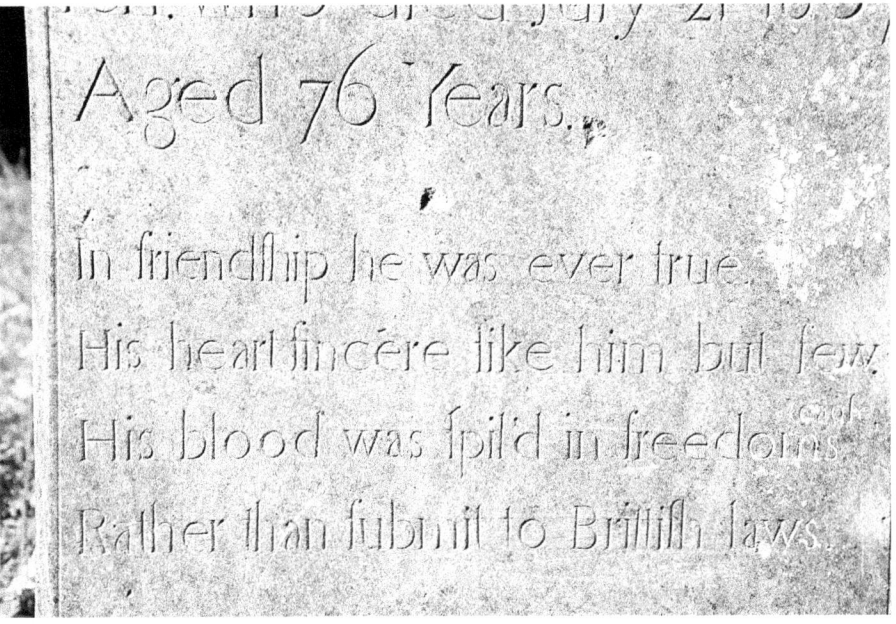

Spratt's tombstone in Fort Mill, with the inscription *"His blood was spil'd in freedom's cause/Rather than submit to British laws"* **(photograph by the author).**

Spratt's grave, ten or so feet away from Harris', gives an equally pithy account:

> In friendship he was ever true.
> His heart sincere like him but few.
> His blood was spil'd in freedom's cause,
> Rather than submit to British laws

Surely the best possible epitaph anywhere of the "crackers" that Hanger and the British feared so much.

3

No Surrender: The Rev. Alexander Craighead and the Presbyterians

"No War is proclaimed without a drawn Sword."
—Alexander Craighead, November 1743

Settlers such as Spratt came south into the Piedmont for a variety of reasons. In Spratt's case, it was the opportunity for free and abundant land, and the ability to live away from English laws. For many others, the reason was religion. They intended to get away from Anglican bishops and a secular, most unholy civilization. They intended to create a new and more pure society in the pinewoods and barrens between the Yadkin and Catawba rivers.

Many who came to Mecklenburg in the beginning were followers of an obscure (even then) and militant sect of Scottish Presbyterianism known as "Covenanting." Now it is little known, but at the time, Covenanting (and even Presbyterianism generally speaking) was viewed by the English as little more than a seditious and dangerous doctrine. It was associated with anti–English, anti-monarchical activities. In 1768, Anglican clergyman Woodmason snarled at the "vile, leveling common wealth Presbyterians" in the Carolina backcountry who were infused with "Republican Spirit."[1]

This was not a compliment. Republicanism was a synonym for treasonable activities and sympathies.

In fact, the entire American Revolution, many believed at the time, was simply another chapter in the centuries-old war of Scottish Presbyterianism against English Anglicanism. In the seventeenth century the battleground had been Britain, but now it was North America. "I fix all of the blame for these extraordinary proceedings on the Presbyterians," one English monarchist wrote as the American Revolution began. "The Presbyterians have been the chief and principle instruments in all of these flaming measures. They always do and ever will act against government from that restless and turbulent anti-monarchical spirit which has always distinguished them everywhere."[2] Another wrote, "Presbyterianism is really at the bottom of this whole conspiracy, has supplied it with Vigour, and will never rest, till something is decided on it."[3]

There was some truth to that, as the essence of Covenanting, and in many respects of Presbyterianism in general, was a republican belief that God, not monarchs, ruled, and that the will of God could be determined by honest and devout men reading scripture. This was a democratic view, in contrast to the Anglican belief that God reigned through one supreme emissary on earth: the king. Presbyterian reading of scripture taught that the City of God would be built in accordance with a holy contract (hence, "covenant") that God promised his followers. Irish ministers, complained one Anglican, "press it on [their followers], and say that [it] is as binding ... as the Gospel it Self, for it is a Covenant enter'd into with God, from which they cannot recede."[4] These two views—republican Presbyterianism, on the one hand, and Anglican monarchism, on the other—would collide in the Carolina backcountry.

The Covenanters

The Covenanting movement arose in Scotland in the 1660s as a rebellion by Presbyterians against the attempt by the English Crown to Anglicize Scotland. Its basis was national revival based on a relationship—the Covenant—between a reformed Presbyterian community and God. They looked to Jeremiah 50:5: "They shall ask the way to Zion with their faces thitherward, saying, Come, and let us join ourselves to the LORD in a perpetual covenant that shall not be forgotten." To Covenanters, this was literal truth.

The movement was embodied by the Solemn League and Covenant of 1643, a six-point semi-mystical, quasi-religious, and overtly political manifesto that was negotiated between the English Parliament and leading Scottish warlords. They had as their common enemy King Charles I. The motives of the two allies were mixed. The Scots intended nothing less than a wholesale reform of the Church of England, indeed a total religious conversion of the British Isles to Presbyterianism. The English Parliamentarians, on the other hand, were engaged in a war with the Crown and needed military aide from the Scots to smash the Royalists. Over time it became clear that the English had little intention of permitting a Presbyterianization of England. When the balance of power shifted, the English Parliamentarians reneged on the Solemn League. The Scots were double crossed.

After the beheading of King Charles I and the triumph of the Parliamentarian party, the Covenant leaders turned to the deposed son of the dead king, the future Charles II (founder of Carolina), as the only means of enforcing a Presbyterian settlement. They forced the young prince to swear allegiance to the Solemn League. When the Scots were crushed by Cromwell, Charles II fled the kingdom and Cromwell expelled all Presbyterians (both English and Scottish) from Parliament. The Covenanters had lost, and lost badly.

Repression of the Presbyterians in Scotland began in earnest. In 1662, all clergyman and teachers were compelled to swear allegiance to the Anglican Book of Common Prayer. In 1664 the Conventicle Act was enacted whereby anyone found attending a Covenanting meeting was subject to seven years of exile. In 1665, a "Five Mile Act" banned Presbyterian ministers from coming within five miles of their former churches. Presbyterian church services could only be held in secret, in outdoor services called *conventicles*, sometimes held in mountain passes, highland ravines or remote caves. The repression was successful.

A hardcore militant faction of Presbyterians, however, would not consent to Anglican rule. The apotheosis of the "lost cause" of the Covenanters was a Presbyterian minister named Richard Cameron. Born in Falkland, Scotland, around 1648, Cameron had fled to Holland to resist the repressions of Charles II. There, Cameron preached defiance and rebellion against the "Papist" king of England, Charles II. In 1680 he returned to Scotland to attempt a peasant uprising against the Crown. On June 22, 1680, Cameron issued what was called the *Sanquhar Declaration* on behalf of "the true Presbyterian Kirk and covenanted nation of Scotland." In it, Cameron declared "war with such a tyrant and usurper ... as enemies to our Lord Jesus Christ, and His cause and covenants."

Cameron was hunted down and killed with a small band of supporters in July 22, 1680, at Airds Moss in the Ayr River Valley. His head and hands were hewn off and delivered as a special gift to the English authorities in Edinburgh Castle.

By 1685, James VII of Scotland (James II of England) ascended to the throne and the last act of the Covenanting Movement began to play itself out. James II publicly avowed his conversion to Roman Catholicism—a final, bitter betrayal of the Scots. Final and irreconcilable war on the remnants of the Covenanting movement was launched. The Lord Chancellor, the Earl of Perth, in a speech to the House of Lords declared: "we have a new sect sprung up among us from the dunghill, the very dreggs of the people who kill by pretended inspiration ... whose idoll is that accursed paper the Covenant."[5] Episcopacy was declared the final—non-negotiable—word on Scottish church government. The Solemn League and Covenant was publicly burned by the royal hangman. To be caught attending a conventicle, punishable by death. Covenanting was synonymous with high treason. The Cameronians—the last diehard extremists of the "lost cause"—were now to be finished off once and for all.

Covenanting leaders were hunted down and hanged, drowned or beheaded. During a period known as "the Killing Time" in Scotland, there was widespread "bloody butchering, beheading, mangling, dismembering alive, quartering upon scaffolds, imprisoning, laying in irons, torturing by boots, thumbkinds, fire-matches, cutting pieces out of the ears of others, banishing and selling as slaves old and young men and women in great numbers," wrote one observer of the period.[6] The lucky ones fled to America, where they could carry on their anti-English campaign at a safe(er) distance from English authority, usually in the remote backcountry or frontier areas.

One such political-slash-religious refugee was a Presbyterian Minister named Thomas Craighead, whose son, Alexander, would leave an indelible impression on Mecklenburg County, and the fiery, militant, and uncompromising character of its earliest settlers.

"Steadfast in the Faith"

Alexander Craighead (sometimes given as *Craeghead, Creaghead* or *Creghead*) was born in March 1707 in Donegal, Ireland into a well-known Presbyterian family. According to the historian William Foote: "The name of Craighead is of frequent occurrence in the history of the Church of Scotland and of Ireland, and holds an honorable place among the ministry…. Thomas Craighead was among the first ministers of Donegal Presbytery,—a native of Scotland, ordained in Ireland."[7]

The Craighead family arrived in the American colonies in October 1715. Alexander was seven or eight years old. According to family tradition, both his father and grandfather, writes Foote, "and perhaps his ancestors further back, were ministers of the gospel, strongly attached to the church, and reputed as truly pious." As a minister, Thomas was known for his "impassioned sermons" which reduced his audience to tears.[8] *Pious* he may have been, but Thomas Craighead was also erratic, angry and volatile. According to one later writer, he "had the unhappy gift of discord" and led "a somewhat stormy life."[9] He was an unforgiving and intolerant man; today we might call him a fanatic. He seemed to have been equally hard (or harder) on his own family and their perceived failings, at one point barring his own wife from receiving communion. This act was so "excoriating and unconscionable" according to records of the Presbytery, "that we cannot forbear supposing that he is under some dreadful delusion of Satan, if not a delirium in his head."[10]

Delirium in the head was, to some contemporary observers, considered a Craighead family trait.

In 1735, Alexander Craighead became minister at Middle Octorara Presbyterian Church in Lancaster County, Pennsylvania. He quickly adopted his father's strident Presbyterianism, unwillingness to compromise, and overall volatile personality. He meddled in the affairs of other churches; hectored his parishioners; denounced the English government and the Anglican church; and generally acted as an incorrigible trouble-maker. He was accused of "intruding [beyond] ye bounds of his [congregation] without any invitation"[11] and "bad conduct." He required that church members subscribe to the ancient Solemn League and Covenant, and if they would not do so, refused to baptize their children.

He proudly thought of himself as genuine Covenanter; a follower of the martyred Cameron. "True Presbyterians," Craighead explained, "have been frequently termed *Cameronians* by some to this Day," and "continued steadfast in the Faith." (The Synod Minutes of 1746 denounced Craighead as "a rigid Covenanter or Cameronian.") Presbyterians who accommodated with English governance and the Anglican faith, on the other hand, he said, "were corrupt."

One eye-witness called him "a mad fellow" and "furious leveler who labors to confound their opinions both Religious & Civil."[12] Like a surviving Confederate soldier in the early 20th century, he was a living reminder of a "lost cause"; a throw-back to a distant, uncompromising former age. "[S]ome may take liberty to say that I am very fickle," Craighead wrote of himself, "and want to promote divisions."[13]

In December 1740, Presbyterian Church elders visited remote Middle Octorara to speak with Craighead and look into the numerous complaints against him. In no mood for reconciliation, Craighead accused them of "whoredom, drunkenness, Swearing, Sabth breaking, lying &c."[14]

"Mr. Craighead utterly and absolutely declined our authority," concluded their report on Craighead. His "notorious and disorderly conduct," resulted in:

> [L]itigiously interrupting the [meeting] for a long time in their proceedings ... & conniving at ye peoples tumultuous behavior, whereby we obliged to break up in an abrupt manner. In sum, we cannot but look on Mr. Craighead's whole conduct on ye above instances to be extremely irregular and disorderly, So that we have not known a parallel instance Since we have been capable to mark anything in the world.[15]

Craighead's "irregular and disorderly" conduct was more than just an irritating behavioral problem, however. The Covenanters believed in the sovereignty of Christ over all men; including princes, Kings and other officials. This ran contrary, of course, to the theory of the "divine right of Kings," which held that the supreme authority, on Earth anyway, was God's representative— His Majesty King George III. As such, subjects owed a duty of loyalty to the Sovereign. But he owed no obligations to them. Not so, said Craighead. The King and his subjects, Craighead wrote, "As both of them are tied to God, so each of them is tied the one to the other for the performance of mutual and reciprocal duties."[16] It followed then that the subjects' loyalty to government was conditional. If the leaders were corrupt or unholy, then the citizens, as true Christians, had a duty to resist. The Protestant leader John Knox had arrived at this logical conclusion in 1560, asserting in his first confession of faith of "the right and duty of the people to resist the tyranny of their rulers."[17]

And because the English Kings had strayed from true Christianity, Craighead believed, they were no longer legitimate monarchs, and lacked legal right to rule. King James I was "[without] any legal Right to rule over this Realm, by Reason of his Popish Principles."[18] King George I he called "an outlandish Lutheran" and King George II "the Head of Malignants, and Protectors of Sectarian Heretics."[19] Craighead saw himself as engaged in a struggle against a bastardized form of Catholic popism.

Some of his parishioners must have nervously thought to themselves—*if I agree with him, aren't I required by my faith to take up arms against the British?*

"Some say," Craighead answered, "that if they adhere unto the Covenants, that they are obliged to rise in Rebellion against his present Majesty King George."

"However," he explained, "the Covenants relate to Things spiritual, and consequently the Warfare for the upholding of them, ought to be spiritual." This was an unconvincing answer. The reality was that, as a devout follower of Cameron, Craighead had no practical objection to armed resistance; indeed his sermons practically demanded it. As he put it, "no War is proclaimed without a drawn Sword."[20]

Drawn swords, even metaphorical ones, implied rebellion; rebellion implied treason. These incendiary preachings were no laughing matter for the moderate faction of the Presbyterian church. As "dissenters," and worse as dissenters associated with the losing, rebellious Scottish Kings in the English Civil Wars, it was imperative for the establishment Presbyterians to disassociate themselves with rebels like Craighead, lest the English authorities enact punitive measures against them.

In 1743, the Royal Governor of Pennsylvania reported one of Craighead's sermons to the Philadelphia Presbyterian Synod. The Governor was not amused, and nor was the Synod. They "unanimously agreed" that the paper:

> is full of treason, sedition, and distraction, and grievous perverting of the sacred oracles to the ruin of all societies and civil government … we hereby unanimously, with the greatest sincerity, declare that we detest this paper, and with it all principles and practices that tend to destroy the civil and religious rights of mankind, or to foment or encourage sedition or dissatisfaction with the civil government that we are now under, or rebellion, treason, or any thing that is disloyal.[21]

In due course, Craighead was expelled from the Presbyterian church "by Reason of [his] divisive, censorious and uncharitable Doctrine and practices."[22]

He retaliated in a series of pamphlets and sermons. He also began to make plans to take his teachings south, into the wilderness, where he and his followers could live a true, Godly life, far from the corrupt cosmopolitan ways of Pennsylvania.

Militants in the Backcountry

A logical destination was the sparsely settled backcountry. Scots-Irish settlers, many of them hard-core Presbyterians of Craighead's persuasion, were moving there in droves. Numerous itinerant, evangelical ministers like Craighead—called "New Lights" during the period—travelled into the area. Far from British officials, among their own people, they could preach as they liked without fear of being arrested.

The New Light ministers rode from Irish settlement to settlement, preaching under large oak trees, canopies or tents, strung up for the purpose. Often they preached three or four times a day to audiences of several hundred people. Their preaching style was emotional, even hysterical. Onlookers were known to have "incidents of weeping, screaming, fainting" and other "bodily commotions like 'epileptic fits.'"[23]

"The Country is very much over spread with New Light Whitefield followers," complained one Anglican in 1747, particularly "covenanters who receive their Sacrament with a gun charg'd and drawn sword; & profess they'l fight for Christ against Civil Magistrates."[24] Another complained that the Carolina backcountry had been infested with "Irish Presbyterians from Belfast,

The Rev. Alexander Craighead preaching in the Carolina backcountry, as imagined by artist Will Puckett. One writer in the 1760s complained that the Carolinas were overrun with "Covenanters who receive their Sacrament with a gun charg'd and drawn sword; & profess they'l fight for Christ against Civil Magistrates" (courtesy William Puckett).

or Pennsylvania."[25] Craighead was one of a number of "roving Teachers that stir up the Minds of the People against the Establish'd Church, and her Ministers."[26]

Towards the end of 1743, Craighead gathered his followers together and gave his reasons for leaving Pennsylvania. They had, he said, a "Duty to separate ourselves from the corrupt Constitution of both Church and State, and not to touch, taste, or handle these Abominations, lest by partaking with them in their Sins, we be made Partakers with them in their Plagues." He found it impossible to tolerate "the apostate, perjured and blood-guilty Condition of Church and State," as well as the "Errors and Immoralities that abound in this corrupt and apostate Age."

Together, in Covenanter fashion, they drew swords in a symbolic renewal of the Solemn League and Covenant, just as their "spiritual forebears had done."[27]

"[O]ur renowned Ancestors were constrained to draw the Sword in the Defense of their own Lives," he said. "Our drawing of the Sword is to testify to the World; that we are one in Judgment with them, and that we are to this Day willing to maintain the same defensive War in defending our Religion and ourselves against all Opposers thereof, although the Defense of these should cost us our Lives."[28] They resolved to head south, where they could live free.

Craighead and his parishioners first went into the Shenandoah Valley in Virginia, but within two years he again caught the attention of English authorities. In June 1752, complaints were made against "the Revd Mr Alexander Creaghead [who] has taught and maintained treasonable positions and preached and published pernicious doctrines."[29] They were forced to move on, southwards, into North Carolina.

The timing was fortuitous, for the Virginia frontier was no longer safe. The slaughter of Braddock and his men at Fort Duquesne that summer rent open the whole of the western flank of the Piedmont as cleanly a hunting knife across a man's scalp. Indians began frequent and brazen attacks on settlers in the Virginia Valley, burning homesteads, abducting women and massacring men. According to the historian Waddell, "there was no peace on the frontiers, and no feeling of security by any of the white settlers west of the Blue Ridge."[30] The Rev. Hugh McAden, who rode through the frontier in the summer of 1755, would write that Braddocks' defeat, "together with the frequent accounts of fresh atrocities being daily committed upon the frontier, stuck terror to every heart. A cold shuddering possessed every breast, and paleness covered almost every face."[31]

Sometime in the autumn of 1755, writes Foote, "[c]rossing the Blue Ridge, [Craighead] passed on to the more quiet regions in Carolina, and found a location among the settlements along the Catawba and its smaller tributaries, in the bounds of what is now Mecklenburg county."[32] There he accepted the call to lead a new congregation of what was called "Rocky River."

There were only a handful of settlers living along the scattered small creeks. Materially and spiritually, it was virgin territory. Earlier he lectured his congregation that they had a moral duty to "not to touch, taste, or handle the Abominations" of the corrupt world of Pennsylvania. Here, amidst the silent forest, they could build a world to their own liking. In the historian Foote's famous summary:

> In Carolina, he found a people remote from the seat of authority, among whom the intolerant laws were a dead letter, so far divided from other congregations, even of his own faith, that there could be no collision with him, on account of faith or practice; so united in their general principles of religion and church government, that he was the teacher of the whole population, and here his spirit rested. Here he passed his days; here he poured forth his principles of religious and civil government, undisturbed by the jealousy of the government, too distant to be aware of his doings, or too careless to be interested in the poor and distant emigrants on the Catawba.[33]

"Dissenters of the most rigid kind"

The Scots-Irish may have thought by fleeing into the wilderness they had escaped the British Empire, but the English were not going to give up so easily on the dissenters. In March 1764 Royal Governor Dobbs proposed that the Anglican Church send "a missionary or schoolmaster who might be also established for [M]ecklenburg county, who are mostly now Presbyterians or other foreign Sectaries."[34]

Andrew Morton was selected on the Governor's recommendation to act as a missionary. In the summer of 1766 he set out on horse from New Bern into the wilderness. He got as far as Brunswick when he received a report that gave him pause. Mecklenburg County, he was told, "abounded with Dissenters of various denominations and particularly with Covenanters[,] Seceders[,] Anabaptists and New Lights." Morton was warned that "he would meet with a very cold, if any reception at all have few or no hearers and lead a very uneasy life—Such disagreeable relations quite discouraged Mr. Morton from proceeding."[35]

Later that summer Morton reported on his aborted mission:

> I wrote to you in June last informing you of my Journey to my new mission in Mecklenburgh County—From Newbern I pursued my Journey to Cape Fear where I received such Intelligence as discouraged me from proceeding any further—There I was well informed that the Inhabitants of Mecklenburg are entire dissenters of the most rigid kind—That they had a solemn leage and covenant teacher settled among them[.] That they were in general greatly averse to the Church of England—and that they looked upon a law lately enacted in this province for the better establishment of the Church as oppressive as the Stamp Act and were determined to prevent its taking place there,

by opposing the settlement of any Minister of the Church of England that might be sent amongst them...[36]

Despite the failure of Morton's errand, Anglican influence continued to spread. A series of regulations called the Marriage and Vestry Acts required Anglican ministers to officiate weddings. The British levied an annual tax of 10 shillings per "taxable soul" on each settler to build Anglican churches and hire priests. These actions infuriated the Scots-Irish.

In a series of petitions to the Governor in this period the settlers protested, time and again, these unjust laws. For example, the free citizens of Mecklenburg County, in a 1769 petition to Governor Tryon, argued:

> [W]e think it a grievance that we are liable to a burthensome taxation to support and Episcopal clergy. [...]
>
> We think it as reasonable that those who hold to the Episcopal Church should pay their clergy without our assistance as that we, who hold to the church of Scotland should pay our clergy without their assistance.
>
> We now support two settled Presbyterian ministers in this Parish, we, therefore, think it a grievance, that the present law makes us liable to be still further burthened with taxes to support an Episcopal clergyman: especially as not one twentieth part of the inhabitants are of that profession.
>
> We think that were there an Episcopal clergyman in this Parish, his labours would be useless.
>
> We think ourselves highly aggrieved by the exorbitant power of the vestry, to tax us with the enormous sum of ten shillings each taxable; which is more than double the charge of Government: And that for purposes to which we ought by no means to pay anything by compulsion. [...]
>
> We conceive ourselves highly injured and aggrieved by the marriage act, the preamble whereof scandalizes the Presbyterian clergy, and wrongfully charges them with celebrating the rites of marriage without license or publication of banns[...]
>
> We declare that the marriage Act obstructs the natural and inalienable right of marriage and tends to introduce immorality.[37]

Other petitions in Rowan and Tryon Counties in this period made similar arguments.

But the British were not swayed. Although Governor Tryon recommended a repeal of the Marriage and Vestry laws in 1771, he was overruled in London. And by that time it was too late anyway. The Presbyterians of Mecklenburg, who considered themselves "highly injured and aggrieved," were ready to resist. And in May of 1775, when the opportunity presented itself to them, they did so.

Craighead's Legacy

Craighead died in Mecklenburg County in March 1766 at the age of eight. He left behind two sons and six daughters. His remaining possessions

(9 horses, 30 cows, 19 sheep, 14 hogs, assorted furniture, plates, cutlery, pots and pans, two punch bowls, three saddles, one wagon, one plow, three guns and five slaves) were left to his heirs. It is interesting to speculate what role he would have played in the American Revolution had he lived another decade.

By legend, Craighead's was the first marked grave in Mecklenburg County, in the old cemetery at Sugaw Creek. His headstone stands to this day behind a chain link fence, very near that of Hezekiah Alexander and other early settlers. Also per legend, two sassafras saplings used as poles to carry his coffin were stuck in the ground near his grave, sprouted and later towered over his tomb. "A storm about one hundred and twenty-five years later uprooted one and the other was broken off about 20 feet about the ground. The people all around, hearing of the destruction of the trees, came and cut them up for souvenirs."[38] The present pulpit, it is said, is made from the wood of these trees, as is a gavel that was given to the synod.

The Sugaw Creek congregation "loved Craighead," states the history of the church, so much so that in 1778 they invited his son to be their pastor (an offer he refused), and later, in 1791, his grandson (he accepted).[39] The congregation's love for him tells us something about the character of the people who lived here then. Craighead, writes one historian, "was the foremost American of his day in advocating those principles of civil liberty under a republican form of government, to confirm which the Revolutionary War was fought."[40] Another believes, "Craighead's principal legacy was to instill among the people of his congregations a fierce determination to resist the imposition of unwanted authority from outside the community, especially from the State Capital in New Bern or from London."[41]

Although Craighead did not live to see the Revolutionary events of May 1775, he was there in spirit, covenanting sword held high.

4
The Founding Father: Thomas Polk

> "No man possessed more influence in that part of North-Carolina."
> —Joseph Johnson, *Traditions and Reminiscences, Chiefly of the American Revolution in the South*

Thomas Polk is the answer to the often-asked question: *Why is Charlotte where it is?*

After all, there is no geographically obvious reason that the center of town should be located where it is. It is not near a large body of water nor other landmark. Although the main thoroughfare of Tryon Street, once part of the Great Wagon Road, runs along a very modest hill, that could be said of any other location a dozen miles north or south of where the city center now lies. Surrounded by rivers north and south of town, one wonders why the city was not founded there, say near what was Cowan's or Beattie's Ford over the Catawba River, or for that matter further south near the Catawba Indian settlements.

Charlotte *is where it is* because Thomas Polk's house sat alongside the north-east corner of the cross-roads. Through Polk's clout and connections, that is where they put the courthouse. In fact, the founding deed of the city, dated January 15, 1767, defines the town boundaries as "beginning at a White Oak about 150 yards from Thomas Polk's line."[1] A year later, the town was established.

Polk was also one of the three "Trustees and Directors" named in the page and a half long founding deed. In fact, if you look closely, Polk is everywhere in early Charlotte history, his name synonymous with the county itself. He was a local leader, merchant and politician. He was a commander of the local militia, owned three grist-mills and received local dignitaries, such as Governor William Tryon. Polk's name is associated with the great events of the period, from the chartering of the town, to the Mecklenburg Declaration, to the American Revolution.

We see Polk everywhere in this period. On January 4, 1768, he introduced the bill that led to the legal creation of the town of Charlotte ("An Act for establishing a Town in Mecklenburgh County"). By "Reason of the Healthiness" of the area and its "convenient Situation thereof for Trade" the town, they hoped, "might soon become considerable."[2] He was named one of three trustees whose job it was to populate the new town by granting property deeds to would-be settlers. In exchange for a grant from the trustees, each recipient was required within three years to "erect and build on each Lot so conveyed, one well framed sawed or hewed Log House, twenty Feet in length, and sixteen Feet wide, and Ten Feet high in the Clear, with a Brick or Stone Chimney."[3] He was a member of the General Assembly and widely known across the Province. (In connection with the October 1769 legislative session Polk spent 18 days travelling on horseback to and from New Bern for which he was reimbursed £12, 14 shillings, 10 pence).

He was, in short, a man to be reckoned with; a man whose counsel was sought; a man who knew the movers and shakers in the region; a man who could get things done.

Not that he was universally popular. Some found him to be arrogant, aggressive and opinionated, qualities that he himself acknowledged. "I was not a little obnoxious to a vast majority of the Province in which I lived," he would later write.[4] Between Polk and the Alexander clan, it was said by others, "some jealousy" existed, and their views had "not always coincided."[5] His role and power as a trustee of the city and as an elected delegate; his relationships with the power brokers in New Bern; his commercial success and growing wealth (in the first U.S. Census of 1790, Polk was recorded as owing 47 slaves—the most in the county), and his outspoken views made enemies.

Whispers were heard in the taverns and ale-houses around Charlotte that Polk abused his political offices—even that he might be corrupt. One critic in 1771 noted that Polk "has been much employed in public services," but in his civic roles was "ever mindful of his own private emolument." The same anonymous critic said that he "is something like the *novus homo* of the Romans, having risen to wealth and honour from a state of poverty & meanness."[6] This was not meant as a compliment.

Whether these criticisms were fair or not, there was no gainsaying Polk's power and notoriety. He may have been an "ungrateful and brutal SOB," as another contemporary described him, but he was not a man to be trifled with. "No man possessed more influence in that part of North-Carolina," concluded historian Joseph Johnson in *Traditions and Reminiscences, Chiefly of the American Revolution in the South* published in 1851.[7] In short, if you wanted something done in Mecklenburg, you first had to talk to Thomas Polk.

Polk's life and career are a tangle of contradictions. He was a local Scots-Irish leader, but one aligned with Governor Tryon, most notably in Tryon's suppression of the Regulator Rebellion. He was an ardent Whig and believer in liberty, but also a slave owner. His name is forever associated with the Mecklenburg Declaration of Independence saga, but there is some confusion on his involvement. He fought with the American Continental Army, was even at Valley Forge, and by one account saved the Liberty Bell from capture by the British, but, incredibly, was later brought up on charges of suspicion of collaborating with the English. He is even mentioned in Cornwallis' papers as being a man eager to turn. Who was Thomas Polk, really?

The Sugar Creek War

Polk was born in Cumberland County, Pennsylvania around 1730. He came to Mecklenburg, as so many of the settlers from that area seemed to, around 1753, along with two of his brothers. Two years later he married Susanna Spratt, by legend the first European born in the area. Over the years, they had eight children.

Polk rose to eminence as a leader of the Scots-Irish settlers living along the small muddy creeks of Mecklenburg County in the 1760s as a result of a land dispute and quasi-riot that became known as the Sugar Creek War.[8] It was not a real war, of course, but it did result in a few beatings and personal injuries over a period of several months. The affair began with a young Englishman named Henry McCulloh. The clannish settlers led by Polk banded together to resist him. Polk, McCulloh was later begrudgingly forced to admit, was "the only Man who has any pretense to sense or weight among these deluded People."[9]

Mecklenburg County, like most of the surrounding area, was difficult to get to and sparsely settled. Most of the land was unmapped and unsurveyed, and thus it was not clear who owned what. In short, it was a perfect area for squatters. Technically and legally, much of Mecklenburg County was owned by a wealthy English merchant named George Augustus Selwyn. Selwyn could only recoup his real estate investments if the settlers bought the land from him or paid him an annual lease called a "quit-rent." But the settlers living on Selwyn's lands had no intention of making any such payments unless compelled to do so. And Selwyn and his business associates were far away in England.

So they sent Henry Eustace McCulloh to the colonies to do their dirty work for them. McCulloh was, as he put it, "Young in Life, Knowledge, and Experience" when he arrived in this "strange Country" in 1761.[10] He also was a bit of a louche twat; spending his father's money on booze and women, and whining melodramatically about the difficulty of his assignment.

When he first arrived in the area in 1765, McCulloh got a foretaste of the animosity against him. He noted that "many of the Settlers upon Mr. Selwyns Lands ... oppose their running any [boundary] Lines." He received anonymous warnings and "the greatest threats against his Life and Person." Despite these obvious signs, he did not anticipate that he "should meet with the least opposition from the Settlers," and made plans to return for a formal surveying project in the spring. His intention was to draw up formal boundaries on each of the settler's lands, and then sell them back to them at a per acre price. As one could imagine, the residents were not keen on this idea.

McCulloh was nothing if not persistent, however, and when he returned to Mecklenburg in March 1766, he faced "30 & 40 of the Settlers" gathered "with a design to oppose his coming upon the Tract." He guessed that there were a hundred and fifty settlers, maybe more, angrily awaiting his arrival. Ominously, they carried knives, axes and firearms, not surveying tools. Polk was leading the mob.

Polk and his armed associates "surrounded him," McCulloh recalled, with "the utmost insolence [and] manifest designs of terrifying him." The settlers confronted him on all sides, "more like Wolves than rational Beings." They shouted at him, brandished their weapons and jostled him "in the most insulting manner." If McCulloh wasn't terrified, he should have been, and the next day it got worse.

Arriving to begin his surveying work, he saw two men "sitting upon the Fence with Guns in their hands." In "taunting Language and insolent Behavior," Polk told the young man that "neither he nor the People would ever suffer any Sheriff or other Officer" to permit the boundaries to be run. Polk was not kidding around, and with him stood "100 more of his Gang many of whom were Armed with Guns," McCulloh recalled. They surrounded him "in a most ignominious and taunting manner; and among other pieces of Insolence some of them asked [him] whether he had not great honor done him, and whether he thought he would have as many Men attend him to his Grave or not?"

The crowd "contemptuously seized and broke the Surveying Chain in several pieces," and Polk himself "took the Compass off the Staff."

"For many hours," McCulloh was not sure, he said, "whether that day was to have been the last of his Life or not." Terrified, McCulloh fled the county. He was persistent, however, and he returned more fully prepared and armed a few months later. This time, as they attempted to run boundary lines, McCulloh's henchmen were attacked and beaten by unknown assailants, who had blackened their faces with tar to avoid identifying them.[11] Was Polk one of them?

"More adventures yet," McCulloh reported to a friend.

One of his men "got one damnable swipe across the Nose and Mouth." And of the others: "Abraham they say is striped from the nape of his neck to the Waistband of his Breeches, like a draft Board; poor Jimmy Alexander had very near had daylight let into his skull."[12]

"[H]ad I been present—I most assuredly & without any ceremony had been murdered." The attackers had brought guns "for that particular purpose.—They declare solemnly—publicly, they will put me to Death."[13]

"Shall not the war of Sugar Creek be handed down to posterity? Can the annals of the history of this Country, parallel this affair?"[14] Polk had won the battle, although the so-called "Sugar Creek War" was not yet at an end. "Damn thee, Tom Polk," McCulloh said, "if I don't conquer thee."[15]

Complaints about the riots in Mecklenburg made their way to then-Lieutenant Governor Tryon.

On May 18, 1765, Tryon announced:

> [I]n the County of Mecklenburg several Rioters to the number of twelve or more, blacked and disguised and armed with Guns and Clubs to the Great Breach and Disturbance of His Majestys Peace and Government, did violently outrageously and riotously assault and beat John Frohock Esqr and others employed by the Honble Henry Eustace McCulloh in surveying and running out some surveys for persons settled in the Lands belonging to George Augustus Selwyn.[16]

Unable to locate or identify the perpetrators, no one was punished.

In the years that followed the Sugar Creek War, Polk's reputation and standing among the Presbyterian settlers continued to grow. He served as a magistrate, as the town's first treasurer and as Mecklenburg's representative in the House of Commons from 1766 to 1771 (and again from 1773 to 1774). Like them, Polk was culturally Scotch-Irish and had an inbred dislike of being told what to do—particularly by anyone with an English accent. Like them, Polk was self-made. He had arrived in the backcountry with nothing. Whatever bread he ate, or money he earned, it was gained through sweat, toil and tears. Like them, Polk was accustomed to a life of grueling, physically demanding labor on the frontier. Like them, Polk was tough.

The Mecklenburg Declaration of Independence

The other local story that Polk is forever associated with is that of the Mecklenburg Declaration.

In fact, every year on May 20 in Charlotte, a man dressed in Revolutionary War garb playing Colonel Thomas Polk stands on the square, on the corner of Trade and Tryon Streets, and reads the five stanzas of the Mecklenburg Declaration to the delight and confusion of passersby. It is a storied tradition, going back decades (or possibly centuries?) Other than Captain Jack, Polk is the man most firmly associated with the MecDec story.

For it was he, it is said, as senior commanding officer of the county, that

The MecDec legend. Colonel Thomas Polk reading the Mecklenburg Declaration from the County Courthouse steps on May 20, 1775 (courtesy Dan Nance).

called the meeting of militia leaders on May 19, which led to the county's declaration of independence on the day following. And it was he who read the document from the courthouse steps at noon; a fact that no less a credible personage than Joseph Graham attested to. But there is one small problem with this.

That is *not* what the surviving papers say.

The MecDec paperwork, like much of the story, is complicated and confusing, but can be summarized as follows. The original minutes and papers of the meeting were kept at the home of John McKnitt Alexander, who by virtually all accounts acted as secretary of the convention. In April 1800, a fire at Alexander's home destroyed most—but not all—of these original records. It can be surmised, but not proven, that the original copy of the Mecklenburg Declaration, the literal text, as well as the signatures of those who signed it (if they in fact did so) was thus forever lost.

But ... but ... not all the relevant paperwork was destroyed in the fire. In fact, Alexander's son, Dr. Joseph McKnitt Alexander, found, sometime around 1818 or 1819, several other "papers on the above subject."

The first was a series of hand-written notes by his father, later called the "rough notes." These were torn in places, marked up, but otherwise legible and clear. They gave a succinct account of the entire MecDec story.

The second paper Dr. Alexander had was, as he put it, a "full sheet." This paper (called the "copy in an unknown hand") ran several pages in length and gave the full account and text of the MecDec. It was this paper that Dr. Alexander copied word-for-word and had published in the *Raleigh Register*, setting off the MecDec historical firestorm.[17] This paper was unsigned and undated. And to this day, it cannot be proven who is its author (although it clearly was not John McKnitt Alexander). (A third paper, known as the "Davie Copy" was also later found, although it is identical, at least insofar as its remaining text goes, to the "copy in an unknown hand.")

Dr. Alexander said that he found these two papers bound up with a roll of Revolutionary War era pamphlets. As he put it, "the roll of pamphlets with which these two papers were found" (meaning the "copy in an unknown hand" and the "rough notes") "were amongst his old surveying and other old papers [not found] until after his [father's] death." He guessed that the papers "may have been unrolled since 1788."[18] (Dr. Alexander was wrong on this point, as the second of the two papers must have been written after 1792).

In any case, the entire veracity of the MecDec saga comes down to what credibility one gives these two papers. The believers will argue that although these papers suffer certain evidentiary flaws, namely the impossibility of dating them, and in the case of the second paper, even identifying who wrote it, they still present a credible and convincing circumstantial case in favor of the story. In their view, these papers, corroborated by other eye-witness accounts of the events in May 1775, are excellent evidence of what was said and done. Despite the doubters, there is no reason to disbelieve the written testimony. As Dr. Alexander summed up the questions of who wrote the "copy in an unknown hand," and when: "it matters not."

Critics, however, contend that the papers are worthless as evidence. The "rough notes" could have been made at any time, and importantly, after the original papers were lost in the 1800 fire. As such, they only reflect McKnitt Alexander's aged and confused recollections of things that were said and done over twenty five years before. As to the "copy in an unknown hand," the skeptics argue, the fact that it is unsigned and undated speaks for itself. Unless it can be shown that these papers were "true copies" of the originals, which cannot be done at this point, their value is scant.

One late Nineteenth historian and MecDec arch-skeptic named A. S. Salley, Jr., even made the case that one of the Alexanders must have forged the "copy in an unknown hand," as part of an elaborate hoax: a charge that has survived in certain quarters to this very day. "As a matter of fact," Salley wrote in a widely read scathing article in 1908, the Alexanders "never did have a single original record" and none of these papers "came from original sources."[19]

The arguments over the MecDec paperwork are arcane and can never at this point be resolved to everyone's satisfaction. But amidst the debate over whether the surviving papers are in fact legitimate records, forgeries, or some combination of both, one interesting fact has largely gone unnoticed and uncommented on.

In the case of both of the papers, they do *not* say that Thomas Polk called the initial meeting of the militia leaders. In both cases, they say that Adam Alexander did. And in both cases, Alexander's name has been crossed out, and the name "Thomas Polk," in someone else's handwriting, has been written over it.

What does this deletion mean? What does it prove?

First, it proves that John McKnitt Alexander thought that his cousin, Adam Alexander, had called the important meeting, not Thomas Polk. We know this because in the "rough notes" McKnitt Alexander had clearly written "Alexander's" name. And the deletion is not in McKnitt Alexander's easily identifiable handwriting. It also means that whomever wrote or copied the "copy in an unknown hand" was of the same view. And that someone, probably the same person, made the same change. But who made this change, and why?

The simplest explanation is that Dr. Alexander did so. After all, he had found the papers and it was he who had them published in the *Raleigh Register*. Nowhere did Dr. Alexander speak to the discrepancy on this matter. Another writer has surmised that before he published them, he showed them to William Polk, Thomas' son, and that *he* made the change. But if William Polk did, why would Dr. Alexander have consented to it? (And of course there remains the possibility that the papers had already been corrected by a person unknown before Dr. Alexander found them.)

The issue is important because it means that Polk, possibly, has been given undue credit for over two centuries in calling the important meeting; credit that was due to Adam Alexander. And for what it is worth, it seems that Alexander, not Polk, was the commanding militia officer at the time. For those who enjoy historical mysteries and unanswered questions, MecDec is the gift that keeps on giving.

Polk in the American Revolution

Regardless of who called the meeting on May 19, 1775, the prominence of Polk in the community and his role in the Revolutionary period that follows is beyond argument.

In the winter of 1775, Polk, and Colonels Rutherford, Martin and Graham, marched into South Carolina with about nine hundred men. Their objective was to suppress a gathering of Loyalists. Polk's son, William, rode with him. The Whig forces, supplemented by rangers and other militia, scoured the Carolinas arresting loyalist leaders. In late December, they located a camp of 200 Tories on the Reedy River. Greatly outnumbering them, the Whigs surprised them at a place called the Great Cane Break, taking prisoners, seizing provisions and scattering the bulk of the loyalists. William Polk was wounded in the fighting.[20] The next day, as Polk and his men made ready to return to Mecklenburg, it began to snow heavily, and hence the punitive expedition was later known as the "Snow Campaign."

When North Carolina raised regiments of continentals, Polk was appointed Colonel of the 4th Regiment. His regiment served along the lower Cape Fear River, then marched north in the spring of 1777 to reinforce General George Washington. The 4th under Polk fought at the Battle of Brandywine and was at Valley Forge in the winter of 1777. Polk's son, William, fought and was wounded at Germantown on October 4, 1777, outside of Philadelphia, where he had his jaw smashed by a musket ball.

During that battle, Thomas Polk was given the assignment of moving the heavy baggage—seven hundred wagons in all—out of reach of the British. The evacuated goods included many of the bronze bells in Philadelphia, which the British would have smelt for cannons. Among these was the Pennsylvania State House bell, later called the Liberty Bell.[21] And thus, Tom Polk of Charlotte saved the Liberty Bell.

"My ungratefull country"

Following the Battle of Germantown, things soured between Polk and his colleagues.

It began when Francis Nash, a Brigadier General of North Carolina continentals, was gravely wounded at Germantown and died shortly thereafter. Polk hoped to succeed Nash, but for whatever reason, General Washington passed him over. Polk was hurt and resigned his commission in an emotional letter to Washington on June 26, 1778, in which he wrote:

> From the earliest Commencement of the present War, I have been actively engaged in the services of my country. I embarqued in it at so early a season as rendered me not a little obnoxious to a vast majority of the Province in which I lived. The timid, the Friends of the established Government, & the moderate, as they were called, at that Period composed the bulk of the Inhabitants—by them was my forward zeal universally condemned.
>
> Thro' innumerable difficulties, from opposition, & inconveniences to my private interest, in the militia and regular service, I continued my efforts for the public good, and doubted not, as I had done more of this kind for the defence of the State than any other member of it, that I had deserved well of my Country; but as soon as an opening for promotion was made by the unhappy fall of Gen'l Nash, the power of a party, over-

looking the merit of these services, procured a recommendation in favour of a Junior Officer.

Such a flagrant demonstration of partiality and injurious preference, without alledging a single article of disqualification against me, has determined me no longer to serve *my ungratefull country* in so painful and so hazardous a capacity.

He concluded, "I rejoice in the prosperity of my country, and am willing, on every occasion, to aid the advancement of its Interests, but choose not to obtrude my services."[22]

The words *my ungratefull country* showed how insulted Polk was. They would later come back to haunt him.

Two years later, in the summer of 1780, the focus of the war had shifted from New York and Pennsylvania to the Carolinas. The British were on the ascendancy. Charleston fell in May 1780. Polk returned to military life that summer, accepting two appointments: one as commissary general of purchases for the State of North Carolina and a second appointment as commissary for the Continental Army. These were difficult, unglamorous and unrewarding jobs; feeding the troops, which was never easy, and, as events would prove, almost impossible once the British army marched through the Carolinas.

Polk was not happy in these roles, nor happy with his commanding officers: especially Horatio Gates. On August 6, just ten days before Gates would be smashed at the Battle of Camden, Polk wrote to Thomas Pinckney. "My Zeal to Serve My Country, and Seeing that the Army is not likely to be well Supplied Otherwise, induce Me to Accept of Genl. Gates's offer of an appointment as Commissary [General]," he pointed out, but "as Mr. Green has been hitherto so inactive as to Suffer the Army to want Supplies that might be had, I cannot think of Acting either under or in Conjunction with him."[23]

Polk felt that he was getting no clear instructions from his superiors. He was also out of supplies, and what was perhaps worse, in his view, he was not being paid. "What provisions has heretofore come to my mills was given out to the Commissaries, So that I have No Quantity at present," he told Pinckney. He reported that he had already "dispatched three waggon loads of flour to your Appointed post, and will, without loss of time, Send a Considerable Quantity for that purpose."

But he wanted to know "how Soon you Could Send my Commission, with particular directions Concerning what kind of provisions I am to purchase, and from time to time what Number of troops I am immediately to Supply[?]"

"I mean to exert my Credit and lay out all my money now; and, as I have ever made it a rule Not to deceive people with regard to payment, *I will expect to be regularly Supplied with Cash*," he concluded. Even with these challenges, he told Pinckney, he could "expect the Next Supply Very Soon."[24]

Then came the catastrophe at Camden. Cornwallis' entire army now advanced towards Charlotte and Polk's home. The Continental army was on the ropes, supplies were scattered, and communications broken. The situation was a mess. In Polk's letters one can tell he is fed up, and sick of the incompetence. He probably complained widely to his neighbors and colleagues.

On September 10, 1780, the British army lay virtually on Charlotte's doorstep. Polk had been told by Major Rutherford that "Corn Wallis Was on his March. If so it Wood be a Good time to through sum troops in their Reer. As their force is said to be 1,000, their Cannot be Many behind. We Intend to Meet them and scrimedg with them, & hop for Relieffe from you as soon as Possable; but I am afraid We air Ruened if they Come on."[25]

No response from Gates. The next day, clearly alarmed, Polk wrote again to the MIA Gates:

> After the unhappy Fate of our Army [following Camden] almost every man took the Liberty of conjectureing what might probably be the Consequence as to this State. With your Approbation I formerly troubled you with my Sentiments on this subject. You must pardon me if my Desire of doing public Service prompts me again to trouble you with Accounts of Danger impending over this country, & submit to you the mode of Relief.
>
> From the present motions of the British Armies, We have nothing less to expect than an Attack on the Western Counties of this State.... Cornwallis is in the line—his Force not yet well known. Coll. Ferguson, with an Army composed of British & Tories have penetrated into one of the Western Counties of this State, and from their mode of march intend to pursue their Rout thro' the Frontiers where their party must increase & probably Overun some of the interior Counties of this District on their Return.

Polk added, as a post-script, "We have had no Relief from Sumner [Sumpter] or Virginia, & believe we shall be reduced to the Necessity of fighting in two or three days, or passively suffer the Enemy to ravage the Country."[26]

Things looked bleak. Gates did nothing. The Mecklenburgers were on their own. Local militia, under Davidson, Davie, Graham and others, organized to resist, but without an American army the war was men against boys. In late September, the British took Charlotte and planned their next move. They seized Polk's mill, among others, and stripped the countryside bare of corn, pigs, cattle, chickens and anything else they could get their hands on. The area, and Polk, were ruined. Gates was also on his way out, but until Congress acted to replace him as commander, and confirm his appointments, other states refused to provide North Carolina with supplies or men. To add insult to Polk's injury, Cornwallis had taken Polk's home and was using it as his headquarters.

With the British encamped in Charlotte, Polk reported to Gates that "the Provision I had laid up in Charlotte was taken by the Enemy. My own Money is entirely expended; am therefore reduced to the Necessity of calling on you for a supply.... My Property is chiefly lost; [I] cannot therefore Venture to extend my Credit."[27]

Things changed drastically the next day, with news that Ferguson's expeditionary force had been killed or captured, to a man, at Kings Mountain, just over forty miles from Charlotte. It was clear that Cornwallis would be forced to withdraw.

"I have the pleasure to inform you that on Saturday last the noted Col. Ferguson with 150 fell on Kings Mountain, 800 taken Prisoners with 1500 Stand of Arms," Polk wrote to the North Carolina Board of War. "A glorious affair. In a few Days doubt not but we will be in Charlotte & I Will take Possession of my house & his Lordship [Cornwallis, shall] take [to] the Woods."[28]

The dramatic and unexpected success at Kings Mountain did not cover up the fact that patriot resistance to the British invasion had been largely a total shambles. The Americans had been routed at Camden; Gates had fled and despite a fighting retreat against overwhelming odds the British had taken Charlotte-Towne with little loss; and there were no supplies to be had.

Someone had to take the blame for these failings, and for a time the clear scapegoat was the commissary, Thomas Polk. Polk, after all, had time and again refused to extend credit for purchases and requested cash from the authorities to make payment.

William Smallwood, a Brigadier General of Maryland continentals, complained to the Board of War that "Colo. Polk refuses to supply any but the regular Troops." He implied that Polk was acting selfishly. Polk, Smallwood wrote, believed those to whom he was selling might have "great difficulty in settling their Accounts, which may eventually involve him."[29] At the same time, Smallwood complained to Gates about a "great Scarcity of Provision. [and] Colo. Polk has not even supplied the regular Troops."[30]

Gates and the Board of War took these complaints seriously. The next month, in a summons dated November 12, 1780, Polk was "directly Ordered to Salisbury to answer his Conduct" before Gates concerning "a number of Suspicious Circumstances respecting [his] Conduct & behavior" in connection with "provisions for the State of No. Carolina, & Commissary of purchases for the Continental Troops."[31]

Polk arrived in Salisbury on November 16. Gates confronted him with Smallwood's complaints against him, alleging "that his conduct was deemed doubtful and suspicious; and requested to know if I [Gates] might depend upon his continuing as Commissary to the Troops." Polk was no doubt infuriated. He told Gates that "since he found his Countrymen suspected his Fidelity; he would no longer act as Commissary." Once Polk had delivered 500 cattle and 1,000 bushels of corn, which he had promised earlier and was now collecting, "it might be understood he resigned his Office."[32] Polk had had enough.

Nathanael Greene took over command of the American forces in the south on December 3, 1780, near Polk's home in Charlotte. Greene had no doubts about Polk's honorable intentions or his qualities refused Polk's resignation. He wrote to Polk on December 15, 1780, and "I find it will be impossible to leave camp as early as I intended.... I must, therefore, beg you to continue the daily supplies of the army, and keep in readiness the three days' provisions beforehand."[33]

The incident passed over, and contemporaries and others later spoke highly of Polk. But is it possible that Smallwood's suspicions about Polk and his loyalties were, in fact, correct? Just how upset was he with his *ungrateful country*? There is one mysterious allusion to this in the papers of Cornwallis.

During the same period when Smallwood was complaining of Polk, with the British encamped in Charlotte, Lord Balfour wrote to Cornwallis on October 1, 1780: "There is a Colonel Paulk of the North Carolina militia. I am desired to assure you [he] is to be got easily and that *he wishes to come in*. He is represented as a man of great influence and living in Charlotte."[34] Was Thomas Polk considering switching sides?

Snow covered graves of Thomas Polk and his wife Susannah in uptown Charlotte (photograph by the author).

There is a hint that this could be the case.

Earlier that summer, on July 12, 1780, Balfour had made another allusion to Cornwallis. "I believe I can establish a good channel for intelligence from this quarter, and at little or no expense, except that of assuring *a man of considerable consequence* that he will have merit with you in getting it."[35] It is not known who Balfour refers to, but Ian Saberton, the editor of the Cornwallis papers believes, "*Balfour had in mind Colonel Thomas Polk*."[36]

Is Saberton right? Was Polk about to turn?

It is possible that Polk sent out feelers to the British, after his fall out with his superiors. *Perhaps* he considered switching sides, and *perhaps* he changed his mind after the battle of Kings Mountain, when British momentum in the south was abruptly halted. We will never know for sure. Whatever the truth, General Greene was satisfied in his investigation, and there the matter lay. After the War, Polk continued to serve in numerous public roles. The General Assembly appointed him to the Council of State in 1783 and 1784. After the War, he entertained Washington and Lafayette at his home. He became a wealthy, prominent and powerful private citizen; the founder of Charlotte, as he was known.

Polk died at his home in January 1794, and he was buried in the town cemetery. His wife, Susannah, lies beside him. The graveyard is almost always in shade, not only because of the old oaks, but largely as a result of the towering urban buildings nearby, which cast long shadows even in midday, over the first settlers, and the contradictory founder of Charlotte himself.

5

Charlotte's Paul Revere: Captain James Jack and the Mecklenburg Declaration of Independence

> "Gentlemen, you may debate here about 'reconciliations' and memorialize your king, but, bear it in mind, Mecklenburg owes no allegiance to, and is separated from the crown of Great Britain forever."
> —Captain James Jack, as quoted in Hunter's "Sketches" (1877)

The ancient Greek poet Archilochus observed, "a fox knows many things, but a hedgehog knows *one big thing*." So it is with Captain James Jack, for in the history of Mecklenburg County he is known for one thing and one thing only, but it is a very big thing indeed. For Jack was the messenger who, in the summer of 1775, delivered the Mecklenburg Declaration of Independence to the Second Continental Congress in Philadelphia.

The Mecklenburg Declaration (or "MecDec" as it's known) was, for many decades, the most important historical commemoration in North Carolina. In many ways, it gave the state a distinct identity. The date of its adoption (May 20, 1775) was put on the North Carolina state flag, where, to the bemusement of some, it remains to this day. MecDec Day was once a city and county holiday, and four sitting American Presidents (Taft, Wilson, Eisenhower and Ford) travelled to Charlotte to celebrate it. The fact that the original papers were later lost did nothing to diminish North Carolinians enthusiasm for the MecDec story. Nor, for that matter, did the fact that Thomas Jefferson later called the entire episode "spurious." If the story of Captain Jack valiantly riding to Philadelphia to deliver the "first" American declaration of independence was not true, well, it should be. It was too good not to be.

The Solitary Rider

The solitary rider, bringing word of impending menace, is a Jungian archetype of the American Revolution, and, as such, a part of our collective historical memory. The most famous of course is Paul Revere, his familiar silhouette at dusk, candle-lit lantern in hand, delivering word that *the British were coming*. The poem "Paul Revere's Ride" by Longfellow crystallized the mood and launched the Revere legend:

> So through the night rode Paul Revere;
> And so through the night went his cry of alarm
> To every Middlesex village and farm,
> A cry of defiance, and not of fear,
> A voice in the darkness, a knock at the door,
> And a word that shall echo forevermore!
> For, borne on the night-wind of the Past,
> Through all our history, to the last,
> In the hour of darkness and peril and need,
> The people will waken and listen to hear
> The hurrying hoof-beats of that steed,
> And the midnight message of Paul Revere.

It was a legend grander than reality, however. In the first place, Revere was captured by the British and his ride aborted. In addition, he was only one of many Massachusetts riders who went out on the night of April 18, 1775, warning colonists about troop movements. Others, now largely forgotten, were Samuel Prescott, Israel Bissell, William Dawes, and—a woman—Sybil Ludington. Paul Revere had something they lacked however: an excellent publicist in Longfellow.

Still, despite some arguable historical blemishes, Revere's image of a selfless messenger risking his life for the patriotic good of his country, captured something essential and vital. As with Paul Revere, Captain Jack seemed to represent the bravest and best of us, the Paul Revere of the south, as Jack was later called.

"A Declaration of their Independence, which was unanimously adopted"

The story of Captain Jack begins with yet another horse-messenger, but this one is anonymous. Sometime on Thursday, May 19, 1775, an express rider arrived in the muddy, cross-roads backcountry trading town of Charlotte. In the center of town, in the town commons, was the Mecklenburg County Courthouse. That afternoon, the county's local militia leaders were meeting to discuss the deteriorating state of affairs in the American colonies.

By the spring of 1775, the American colonies were, in the words of one British official, in a "state of general frenzy."[1] The purpose of the meeting that day, as one participant later put it, was "devise ways & means to extricate themselves and ward off the dreadful impending storm bursting on them by the British Nation."[2]

Taxation without representation was the issue of the day. For those in Mecklenburg, however, their grievances went beyond that. They were largely Scots-Irish and Presbyterian, which was considered a deeply seditious, Republican and alien religion by the British Anglican authorities.

The express rider delivered a distressing message to the assembled delegates. American colonists had been fired upon by British regulars at Lexington and Concord, Massachusetts. The long anticipated revolution had begun.

The effect on the meeting was electric. According to one eye-witness, Joseph Graham, when news of "the Battle of Lexington, the 19th of April preceding [was delivered] ... There appeared among the people much excitement."[3] Another participant, John McKnitt Alexander, recalled in more vivid terms: "We *smelt* and *felt the Blood* & carnage of Lexington, which raised all the passions into *fury* and *revenge*."[4]

In the meetings that followed, over the course of May 19 and 20, the civic leaders of Mecklenburg debated and adopted a series of anti-British resolutions. Several eye-witnesses accounts, such as Graham, describe what happened next:

> After reading a number of papers as usual, and much animated discussion, the question was taken, and they resolved to declare themselves independent. One among other reasons offered, that the King or Ministry had, by proclamation or some edict, declared the Colonies out of the protection of the British Crown; they ought, therefore, to declare themselves out of his protection, and resolve on independence.[5]

Another witness, Isaac Alexander, recalled:

> I was present in Charlotte on the 19th and 20th days of May, 1775, when a regular deputation from all the Captains' companies of militia in the county of Mecklenburg ... met to consult and take measures for the peace and tranquility of the citizens of said county, and who appointed Abraham Alexander their Chairman, and Doctor Ephraim Brevard Secretary; who, after due consultation, declared themselves absolved from their allegiance to the King of Great Britain, and drew up a Declaration of their Independence, which was unanimously adopted.[6]

As Graham put it:

> It was unanimously adopted, and shortly after it was moved and seconded to have [the] proclamation made and the people collected, that the proceedings be read at the court house door, in order that all might hear them. It was done, and they were received with enthusiasm. It was then proposed by some one aloud to give three cheers and throw up their hats. It was immediately adopted, and the hats thrown. Several of them lit on

the court house roof. The owners had some difficulty to reclaim them. The foregoing is all from personal knowledge.[7]

This episode became known as the Mecklenburg Declaration of Independence. According to many later accounts, the county declared itself "free and independent" of the British Crown, which, if true, was an astonishing development as it occurred over a year before the National Declaration of July 4, 1776.

Exactly *what* resolutions were adopted has been much debated (for two hundred-plus years, in fact) and can at this late date never be proven to the satisfaction of everyone. Nonetheless, it is beyond debate that they were anti-English, treasonable and sufficiently important that the delegates decided that the Mecklenburg resolutions were to be delivered to Congress, post-haste.

The original papers were later lost in a fire at the home of McKnitt Alexander, keeper of the records, in April 1800. Therefore it is impossible to know exactly what was resolved in Mecklenburg that May. Later historians would disparage the entire story, saying it arose from the aged and confused mind of McKnitt Alexander, or was simply a hoax. Presidents John Adams and Thomas Jefferson would famously debate one another about the story's authenticity (the former calling it "the genuine sense of America," the latter, that it was "spurious").

With the involvement of Jefferson and Adams, the MecDec story engendered a national controversy entirely out of proportion to its historical importance, even if the story were true. And because even its most ardent supports conceded that the original papers were irretrievably lost, the story could not ever be decisively proven. Regardless, it had a richer, more symbolic importance.

A small, poor and isolated rural community had unilaterally seceded from the largest imperial power in the world. In the words of commentator George Will, "Thus did a settlement on the fringe of the British Empire declare war on that Empire."[8]

But declaring war was in a sense the easy part. Now the war actually had to be fought. No doubt many in Mecklenburg, following the rash days of May 20, must have gulped and thought, *Now what do we do?* And that is where Captain Jack comes in.

The Ride of Captain Jack

In May 1775, Jack was forty-four years old. The Jack surname may have derived from *Jacques*, a common family name of French Huguenots, many of whom came to Scotland and Ireland in the 1600s. The Jack family was just one of many impoverished Scots-Irish refugees who found their way to the

New World during the mass migrations in the first quarter of the eighteenth century. High taxes, poverty and religious oppression drove tens of thousands across the Atlantic. Indeed, so many flooded into Pennsylvania during this time that one observer noted, "it looks as if Ireland is to send all its inhabitants hither."[9]

Nor did they receive a warm welcome. The English, of course, despised them, but so did other minorities, such as the Baptists and Quakers. By common consent they were quarrelsome, aggressive, smelly and violent. One Anglican minister described them as: "Ignorant, mean, worthless, beggarly Irish Presbyterians … the Scum of the Earth, and Refuse of Mankind."[10]

James was born in 1731 probably in the Lancaster area of Pennsylvania, where the family had settled after departing Ireland around 1730. He was the eldest of nine children. Although he is now known as "Captain Jack" due to his rank in the county militia, in 1775 he would have been simply James, Jim or even Jimmy.

His grandfather may have been a dissenting minister, removed from his benefice due to "nonconformity to the Church of England."[11] If true, this would put Jack in good company with many future settlers to the Carolina Piedmont, who considered anti-Anglicanism as part of their DNA. His father, Patrick Jack, Jr., had been born in Ballykelly, County Derry, Ireland, on September 19, 1700. His mother, Lillis (or Lillie) McAdoo, was born in Ireland in 1714. They married when she was just 16 years old, which was not uncommon at the time. Lili was later described by some who knew her as "one of the best of women," amiable, charitable and pious.[12]

We know that around 1760, Patrick and Lili were settled in a Presbyterian community west of Salisbury called Thyatira. All that remains of it now is an evocative cemetery at a church of the same name. In November 1766, James married Margaret Houston, and in 1772 the family moved to Charlotte.[13] There, the Jack family owned and operated a tavern, known as Pat Jack's, a few hundred yards west of the county courthouse.

In 1772, the town of Charlotte consisted of little more than a dozen or so log cabins near an Indian trading path, surrounded on all sides by thick and ancient forest. The same year that the Jack family started their tavern, one surveyor passing through gave the following account: "The town has a tolerable Court-House of wood about 80 by 40 feet, and a Gaol [jail], a store, a tavern, and several other houses say 5 or 6, but very ordinary build of logs."[14] A few years later a caustic lawyer from South Carolina had a more critical view of Charlotte, writing: "This place does not deserve the name of a town," as the village "consists only of a wretched courthouse, and a few dwellings falling to decay." And of course the most famous visitor to Charlotte, President George Washington, was to sum up the scrappy village in three infamous words: "a trifling place."[15]

Trifling, perhaps, but it consisted of some angry, prickly and motivated citizens; citizens outraged by the increasing aggressiveness of the British government and prepared to do something about it, as events in May 1775 would demonstrate.

Jack himself was not a leading participant in the meetings that resulted in the Mecklenburg Declaration, which is ironic given that no one is now more commonly associated with that story.

Following the meetings in the county courthouse in May and the adoption of various anti–British resolutions, it seems that the people in the area were divided as to their next course of action. Indeed, there are some indications that they began to have second thoughts entirely, and described their actions as "rash." So a few days later, recalled McKnitt Alexander, "a considerable part of [the] Committee Men convened" to decide what to do next.[16]

The logical course of action was to send their resolutions to their elected delegates in Congress and ask for their approval and advice. The more militant delegates might even have hoped that their actions would compel Congress to move immediately towards a national declaration of independence.

Whatever their intentions, they agreed to send a messenger "to go express to Congress (then in Philadelphia) with a copy of all S^d. resolutions and laws &c and a letter to our 3 members there, $Rich^d$. Caswell, W^m. Hooper & Joseph Hughes, in order to get Congress to sanction or *approve* them."[17] The "3 members" were North Carolina's delegates to the Second Continental Congress: Richard Caswell, William Hooper and Joseph Hughes.

As Jack later put it, he was "solicited to be the bearer of the proceedings to Congress."[18] Exactly why he was chosen has been the subject of much subsequent speculation, but the truth is no one really knows. Clearly Jack was sympathetic to their cause, and considered trustworthy, or he would not have been chosen for such a dangerous errand. As a tavern owner, he might have been familiar with the road to Philadelphia and perhaps had traveled it often enough that his presence would not arouse suspicions.

Whatever the reason, Jack agreed to ride to Philadelphia and deliver the Mecklenburg papers. This is confirmed by numerous accounts of the period such as this one: "a few days after the Delegates adjourned, Captain James Jack, of the town of Charlotte, was engaged to carry the resolves to the President of Congress, and to our Representatives—one copy for each."[19]

According to Jack, "I set out the following month, say June."[20] The distance to Philadelphia was approximately 1,100 miles. It is estimated that he could have covered about 50 miles a day if the weather was good. The weather that summer was stormy, as journals of the Moravians attest. "There has recently been much rain," the entry for June 7, 1775, states. "Last night there was a very hard rain; about noon today the sun came out and it was oppressively

Captain Jack, known as "Charlotte's Paul Revere," riding north to deliver the Mecklenburg Declaration of Independence to the Second Continental Congress (courtesy Chas Fagan).

hot, but about sunset there were more storms, and it rained heavily for three hours."[21]

The road Jack would have travelled to Philadelphia was known as the Great Wagon Road (or sometimes called the *Philadelphia Road*). At the time it was the main artery of travel along the East Coast. Some accounts suggest that Jack first stopped in Salisbury, roughly forty miles from Charlotte. Jack himself reports: "In passing through Salisbury, the General Court was sitting. At the request of the court I handed a copy of the resolutions to Col. Kennon, an Attorney, and they were read aloud in open court." The following evening, Major William Davidson and Waightstill Avery called on Jack at his lodgings, "and observed, they had heard of but one person, (a Mr. Beard) but approved of them."[22] Court records of the period do not show any evidence of this, but there is no reason to disbelieve Jack's story.

From Salisbury, the Great Wagon Road crossed the Yadkin River at a place known as the Trading Ford. From there, the road continued on through the flat Piedmont countryside. The largest settlements in the area were those of the Moravians, in small hamlets named Bethania and Bethabara in what was called the Wachovia tract (near present Winston-Salem, North Carolina).

After the Moravian settlements, the Wagon Road crossed the Dan River in Virginia, turned west to cross a gap in the Blue Ridge Mountains, then ran northeast towards Staunton. Jack's path continued through the Blue Ridge, passing through much Indian country, before reaching a series of scattered Quaker farms and Irish mud and daub houses, places then known as the "Irish Tract" or the "Quaker Meeting place." Jack's ride continued through the rolling hills near Winchester, Virginia, then into land familiar to him, York and Lancaster, Pennsylvania, from whence the Jack family had moved a few decades before, and where many of their kin still lived. Next stop: Philadelphia.

It is estimated that it would have taken Jack ten to twelve days to complete the journey from Charlotte to Philadelphia. Factoring in the weather, and perhaps a great motivation to get there quickly with his urgent message, it might have been as quick as a week. Since we can date his return trip as July 7, and he states that he left in June, the best guess is that it took Jack approximately two weeks.

As one later historian put it, Jack's ride was "long, lonesome and perilous."[23] Had he been stopped and searched by loyalists or British soldiers, the papers he carried would have been a death warrant. And although Jack probably did not know this, spies or informers had in fact made the British aware of his mission. In August 1775, for example, Royal Governor Josiah Martin sent the following letter to his superior in London, the Earl of Dartmouth.

> The Resolves of the Committee of Mecklenburgh, which your Lordship will find in the enclosed Newspaper, surpass all the horrid and treasonable publications that the inflammatory spirits of this Continent have yet produced, and your Lordship may depend its Authors and Abettors will not escape my due notice, whenever my hands are sufficiently strengthened to attempt the recovery of the lost authority of Government. *A copy of these Resolves I am informed were sent off by express to the Congress at Philadelphia as soon as they were passed in the Committee.*[24]

The "enclosed newspaper" referenced in this letter has never been found (which is quite another story, and a good one at that), but be that as it may, the fact that as early as August, Jack's papers were already characterized at a very high level of the British government as "treasonable" is of great interest. It also decimates the argument, made by many nineteenth century historians, that whatever resolutions were passed in Mecklenburg in May 1775 were of no consequence. The British certainly thought otherwise.

Many years later, a handful of eye-witnesses gave corroborating testimony that Jack had been seen in Philadelphia. For example, in 1830 several witnesses recalled that they had "frequently" heard William Alexander, who was then deceased, say that he was in Philadelphia "on mercantile business, in the early part of the summer of 1775, say in June," and that on the same day that "Gen. Washington left Philadelphia to take command of the Northern army," (June 23) he "met with Capt. James Jack, who informed him" that he had been sent on behalf of the Committee of Safety in Mecklenburg "as the agent or bearer of the Declaration of Independence made in Charlotte, on the twentieth of May [1775] by the citizens of Mecklenburg." Alexander said that Jack had told him that he had been given "instructions to present the same to the Delegates from North Carolina."[25] Beyond this testimony, however, we don't know much about when Jack arrived, whom he spoke with, or how his meetings went.

The Moravian journals do allow us to pinpoint the date of Jack's return from Philadelphia. On July 7, 1775, the Moravian diary records: "This afternoon a man from Mecklenburg, who had been sent from there *Express* to the Congress in Philadelphia, and was now returning, brought a circular, addressed to *Mr. Traugott Bagge*."[26] Bagge was a leading merchant amongst the Moravians, and the "circular" being delivered was an open letter from North Carolina's delegates (Caswell, Hooper and Hughes) proving that Jack had met with them. Although the name of the rider is not given, the circumstantial evidence that it is Jack is beyond refute. A footnote in the *Records of the Moravians* sums it up perfectly: "Undoubtedly Captain Jack."[27]

Jack's own account of that summer, given in 1819, is tantalizing minimalist, less than a page long in total. It begins:

> Having seen in the newspapers some pieces respecting the Declaration of Independence by the people of Mecklenburg county, in the State of North Carolina, in May, 1775, and being solicited to state what I know of that transaction; I would obverse, that for some time previous to, and at the time those resolutions were agreed upon, I resided in the town of Charlotte, Mecklenburg county; was privy to a number of meetings of some of the most influential and leading characters of that county on the subject, before the final adoption of the resolutions—and at the time they were adopted....
>
> When the resolutions were finally agreed on, they were publicly proclaimed from the court-house door in the town of Charlotte, and received with every demonstration of joy by the inhabitants.[28]

Other than the brief passage where Jack describes reading the Mecklenburg Declaration aloud in open court in Salisbury (noted earlier), Jack gives no details on the ride itself, where he went, how long it took, or what the document itself said.

And of the most critical part of the story, his arrival and meeting with the North Carolina delegates, all he tells us is this: "I then proceeded on to Philadelphia, and delivered the Mecklenburg Declaration of Independence of May, 1775, to Richard Caswell and William Hooper, the Delegates to Congress from the State of North Carolina."[29]

Conspicuously absent from that sentence is Joseph Hughes, who was the third N.C. delegate. Jack also says he "delivered" the document, but he does not state that he met with the delegates, advocated for its adoption, or even for that matter spoke with them at all. The silence is pregnant.

Jack's short testimony quoted above is all he is known to have ever written about his famous ride.

The ensuring controversy about the veracity of the Mecklenburg Declaration can be summed up with this question: *What papers was Jack carrying?*

Jack himself was in no doubt, stating unequivocally that he carried the Mecklenburg Declaration among the "proceedings." Later historians were not so sure, arguing that since the only papers extant from the period were a series of twenty resolutions from "Charlotte-Towne" dated May 31, 1775 (and known as the Mecklenburg *Resolves*), that Jack must have been carrying these, and gotten these true (and uncontested) resolutions confused with a fictional "Declaration." Many other historians have continued this line of argument, which remains unresolved to this day. Since Jack doesn't give us the exact text of the resolutions, nor seemingly kept a copy, the argument is unresolvable.

According to perhaps the best eye-witness in the entire story, John McKnitt Alexander, Jack carried "a copy of all S[ai]ᵈ resolutions and laws &c" as well as a "a letter to our 3 members there [in Philadelphia]."[30] McKnitt Alexander believed that "all S[ai]ᵈ resolutions and laws" *meant* the Mecklenburg Declaration, not the Mecklenburg Resolves. The latter document, it is argued, is what McKnitt Alexander meant by his catch-all concluding expression, "*and laws &c.*"

The sad fact is that beyond Jack's brief account, the corroborating (second hand) testimony of those who claimed to have seen him in Philadelphia, and the (unnamed) reference to his return ride in July 1775 in the Moravian diaries, we don't know anything else about the ride of Captain Jack. Critics of the story go a step further, pointing out that not only is there no direct evidence, but that *the absence of evidence* tells its own story. That absence of evidence includes no reference to Jack's arrival in Philadelphia in the records of the Second Continental Congress; no reference to Jack in the letters and papers of Representatives Caswell or Hooper; not even a bar bill. The historical record presents an almost complete evidentiary vacuum.

That vacuum was filled, as scientists tell us vacuums are inclined to be, by the historian Cyrus Hunter who gave a full account of Jack's story in *Sketches of Western North Carolina*, albeit a century after the fact. Where Hunter got this account is not clear, as Jack and all of his contemporaries were dead by the time he wrote it. But giving Hunter the benefit of the doubt, he was memorializing the local legend of those in Mecklenburg familiar with the story. Hunter's account of Jack's meeting in Philadelphia with the Congressional delegates went as follows:

> Upon his arrival [Captain Jack] immediately obtained an interview with the North Carolina delegates (Caswell, Hooper and Hewes [sic]), and, after a little conversation on the state of the country, then agitating all minds, Captain Jack drew from his pocket the Mecklenburg resolutions of the 20th of May, 1775, with the remark: "Here, gentlemen, is a paper that I have been instructed to deliver to you, with the request that you should lay the same before Congress."
>
> After the North Carolina delegates had carefully read the Mecklenburg resolutions, and approved of their patriotic sentiments so forcibly expressed, they informed Captain Jack they would keep the paper, and show it to several of their friends, remarking, at the same time, they did not think Congress was then prepared to act upon so important a measure as *absolute independence*.
>
> On the next day, Captain Jack had another interview with the North Carolina delegates. They informed him that they had consulted with several members of Congress, (including Hancock, Jay and Jefferson,) and that all agreed, while they approved of the patriotic spirit of the Mecklenburg resolutions, it would be premature to lay them officially before the House, as they still entertained some hopes of reconciliation with England.
>
> It was clearly perceived by the North Carolina delegates and other members whom they consulted, that the citizens of Mecklenburg county were *in advance* of the general sentiment of Congress on the subject of independence; the phantasy of "reconciliation" still held forth its seductive allurements in 1775, and even during a portion of 1776; and hence, no record was made, or vote taken on the patriotic resolutions of Mecklenburg, and they became concealed from view in the blaze of the National Declaration bursting forth on the 4th of July, 1776, which only re-echoed and reaffirmed the truth and potency of sentiments proclaimed in Charlotte on the 20th of May, 1775.
>
> Captain Jack finding the darling object of his long and toilsome journey could not be then accomplished, and that Congress was not prepared to vote on so bold a measure as *absolute independence*, just before leaving Philadelphia for home, somewhat excited, addressed the North Carolina delegates, and several other members of Congress, in the following patriotic words: "*Gentlemen, you may debate here about 'reconciliations' and memorialize your king, but, bear it in mind, Mecklenburg owes no allegiance to, and is separated from the crown of Great Britain forever.*"[31]

In a sense, Hunter was doing for James Jack what Longworth and his poem had done for Paul Revere, although in Longfellow's case there was no pretense that what he was doing was writing history. Ironically, of course, Longfellow was doing exactly that—*his own* preferred history.

That being said, and to be fair to Hunter, his work was entitled "Sketches," which was a form of historiographical *caveat emptor*. The fact that Hunter's account contradicts Jack's in a few places, such as who he says Jack met with (Hunter says he met with all three N.C. delegates; Jack says he only met with two), says a great deal. And of course there is the fact that Hunter's vivid account is given one hundred years later.

But no matter. What Jack said or did not say to Caswell and Hooper, the absence of proof in the Congressional records, the lost papers, all of this is only of secondary importance, given the outcome of the story.

For in the end, the N.C. congressional delegates failed to promote or take any action on the Mecklenburg resolutions. They concluded that Mecklenburg's actions had been "premature." As the papers of McKnitt Alexander describe it, "Captn. Jack returned" to Charlotte carrying a "long, full, complasent letter from [the] 3 members"—Caswell, Hooper and Hughes—"recommending our *zeal, perseverance, order & forbearance.*"[32] But "Congress never had our S[ai]^d. laws on their table for discussion, though [a] copy was left with them by Captn. Jack."[33] If the purpose of Jack's mission was to rouse Congress to declare independence, then that mission ended in failure, just as Revere's mission ended in ignominious capture by the British.

Failure, yes, but whose? Surely not the patriots of Mecklenburg who took action to liberate first themselves, and by example the country? Nor Jack's failure, as he successfully completed his errand and delivered the document? The failure, then, must have been that of North Carolina's delegates, who through prudence or timidity, failed to take any actions, and indeed thereafter shushed up the entire story.

Statue of Captain James Jack on the Little Sugar Creek Greenway in Charlotte. Was he carrying the Mecklenburg Declaration or is the story a myth? (photograph by the author).

John Adams and Thomas Jefferson both reached this conclusion, although in entirely different ways. As Adams put it in a letter to a friend on July 15, 1819, the Mecklenburg Declaration's "total concealment from me is a mystery, which can be unriddled only by the timidity of the delegates in Congress from North Carolina."³⁴ Jefferson corroborated this explanation: "You remember as well as I do," he wrote Adams in July 1819, "that we had not a greater Tory in Congress than Hooper" and "that Hughes was very wavering, sometimes firm, sometimes feeble, according as the day was clear or cloudy."³⁵

How else could these resolutions, which the British themselves called "horrid and treasonable," have remained entirely silent, except for the malfeasance of the politicians? The failure of Jack's ride must be laid at their feet.

"The claim to him was lost"

Captain James Jack died on the Jack Plantation in Elbert County, Georgia on December 18, 1822. He was eighty-four years old. Today it is not known where the Jack Planation was located, or even for that matter where Jack himself lies buried. Jack's obituary in the *Raleigh Register* noted:

> He was born in the State of Pennsylvania, from whence he removed to North Carolina and settled in the town of Charlotte, where he remained till the end of the Revolutionary War, in which he took a decided and active part from the commencement to the close, after which he removed to Georgia with his family, whom he supported by the sweat of his brow. He spent the prime of his life and his little all in the glorious struggle for independence, and enjoyed it with a heart warmed with gratitude to the God of battles. In the spring of '75 he was the bearer of the Mecklenburg Declaration of Independence to Congress.

His epilogue further noted that Jack was entitled to a revolutionary pension worth £7,646 pounds, but, "[t]hose papers being of little value at that time, he left them in the hands of a friend, who dying some years after, the claim to him was lost." These important papers, which meant financial security for Jack and his family, went missing, and had fallen "possibly, into the hands of some speculator, who may by now faring sumptuously on the fruits of [Jack's] toil." It was a fitting epitaph, albeit a bitterly ironical one, given that Captain Jack had again been cheated by others, the papers lost, the historical record uncorrected.

Nevertheless, it concluded, "Some few of his old comrades who bore the burden and the heat of the day are still living. Should this notice catch the eye of any one of them, it may draw forth a sigh or elicit a tear to the memory of their friend, more to be valued than a marble monument."

Jack got a monument anyway. Today, an equestrian statue of Captain Jack, horse turning at a gallop, north, towards Philadelphia, stands near Central Piedmont Community College in central Charlotte. It is over twelve feet tall and made of 3,000 pounds of sandy-gray bronze. So perhaps Jack had the last laugh, the politicians, crooks and missing papers notwithstanding.

6

Freedom for Slaves: Ishmael Titus and African Americans in the American Revolution

"After the year was expired for which I was to have my freedom, I enlisted into the Army."

—Ishmael Titus, 1832

On October 10, 1832, an elderly African American named Ishmael Titus appeared in the courtroom of Probate Judge William P. Walker, in Williamstown, a small village in the northwest corner of Massachusetts. As he entered Judge Walker's courtroom Titus was, or at least he believed he was, eighty-nine years old. His voice still carried the lilt of southern Virginia, where he had born (although it was impossible to know for certain) eighty-nine years earlier. According to one who knew him, Titus had a "large wen" (that is, a growth or boil of some kind, or possibly a tumor) on his neck.[1] "His mind seemed more than a match for his body," another said of the old man, "[although] physical infirmities crept upon him...."[2]

Williamstown was then, and is today, the home of Williams College. The college had been founded in 1793 with one small building and a mere eighteen students. Other than the college faculty and students, Williamstown was a farming town, set amidst the rolling hills of New England. The writer Nathaniel Hawthorne described the town in 1838 as "a white village and steeple in a gradual hollow, with high mountainous swells heaving themselves up, like immense, subsiding waves, far and wide around it." It was a sleepy, quiet and civilized place to live, amid the autumnal pines and gentle New England brooks.

Titus had lived in the area for fifteen years, but not in Williamstown proper, but rather an area north of town, called White Oaks. He lived in a house near

Broad Brook, which locals called the "Cato Place." His son, Harvey Titus, lived nearby, as did Abraham Parsons, the brother-in-law of George Washington.[3]

Land was cheap in White Oaks, and could be squatted on "with impunity," it was said.[4] The more upstanding locals complained that it "was easy for fugitives from debt and from petty crimes to find a refuge" in White Oaks, where "concealment and permanent harborage" of criminals was common. It was a rough area, on the wrong side of the railroad tracks, where "begging in the street, and thieving everywhere, became hereditary features in a number of families." The area was thus a favorite of petty criminals, prostitutes—and escaped slaves.

Titus was in court that day to apply for a pension from the federal government, to which he was entitled as a result of his Revolutionary War military service. On June 7, 1832, Congress enacted sweeping legislation providing greater benefits to veterans (such as full pay) than previous bills had done. Each applicant was required to attest under oath to the details of his military service. In return, officers and enlisted men who served at least two years in the Continental Line (as well as militia or the navy) were eligible for full pay for life. (Those who served less than two years, were still eligible, but for less than full pay.) The 1832 legislation was the first opportunity for those, like Titus, who had served in the militia to apply for benefits. Previous laws required soldiers or sailors to have served in the federal army or navy to be eligible (*not* the local militia, although it was often they who bore the brunt of the fighting, especially in the Southern campaigns).[5]

As part of his sworn testimony, Titus stated that he was willing to forego any other pension that might be owed to him, saying "he hereby relinquishes every claim whatever to a pension or annuity, except the present, and declares that his name is not on the pension roll of the agency of any State."

In common with many other veterans of the Revolution, after the passage of fifty years, it was difficult for Titus to give specific and detailed testimony. His knowledge of his past was very sketchy. It's not that his memory was bad; one observer later in life noted that Titus' "mental faculties were remarkably active for a person of years, and [even] after the lapse of nearly a century, he was wont to recount the striking impression made upon his young mind by the red costs of the British soldiers, which he supposed were 'colored with blood.'"[6]

His memory he retained; it was the basic facts that failed him. He knew that he had been born "in the County then called Amelia," southwest of Richmond, Virginia, "below Lunenberg," thirty or so miles north of the North Carolina border. He said he had served with, and had known, all the leading American commanders: Greene, Cleveland, Gates. He could not, however, give the date of his birth with any specificity, nor identify his parents. Also, observed the court, he "has no record of his age." Similarly, noted the court,

Titus "has no documentary evidence of his services & knows of no person whose testimony he can procure to testify to his services."

Nevertheless he told the court that he had been a private in the American army, and had fought against the British in several bloody engagements: among them, Guilford Courthouse and Kings Mountain.

But, he admitted, he could not, "by reason of old age and the consequent loss of memory swear when the battles" took place. He was forced to search through history books for validation of his memories. In them, he said, he found "from the History of the Revolution that the Battle of Kings Mountain was fought in October 1780 and that Colonel Cleveland commanded." He also discovered that "the Battle at Guilford was fought in March 1781," which, he said, "I was at."[7]

"I was also at Gates' Defeat [the Battle of Camden]," Titus told Judge Walker, but "did not arrive there till the American Army began to retreat." The battle, he said, "I find from the History was fought in August 1780. I was one of the number who retreated to Salisbury."

The reason Titus had no memory of his early life, no basic knowledge of the facts of his own provenance, or existence, the reason he was forced to consult the history books to know where and when the major incidents of his life had taken place, was quite simple. He knew little about his past, he told the court, due to "His ignorance being brought up as a slave."

The Moral Calculus

"How is it that we hear the loudest yelps for liberty among the drivers of Negroes?" Samuel Johnson, the English writer and wit famously and caustically asked in 1775. It was a good question at the time, and even today it's difficult to articulate a good answer, other than the fact that until it was abandoned by Great Britain in 1732, slavery was common throughout the civilized world. Bondage in various ways existed virtually everywhere. The British continued slavery in the sugar islands of the Caribbean under the fiction of "apprenticeship" even after 1732. By some estimates, as many as half of all white European settlers in America during colonial times were indentured servants—slaves in every way except that they received their freedom at the end of a fixed time. And colonial apprenticeship was, in many respects, indistinguishable from slavery except that upon reaching the age of majority (21 for boys, 18 for girls) they received clothing and perhaps tools or money. Imperial Russia continued serfdom until well into the nineteenth century, and so on. Still, the promise of America (and of the American Revolution) was that it was different and better than the tyrannies of the past. Thus the inherent schizophrenia in the American character on racial issues during the

Revolutionary period. That is, an extreme, and radical passion for individual liberty, existing alongside a pragmatic, wide scale acceptance of enslaving other human beings. The contradiction remains mystifying to this day.

There were approximately 450,000 enslaved African Americans in the thirteen American colonies at the time the American Revolution began. It is difficult to know how many were in the province of North Carolina. Slavery in North Carolina was less widespread then in neighboring Virginia or South Carolina, in large part due to the relative lack of commercial development of the coastal plantations, dangerous coastlines and unnavigable rivers. Governor William Tryon, shortly after arriving in the colony in 1765, observed that "The Negroes are very numerous I suppose five to one White Person[s] in the Maritime Counties, but as you penetrate into the Country few blacks are employed...."[8] The 1790 census reported 100,572 slaves in the state, representing approximately twenty-five percent of the total population.

As Tryon observed, in the Carolina backcountry such as Mecklenburg and Rowan counties, slavery was less common than it was on the coast. It was not, however, non-existent. On April 17, 1773, the Mecklenburg County court minutes show that Elizabeth Penny transferred to William Penny "one negro woman named Findou, one negroe boy named Jacob & one Negro boy named Bob."[9] Similarly, the well-known local patriot Tom Polk had a slave he called "Negroe Joe" and in October 1773 was recorded to have purchased another "negro man named Dick" from John Anderson.[10] But Polk was a wealthy merchant. Other instances of buying and selling slaves are relatively rare in the local records of the period. The Carolina Piedmont was quite rural and relatively poor, and slave owning, while an accepted practice, was not widespread. Indeed, prior to the cultivation of upland cotton caused by Whitney's invention of the cotton gin, black slavery was not profitable on a large scale except on the coast where rice could be grown. In 1800, before the introduction of cotton culture in Mecklenburg County, only one-third of householders owned a slave. And two-thirds of those owned one to three slaves.

The Revolution in the Carolina backcountry began in May 1775. A military government was formed in Mecklenburg County, which rounded up and expelled known loyalists; procured arms and gunpowder for forthcoming military actions; and demanded an oath of loyalty from all local citizens. Battle lines were drawn between Whigs and Tories throughout the American colonies. African Americans in the American South posed a real conundrum for the Whig leaders. After all, how did the perpetuation of slavery square with the supposedly just war to secure the "freedom and independence" of the American colonists?

At first, the Continental Congress was hesitant to permit the widespread use of African Americans in the army, although General Washington allowed the enlistment of free blacks who had prior military experience in January 1776. By early January 1777, with manpower scarce, free blacks were allowed to enlist.

Many African Americans, some free, others enslaved, fought on the American side. Indeed, in a sense the first casualty of the American Revolution was an African American: Crispus Attucks, killed in the Boston Massacre on March 5, 1770. Another African American, a slave named Prince Estabrook was wounded by British gunfire at Concord (Lemuel Hayes, a black Congregationalist minister, also fought at Concord.)

In Rhode Island, the legislature provided in February 1778 that "every able-bodied Negro, mulatto, or Indian man-slave" could enlist. Two years later, a regiment of white and black soldiers, 450 men in total named the Rhode Island Regiment was formed. In August 1790, muster rolls for the Continental army show 755 blacks: 58 of them were from North Carolina (although whether slaves of free blacks, is not known).[11] Another African American unit called the "Boston's Bucks of America," led by George Middleton, served as local guard for the city, protecting property and keeping order. According to one historian:

> North Carolina's most famous black soldier was John Chavis, who spent three years in the Fifth Virginia Regiment. After the war, he won fame as a Presbyterian minister and teacher of both black and white students in Raleigh. In 1832 he declared, "Tell them that if I am Black I am free born American & a revolutionary soldier & therefore ought not to be thrown [e]ntirely out of the scale of notice."[12]

By some estimates, 5,000 African American soldiers fought in the various services for the American cause. Their stories, motivations and enthusiasms vary greatly. For example, Peter Salem was one of twenty or so African American soldiers at the Battle of Bunker Hill and is credited with killing Scottish Marine Major John Pitcairn in the battle. Some believe it is African American Prince Whipple portrayed third from left in the bow, fending off ice floes, just to the right of General Washington, in the famous painting "Washington Crossing the Delaware" by Emanuel Leutze. Then there was the fabulously and historically named Oliver Cromwell, who fought with George Washington at the Battles of Trenton, Princeton and Brandywine. Dozens of other examples could be cited, including many similar stories in North Carolina.

The American cause, whatever it's other appeals, did not of course provide an answer to the issue of slavery, nor was it intended to. James Madison, among others, recognized the dilemma, asking, "would it not be as well to liberate and make soldiers at once of the blacks themselves as to make them instruments for enlisting white Soldiers?" Stating what now seems the obvious, Madison pointed out that it would "certainly be more consonant to the

African Americans fought on both sides in the American Revolution, drawn by competing ideas of freedom. Some believe it is African American Prince Whipple portrayed third from left in the bow, just to the right of General Washington, in Emanuel Leutze's painting "Washington Crossing the Delaware" (1851). Oil on canvas, 149 × 255 in. (courtesy Metropolitan Museum of Art, gift of John Stewart Kennedy, 1897).

principles of liberty which ought never to be lost sight of in a contest for liberty...."[13]

In fact, the moral dilemma of the use of slaves in a war allegedly for "freedom and independence" was laughable to the British, as Johnson's quote above showed. It only underscored the hypocrisy and duplicity of the American cause, which was little more than an ungrateful rebellion of a child against its parents.

African America slaves, whether armed or not, could however serve a direct military purpose, as the British were aware. The idea of slave uprisings in the south brought terror to the Americans. Joseph Hughes, one of North Carolina's signers of the Declaration of Independence, in July 1775 accused the British of planning to "let loose the Indians on our Frontiers, to raise the Negroes against us, and to destroy our Trade."[14] Similarly, James Iredell warned that the British were "exciting [the blacks] to cut our throats, and involve Men, Women and Children in one universal Massacre."[15]

Iredell and Hughes were not, in fact, entirely wrong as the British were to adopt a canny policy to potentially bring all African Americans into the war on their side.

In November 1775, Virginia Royal Governor Lord Dunmore promised freedom to any slaves who could escape to British lines. "I hereby further declare all indented servants, Negroes, or others (appertaining to Rebels) free," if they were "able and willing to bear arms, they joining His Majesty's Troops, as soon as may be, for the more speedily reducing the Colony to a proper sense of their duty, to His Majesty's crown and dignity."

Lord Dunmore's Proclamation, as it was known, was not an act of liberal morality, however, but rather a crafty strategic move by the British. Southern plantation owners were terrified by the potential of slave uprisings. As a consequence, men were required to stay at home to maintain order. And of course, it brought scores of recruits to the British cause. Slaves in the Carolinas deserted en masse to Cornwallis' army in 1780, given any opportunity to do so. As historian Jeffrey Crow, author of *The Black Experience in Revolutionary North Carolina*, puts it, "[w]herever the British appeared, slaves ran."[16] One British unit, known as Lord Dunmore's Ethiopians, with 800 men bearing arms, wore a uniform with the words "Liberty to Slaves" across the chest. Both sides, it seemed, were fighting for liberty in the American Revolution, but not the same idea of it.

The plain truth is that following Lord Dunmore's Proclamation, African Americans had the choice of fighting for a concept—American liberty—or a personal reality—their own freedom. The moral calculus was complex. But equally true, for many African Americans, fighting for the British meant fighting for freedom, while fighting for the Americans meant fighting for slavery. For those, like Titus, caught up in the chaos and choices of the period, there were no easy solutions.

Titus' Story

To have been born an African American slave in the mid-eighteenth century was, it must have seemed, to have lost the lottery of life. "By all accounts," writes Crow, "North Carolina blacks in the colonial period were ill-fed, ill-housed, and ill-clothed. In a frontier society, privation and harsh living conditions were common to all, but in the case of slaves these conditions proved especially acute."[17] A slave had no identity; no views; and little future. Life was in the Hobbesian sense, solitary, poor, nasty, brutish and short (although in Titus' case he broke the odds on the latter).

The account of one Continental officer travelling through the south in 1781 gives an indication of their intolerable and wretched lives. "Their Negros tho' at this Season of the year [late November] are almost Naked in General.... Some of them Quite as Naked as they were born Have Come into our Camp to look for peices [sic] of Old Clothes.—I don't Know how they Reconcile this treatment of their Slaves with their Liberal Principles of Hospitality." Another traveler saw "five Negroe Children every one dress'd in a

Shirt only—Clothes are not bestowed on these Animals with much profusion—At Johnson's one was Walking abo[u]t. the Court Yard absolutely naked, and in Newbern I saw a boy thro' the Streets with only a Jacket on, and that unbuttoned."[18] Clothing, or the lack of it, was a significant problem, but so was everything else. Little or no food; overwork and constant exhaustion; fear, sleeplessness and brutality. The slave's life was an ongoing nightmare in all respects.

Amelia County, Virginia, where Titus' first masters lived, was rolling, rural, farm country; hot and muggy in the late spring and summer, but bitterly cold in winter.

His master's name was Harry Bluford. According to Titus he lived with Bluford "till he was about 13 years old." Titus was around ten years old or so when he was sent as a wagon rider with a detachment of militia under British General Edward Braddock against the French-held Fort Duquesne at the forks of the Ohio River in the summer of 1755.

Slaves were hired from their masters to clear the grounds for camp at night; to erect tents; to water and feed the horses; and to drive the wagons. Bluford may have served as commissary to the British expedition, or perhaps he simply hired Titus out. In any event, Titus was commanded to ride a third horse to pull the commissary wagon.[19]

Braddock's expedition was a disaster. His men forded the Monongahela on July 9, 1755, where they were instantly ambushed by a combined force of French and Indians. It was a slaughter, not a battle. Braddock himself, shot through the chest and mortally wounded, was carried from the field by a young officer, George Washington, and died four days later. Titus fled with the remainder of the support crew, but survived and returned home.

At some point thereafter, when Titus was around the age of 13, he was "sold to John Muir & Dick Muir who lived on Dan River in the State of North Carolina." The Muirs (or Marrs) owned an interest in the Troublesome Iron Works, in present-day Rockingham County, along a main trading road in central North Carolina. The works, originally named Speedwell Furnace, sat near Troublesome Creek, the waters of which were used to power the machinery and temper the finished iron pieces. The iron works had been constructed around 1770 by Joseph Buffington, a Pennsylvania Quaker and experienced metallurgist. Buffington built a small blast furnace to melt iron, a rock dam to create waterpower, and a forge for finishing products.[20] Likely, Titus worked in all facets of the iron works at some point when he was owned by the Marrs. Most of the work for slaves and other workmen consisted of digging and transporting the iron ore and limestone and in making charcoal—all hard, dangerous and nasty work.

According to Titus he lived with the Muirs "a long while" but did "not recollect how long." At some point, "[I] was then sold to Lawrence Ross."

Ross lived somewhere along the Yadkin River in Rowan County, adjacent to Mecklenburg. Rowan County in 1779 had been spared the direct ravages of the war, but those ravages would not be long in coming. Cornwallis was soon to embark upon a southern campaign, which would thrust Mecklenburg and Rowan into the forefront of the American Revolution. At some point, all able bodied white men were required to serve, and Ross himself (or according to other account's, his son) was drafted, probably sometime in 1779, to serve a one year enlistment. It was permitted for a draftee to send a substitute in his stead. His master made a proposal to Titus, telling him that if he were to serve as a substitute, Titus "was to have his freedom." Titus had, one would think, very little choice.

And thus it was that an enslaved black man joined the American army in a war to fight for freedom and independence from Great Britain, in lieu of his white master.

Titus, per his later recollection, "entered the service on the [Y]Atkin River in the County of Roan [Rowan] & State of North Carolina." He could not later "recollect the day, month or year," exactly, but he said it was "in the spring of the year more than a year previous to Gates' Defeat" (which occurred in August 1780), so it "must have been in the year 1779."

His first year of enlistment, he noted "was previous to any Battles," although "during this time some skirmishes took place among the Tories & Indians." During the winter of 1779–1780 Titus was stationed at a place called Fort Independence, on the Savannah River in South Carolina. The fort was garrisoned principally as a deterrent to the Cherokees and Creek Indians, but also to the Loyalists who were active in the area.

"After the year was expired for which I was to have my freedom," he recalled, "I enlisted into the Army."

He had fulfilled his end of the bargain, so he was, in theory, now a free man. Did he fear that Ross would renege on the deal? Why did he reenlist? Did he have a wife, or friends, or anywhere else to go? It seemed that service in the army was no worse an option than any others he had at the time. He "enlisted under Captain John Cleveland, son of Colonel Absalom Cleveland," he stated.

At the same time, the static civil war in the backcountry between opposing irregular bands of Whigs and Tories was about to change, and change dramatically. The city of Charleston fell after a protracted siege in May 1780, and within the month Tarleton's cavalry was in central South Carolina, chasing the fleeing continental army. Then things got worse.

On August 16, 1780, in a morning battle amidst the pine-barrens and swamps just outside the upcountry colonial town of Camden, the American Continental Army was routed. The debacle became known as "Gates' Defeat" and the General did himself no favors by fleeing north to Charlotte on horseback; riding for his life. Titus missed the battle, arriving just as the Americans began to retreat, joining the throngs of men retreating through Charlotte.

News of Gates' defeat, in the recollections of Joseph Graham, who was there, "spread rapidly, and by noon the next day between three and four hundred militia were collected" in Charlotte, looking for news and leadership. By the evening of August 17, "the village was crowded with troops in retreat from the battle and with the assembling militia."[21] Most of Gates' troops, likely including Titus, took their cue from their leader and hastily left town, headed north. "The success of the enemy at Camden gave the Tories great confidence, and they became more bold, more daring and more numerous," recalled one solider, William Armstrong. "Assisted by detached parties of the British, they marched through the Country almost with impunity, committing every sort of crime. They established posts in various places, and for a while seemed to have subjugated the Country."[22]

Circumstances were auspicious for Cornwallis to move into North Carolina, where he could rally the Loyalists and thus supplement the Royal Army with more troops. In his memoirs, Lighthorse Harry Lee recalled that following Camden, "[t]he conquest of North Carolina, before Congress could bring another army into the field, was deemed certain...."[23] In Lee's opinion, Cornwallis now had the momentum and an opportunity "to restore the loyal authority, to lay up magazines, to provide all the necessary horses for the next campaign, and what was very desirable, to fill up his ranks with young Americans."[24]

A month after the Camden debacle, Cornwallis dispersed the American militia in Charlotte and took possession of the now de-populated cross-roads town. There he waited for two weeks, awaiting information from Major Patrick Ferguson, who was heading an expeditionary force of Loyalist militia to the west, pursued by a group of American frontiersmen known as the "over-mountain men." On October 7, after an all-night ride of over forty miles, the patriots found Ferguson atop a steep and rugged hillock known as Kings Mountain. Holding the high ground, Ferguson's position was, in theory, ideal defensive ground; in fact, not dissimilar to Little Round Top in Gettysburg, which the federals were able to hold against repeated uphill Confederate charges over eighty years later. In the recollections of one participant, Robert Campbell, who fought with the patriots:

> The two armies being in full view, the center of the one nearly opposite the center of the other—the British main guard posted nearly half way down the mountain—the commanding officer gave the word of command to raise the Indian war-whoop and charge. In a moment, Kings Mountain resounded with their shouts, and on the first fire the guard retreated, leaving some of their man to crimson the earth. The British beat to arms, and immediately formed on the top of the mountain, behind a chain of rocks

that appeared impregnable, and had their wagons drawn up on their flank across the end of the mountain, by which they made a strong-breast work. Thus concealed, the American army advanced to the charge. In ten or fifteen minutes the wings came round and the action became general.[25]

Although the loyalists had the high ground, it caused them to shoot high. The terrain was also heavily wooded, which gave the advancing patriots cover. After repeated attacks and counter-attacks over the steep slopes, the patriots finally and definitively gained the summit. There they pushed the loyalists into a terrified bunch, surrounded on all sides. Ferguson was shot dead. It had taken just over an hour, but Ferguson's force was entirely destroyed; dead (nearly 300), wounded or captured. Patriot deaths in the battle were approximately a tenth of the loyalists, which also gives credence to later claims that there was a wholesale slaughter of those attempting to surrender. Whether true or not, it was a colossal British defeat; a calamity, the equivalent of Camden, the previous August; arguably even worse, given that Ferguson's loyalist expeditionary force was destroyed en masse.

According to historian Bobby Moss, there were at least five African Americans who fought at Kings Mountain, including Titus. One of them, Essius Bowman, is thought to have been the marksman who shot and killed Ferguson. Another, John Brodday, was the only slave in the patriot army known to be present at the battle (although some later witnesses, including Shelby and Sevier, question his involvement). Two others, Andrew Ferguson and a man known only as Primus (possibly Ishmael's brother), fought in a number of battles (including Camden and Guilford Court House).[26]

Cornwallis was forced to leave Charlotte a few days after learning the news of Ferguson's destruction. Nathanael Greene then took charge of the Southern American forces. During the winter and spring of 1781, he and Cornwallis engaged in a cat and mouse game in the Carolinas, with Greene advancing, then retreating, across North Carolina. The two armies clashed in the woods near a place called the Guilford Courthouse in March (where Titus also claims to have fought), a "victory" so expensive for the British that it was remarked in London that Cornwallis could not survive any more such wins. The end was nigh in any event, and Cornwallis headed for the safety of the Royal Navy, on the Virginia coast, at a deep water port called Yorktown. And the rest, as they say, is history.

Titus recalled that he felt as if he "marched through the [entire] State of North Carolina," when it was all over. "I was discharged on the Holston River at a Log Court House," he said, and although he "cannot recollect the name of the place," he knew it "was at the close of the war."

But his adventures were not yet over. Loyalists continued to roam the Carolina backcountry, burning homes, hanging patriots and ambushing supply wagons. Titus remembered:

After I was dismissed at Holston River after the war was closed, coming home to Yadkin River, I (with ten others) was taken upon the top of the Allegheny Mountains by a party of Tories headed by a man they called Captain Bill Riddle.

I recollect it was on Thursday in the afternoon we were carried back to the foot of the Mountain & there kept all night with our hands tied & a guard put over us the next day a guard was over us all day.... On Saturday they brought to us Col. Cleveland as a prisoner & bound him in the same manner[.]

The next morning, I was sent by the Tories to look for the Tories' horses. I found all but one & took them back to the Tories. Then I was sent to search for the other horse on horseback, while looking after this horse, I discovered two companies under the command of Captains Cleveland, they inquired if I knew anything about their Father Colonel Absalom Cleveland.

I told him where he was & went with them to the place where the Tories had him. Colonel Cleveland as soon as he saw them said ["]Come on my Boys,["] when they rushed forward & shot at the Tories, they wounded one in the back, the rest fled into the Woods we then all of us came home. Some one or two months after this, I saw all but one of the Tories viz. (nine) hung at Rowan Court house.

It was the end of his adventures. But what would he do next? Later in life Titus was to say that he "ran away from his master" at this time. If this were true, it meant that his former master had reneged on his promise to give Titus his freedom, as masters sometimes did. Perhaps Titus knew this would happen, which was why he reenlisted in the first place after his initial one year of service. At some point he moved north, living in several small towns in New York (first New Rochelle, then Ballston, then Troy). He kept moving every few years, possibly fearing recapture by slave traders. From New York he went to Bennington, Vermont "& from there he removed to Williamstown in the County of Berkshire & Commonwealth of Massachusetts," which lay nearly on the border with Vermont.

He married a woman named Thankful Shepherd on November 13, 1805, and later a second wife, Lucy Rogers in Savoy, Massachusetts, on September 5, 1812. Titus died in Williamstown on January 27, 1855, reported the Springfield *Republican* "at the extraordinary age of 109 or 110 years."[27]

A Fight for Recognition

Petition number 10623—Ishmael Titus' application for benefits owed to Revolutionary War veterans—was denied. The official reason given was "not on the rolls—no proof of service." Rejection of petitions was not uncommon. According to one expert on the subject, about 15 percent of applications for ex-continental soldiers were denied because the applicant's name could not be found on the rolls. This percentage was much higher among the militia, where the terms of service were looser, command and reporting structure were more informal and record keeping almost nonexistent. Titus' application could have fallen victim to this latter cause. (In these types of cases, the applicant had to obtain testimony from an officer and two eye-witnesses.)

In Titus' case, as a former slave, the ability to obtain testimony from his former colleagues in rural North Carolina was simply impossible. In this, perhaps, it was another case of an ungrateful nation screwing over the African Americans. As it happened, due to negligence, ungratefulness or malevolence, very "few North Carolina Negroes apparently earned their freedom by fighting for the patriot cause," writes the historian Crow.[28] Indeed, he points out, most of the acreage that the state of North Carolina reserved for black veterans was never distributed to them, for whatever reasons, and ultimately escheated to the University of North Carolina.

It is also possible that Titus was lying about his service. This seems unlikely, as his account was quite detailed, and given his education and background, how could he have come up with the facts and the names that he did? In addition, those who knew Titus thought well of him, and he had a reputation for honesty. One Massachusetts citizen pointed out that his "story has always been consistent, and no one in that place has ever doubted its correctness."[29] Surely, given the totality of facts and circumstances in this case, we can conclude that Titus was telling the truth; and that the verdict must be that, as he well said, "his ignorance being brought up as a slave," was responsible for his inability to give more details.

Not that his case is entirely closed. A bed-and-breakfast owner from Grover, South Carolina, and Revolutionary War enthusiast named Marti Mongiello, along with his wife Stormy, were drawn to the Titus story and began a 2-person campaign to revive his memory and clear his name. On May 20, 2015—MecDec day—a small group of African American men and women, some descendants of Titus, arrived for a reception at The Harvey B. Gantt Center for African American Arts+Culture in Charlotte. The event was sponsored by several local historical groups, including the Mecklenburg Historical Association, the May 20th Society, the local Sons of the American Revolution Chapter, the Presidential Service Center (an organization founded and run by Mongiello), and the Gantt Center. Mongiello presented one of the guests, Solomon Titus Taylor, a direct descendant of Titus, with a Distinguished Service Medal, an award his organization gives to upstanding citizens. The family (and Mongiello) vowed to continue the fight to obtain Titus' pension. Finally, a small bronze plaque was also laid on Tryon Street in honor of Titus on the Charlotte Liberty Walk (a downtown walking tour of Revolutionary War sites); the same road down which Titus, and other retreating patriots, fled in droves in late August 1780, pursued by Cornwallis.

7
The Roman: Joseph Graham

> "As to endeavoring to obtain terms from the enemy, that was out of the question."
> —Joseph Graham, August 1780

Joseph Graham was born in Chester County, Pennsylvania, on October 13, 1759. His father, James Graham, was of Scots-Irish descent. James' family had emigrated from County Down, Ireland, in 1733 and found his way into the rolling farm lands of Pennsylvania.

James died in October 1763. In his will he left the bulk of his estate, such as it was ("fifty pounds and all my wearing apparel") to his son Henry, twenty pounds to his son Charles, ten to his daughter Elizabeth, and to his wife Mary, his snip mare and saddle "and the bed and stead which she lies on" as well as thirty five pounds cash. After two other children were then bequeathed similar amounts, the remaining part of his estate was to be divided between his wife, Mary, and the three other boys: John, George and, finally, Joseph. Not that there was much estate left at that point in any event, beyond the Graham's mare, a saddle, two feather beds, and the pewter dishware and pots.[1]

It is thus fair to say that four-year-old Joseph Graham inherited virtually nothing at his father's passing. In that, Graham's background is typical of many of the settlers who came south along the Great Wagon Road to the sparsely settled Carolina Piedmont in the 1760s. Their journey shows incredible courage and resourcefulness. But as Graham's situation amply shows, they also had virtually nothing to lose.

Three years after James' death, young Joseph, then aged seven, made the journey south to Mecklenburg County through Charleston, South Carolina. As with most of the settlers, his mother brought with her a stern Presbyterianism and an ancestral dislike of the English, aristocracy and the Anglican Church, and not necessarily in that order.

It is most likely they stayed with kin when they arrived, given the children to feed and the lack of a man to support the house. Joseph went to work in the fields and garden, plowing and corralling hogs in the autumn for fattening and butchering. He probably learned to read and write from his mother and attended an academy at their Presbyterian Church. When he reached the age of 14 or so he attended the newly chartered Presbyterian school for young men, near the center of town, called Queen's College. Here, according to later accounts, "[h]e was distinguished among his fellow student for talents, industry and the most manly and conciliating deportment."[2] Whether this is true or not, his later military and political career does indicate he had impressive abilities, and perhaps these manifested themselves at a young age.

According to his own accounts, when he was just a teenager, Graham witnessed the growing discontent and anger among his fellow Mecklenburgers regarding British rule. In the Carolina backcountry, eager citizens waited for passing express riders or traders to bring newspapers or pamphlets about what was going on in Boston and Philadelphia. Graham witnessed this increasingly stormy scene. According to Graham's later accounts of the period, "several popular meetings of the people were held in Charlotte; two of which I attended. Papers were read, grievances stated, and public measures discussed. As printing was not then common in the South, the papers were mostly manuscript.... It is to be regretted that those and other papers published at this period, and the journal of their proceedings, are lost. They would show much of the spirit and tone of thinking which prepared for the measures they afterwards adopted."[3]

Of course, the most famous "lost paper" of all was the fabled Mecklenburg Declaration of Independence, the signing of which Graham himself said he witnessed first-hand. On May 20, 1775, Graham "was then a lad about half grown, [and] was present on that occasion (a looker-on)."

In Graham's written testimony of 1831:

> After reading a number of papers as usual, and much animated discussion, the question was taken, and they resolved to declare themselves independent. One among other reasons offered, that the King or Ministry had, by proclamation or some edict, declared the Colonies out of the protection of the British Crown; they ought, therefore, to declare themselves out of his protection, and resolve on independence.
>
> [A] sub-committee, consisting of Doctor Ephraim Brevard, a Mr. Kennon, an attorney, and a third person, whom I do not recollect [likely the Reverend Balch], were appointed to draft their Declaration. They retired from the court house for some time; but the committee continued in session in it.
>
> One circumstance occurred I distinctly remember: A member of the committee, who had said but little before, addressed the Chairman as follows: "If you resolve on independence, how shall we all be absolved from the obligations of the oath we took to be true to King George the 3d about four years ago, after the Regulation battle, when we were sworn whole militia companies together. I should be glad to know how gentlemen can clear their consciences after taking that oath." This speech produced confusion. The Chairman could scarcely preserve order, so many wished to reply.

There appeared great indignation and contempt at the speech of the member. Some said it was nonsense; others that allegiance and protection were reciprocal; when protection was withdrawn, allegiance ceased; that the oath was only binding while the King protected us in the enjoyment of our rights and liberties as they existed at the time it was taken; which he had not done, but now declared us out of his protection; therefore was not binding. Any man who would interpret it otherwise, was a fool. By way of illustration, (pointing to a green tree near the court house,) stated, if he was sworn to do any thing as long as the leaves continued on that tree, it was so long binding; but when the leaves fell, he was discharged from its obligation. This was said to be certainly applicable in the present case. Out of respect for a worthy citizen, long since deceased, and his respectable connexions, I forbear to mention names; for, though he was a friend to the cause, a suspicion rested on him in the public mind for some time after.[4]

The drafting committee returned to the courthouse, Graham recalled, and read the resolutions, declaring the County "free and independent" of Great Britain.

It was unanimously adopted, and shortly after it was moved and seconded to have [the] proclamation made and the people collected, that the proceedings be read at the court house door, in order that all might hear them. It was done, and they were received with enthusiasm. It was then proposed by some one aloud to give three cheers and throw up their hats. It was immediately adopted, and the hats thrown. Several of them lit on the court house roof. The owners had some difficulty to reclaim them. The foregoing is all from personal knowledge.[5]

Graham's written account of the MecDec saga later became Exhibit A in the case for the defense. At this point, Graham was a bona fide national hero and a Revolutionary War veteran (and a wounded one, at that). His testimony, in short, was above reproach. However, critics pointed out, be that as it may, it was made over fifty years later, and thus if not deliberately tainted (as no one would dare allege) was nevertheless ... well, possibly confused. Indeed hadn't Graham himself stated in that same letter of October 4, 1831, that "I will give you the details of the Mecklenburg Declaration on the 20th of May, 1775, *as well as I can recollect after a lapse of fifty-five years* [?]" Graham's veracity aside, the MecDec skeptics would say, how much weight can we give an eyewitness account after such a lengthy passage of time? And that is where the arguments essentially reside to this very day.

"The militia were ordered out, en masse."

The reason Graham was such a powerful witness in the later Mecklenburg Declaration kerfuffle was due to his service and heroism in the Revolutionary War. He had enlisted in May 1778 when he was just eighteen years old. He served part of his appointment as Quarter-Master Sergeant and part in Captain Goode's company, 4th Regiment of the North Carolina line. The terms of enlistment were to serve nine months from the time of arriving at the place of rendezvous. In the case of the Mecklenburg soldiers, they were told to go to Bladensburg, Maryland, a month hike's away.

Graham recalled that they "by slow movements marched on to near the Virginia line, detaining by the way for the recruits from the other counties to join." They got as far as Moon's Creek, in Caswell County, where "they received intelligence of the Battle of Monmouth, and that the British were gone to New York; that our services were not wanted in the North." The men became restless. They had been on the march for many weeks, away from their families and their farms. But because they had not reached their launching point, in faraway Maryland, the army considered their service to not even have commenced.

"The men became uneasy," recalled Graham. "[A] mutiny took place, which was suppressed with some difficulty; some officers broke their swords, and some of the soldiers were crippled."[6] Such was Graham's initiation into a soldier's life.

The volunteers were allowed to return home until the autumn, when their terms would commence. Graham accepted the offer, as did most of those from the backcountry, and returned home to Mecklenburg "about three months after he had left."[7] He was not home long, for in August he was again called into service and marched with General Rutherford from Charlotte to Charleston "where he drew arms and camp equipage." Afterwards he was assembled into the infantry under a French officer, Colonel Malmedy. Graham served as Quarter-Master sergeant at this point until the end of the campaign, effectively discharging the role of his superior, a Lieutenant Hilton who was "in bad health and dying."[8]

Graham was discharged that August, amidst the heat and humidity of the swamp lowcountry. He was ready to go home.

But before he could make it back to Mecklenburg, however, Graham:

> [W]as taken with the bilious fever a few days before the term of service was up, and had much difficulty, but by the assistance of a friend, after some time got home; and was not fully recovered at the end of two months. The terms on which this [prior military] service was performed were to be exempted from military duties for three years after. [My] spirits were so depressed by the fever and recollections of the hardship of a southern campaign in the summer, along the seaboard, [I] was disposed to avail [my]self of the privilege allowed by the law [to not enlist again].[9]

Events were to chart a different course for Graham.

In May 1780, "Colonel Buford was defeated," he recalled. Buford was not just "defeated," though; in point of fact his men were slaughtered in the Waxhaws, just a day's ride from Graham's home. Retreating from the surrender of Charleston to the besieging British forces, Buford was caught in the open by the fast-moving cavalry of Lt. Col. Banastre Tarleton. The Americans stood and fought, but the speed and aggression of Tarleton were no match for Buford, and the Americans were massacred, many by all accounts after they attempted to surrender. After the debacle "it was announced the enemy were within thirty-five or forty miles; when the militia were ordered out, en masse." Graham had no choice, as he remembered because his native "county, being a frontier, [had] no other force to protect it." Like the hero of ancient Rome, Lucius Quinctius Cincinnatus, who was summoned by the senate from his farm to protect the Republic, Graham was compelled, against his wishes, to leave his farm and family, and reenlist, to repel the coming invasion.

The Battle of Charlotte

Buford's Massacre, as it was later called, was only the first act in the unfolding drama in the Carolinas that summer. The British were coming, and in force. On August 16, 1780, the American Continental Army was crushed in the pine barrens and swampy, sandy flatlands just outside Camden, South Carolina. The time was now ripe for a long planned objective of Cornwallis: the invasion of North Carolina. Indeed, recalled Charles Steadman, a British officer travelling with Cornwallis: "By the victory gained over general Gates at Camden, and the rout and total dispersion of his army ... the provincial force to the southward seemed for a time entirely annihilated; and nothing prevented Earl Cornwallis from proceeding immediately on his long projected expedition into North Carolina."[10] Cornwallis' motivations, according to American cavalry officer Lighthorse Harry Lee, were "to restore the loyal authority, to lay up magazines, to provide all the necessary horses for the next campaign, and what was very desirable, to fill up his ranks with young Americans."[11] In particular, Cornwallis wanted to teach the Carolinians a hard lesson, for as Lee observed, the backwoods settlers there were "distinguished for their firm adherence to their country."[12]

Cornwallis himself gave several different reasons for moving into Charlotte, not all of which were entirely consistent. To Sir Henry Clinton on September 22/23 he wrote: "The post at Charlottetown will be a great security to all this frontier of South Carolina, which, even if we were possessed of the greatest part of North Carolina, would be liable to be infested by parties who have retired with their effects over the mountains and mean to take every opportunity of carrying on a predatory war; and it will, I hope, prevent insurrections in this country, which is very disaffected."[13]

But just a few weeks later (on October 7) he gave a very different and more definitive answer to Major Wemyss. "*The object of marching into North Carolina is only to raise men,*" he wrote, "which, from every account I have received of *the number of our friends*, there is great reason to hope may be done to a very considerable amount."[14] Clearly latent in Cornwallis' mind was the idea of overawing the "inveterate" backcountry rebels with a show of force. This would encourage the friends of the King and, hopefully, lead to a general rising of the loyalists. After taking Charlotte, he wrote, he intended to move on to Salisbury, "*and from thence invite all the loyalists of the neighbouring countys to repair to our standard.*"[15]

Whatever the reasons, Charlotte was the short term objective, unless there was anyone who could slow the British down. Cornwallis left Camden on September 8 moving towards the cross-roads town of Charlotte.

If Cornwallis "was able to reduce to obedience the inveterate inhabitants of the tract of country through which the main army marched," as Graham put it, "a communication may be opened between the friendly settlements on the right and left, a powerful assistance derived from their cooperation, and the speedy reduction of the whole province reasonably expected."[16]

Meanwhile, wounded, leaderless and terrified American militia men, fleeing the British, continued to flood into Charlotte. They brought with them many of the wounded of Hanging Rock and other skirmishes with the British south of town. So many poured in that, per Graham, a "general hospital was now established" in Charlotte-Towne.[17] The site of this hospital was Queen's College, where Graham had gone to school.

Chartered in 1771, the King had revoked its charter less than two years later on the advice of the Board of Trade, who dourly concluded, "from the Prevalency of the presbyterian persuasion within the County of Mecklenburgh we may venture to conclude, that this College if allowed to be incorporated will, in effect operate as a Seminary for the education and Instruction of youth in the Principles of the Presbyterian Church...."

As such, the BOT doubted "whether it may be adviseable for your Majesty to add Incouragement to toleration by giving the Royal Assent to an Establishment, which in its consequences promises with great and permanent Advantages to a sect of Dissenters from the Established Church who have already extended themselves over that Province in very considerable numbers."[18]

The King thus revoked the charter of Queen's College, severely pissing off the local inhabitants. Undeterred, they renamed the place "Liberty Hall" once the war broke out. Now in the autumn of 1780, the wooden floors were crammed with wounded soldiers fleeing from the debacle at Camden.

The defeat of Horatio Gates, the hero of Saratoga, at Camden that August led to "astonishment and surprise" in Charlotte, said Graham. In fact, not only the news of Gates' defeat, *but the sudden appearance of Gates himself* later the same day threw everyone into a tizzy.

Camden was seventy-two miles distant from Charlotte, but Gates had ridden it in a day, as if Tarleton himself were on his very heels. He did not even bother to dismount, Graham recalled with evident disgust, "but stopped two or three minutes while one of his aides called on Col. Thomas Polk to inform him of the disaster [at Camden]."[19] Gates then rode out of town towards Salisbury, leaving behind him confusion and terror amongst the disorganized and now fully demoralized militiamen. General Smallwood of Maryland had commanded Gates' reserve and fought a retreating action against the British. Smallwood was believed dead or captured in the battle. So when he rode unannounced into Charlotte three days after the battle, Graham tells us there was "great joy of the troops he commanded."

He may have brought joy to town, but also fear, confusion and uncertainty. The British were coming, in great numbers, and with their tails up. Smallwood consulted with the militia officers to "make what resistance they could" to the advancing British, but the reality was that the American army in the south had been broken into bits. Until such time as Congress acted to create a new army, the militia were on their own. With this news, Smallwood "and the rest of the officers and privates who had been in the action" at Camden, left town too. Now they were alone. And Cornwallis and Tarleton were coming.

The townspeople were divided about what to do next. Some favored retreating further, while others thought they should stand and fight. In Graham's words:

> The officers commanding the Mecklenburg militia, and some of the most influential citizens, convened to consult what should be done. Theirs being a frontier country, the Regulars and militia who had been in service [with Gates] all passing on [through town], a numerous and victorious enemy shortly expected to invade them, and no expectation of assistance from Rowan County, they had to rely on their own strength and resources.[20]

Not everyone agreed that they should resist the British advance, and in fact it would have been crazy for them to do so. "Several aged and respectable citizens insinuated that further resistance would, under such circumstances, be temerity, and would only produce more destruction for themselves and families." This course was "indignantly repelled by a great majority," many of whom had recently fought at the Battle of Hanging Rock, barely a month earlier. Several of these veterans stated: "that they then had seen the British run like sheep, and many of them bite the dust; that they were by no means invincible; that under suitable commanders and proper arrangements, they would at any time risk a conflict with them, man to man; that their cause was just and they confided that Providence would ultimately give them success, notwithstanding the present unfavorable appearances."[21]

Furthermore, as Graham put it, "[a]s to endeavoring to obtain terms from the enemy, *that was out of the question.*"

"No faith was to be placed in British promises, generosity or honor," he believed. The feeling was that "as long as there remained any part of North American to which British authority did not extend, they would endeavor to occupy that."[22] The conclusion was to resist. General Irwin was to take half the able bodied men south of town, while the other half were allowed to return to their farms, but await readiness to muster if and when Cornwallis advanced. William R. Davie's cavalry was to reconnoiter the flat, pine-barrens between Charlotte and Camden for the appearance of Tarleton's horse.

Manpower was scarce. Not only had the remnants of Gates' army hightailed it out of town, but the entire area from Camden to Salisbury had been bled white by the Civil War. Lord Rawdon, writing from the Waxhaws a few months earlier, in June 1780, had reported that, "The country, tho' thickly settled, is poor in itself and much drained. I am regularly supplied with cattle, tho even in that article they [the local inhabitants] plead poverty, but the neighborhood is totally destitute of grain or any kind of dry forage."[23]

There simply were no more men to be had. A thousand North Carolina militia had been captured when Charleston fell in May, even before the Camden catastrophe, where another five hundred plus had been taken. Hundreds more had left the area to serve with the Continentals, some of whom had also been taken prisoner.

By September 11 Cornwallis' army was just north of present day Lancaster, South Carolina, and Davie was forced to retreat from the Waxhaws to camp New Providence, south of Charlotte. At the time, Brig. Gen. William Lee Davidson estimated the size of Cornwallis' army at 1,200 men, "nearly one half of his number Tories."[24] Tarleton moved up to near present day Rock Hill on the 16th, and the two prongs of the advancing British army sat, one on each side of the Catawba River. Several days passed, while the British foraged for supplies, spread the King's word, and made ready to enter into North Carolina.

On September 24, Cornwallis' army made camp between the McAlpine and Sugar Creeks, only ten miles from Charlotte. Tarleton was dispatched to chase sixty or so South Carolina militia at the Bigger's Ferry Catawba river crossing, but Sumter received warning, crossed the river and evaded them in the woods. Tarleton missed them by an hour.

Davidson knew his militia had no chance of contesting Cornwallis' advance, so when he received word of their approach he had already broken camp and advanced north of town, out of harms' way. At the same time, he sent Davie's cavalry, consisting of one hundred and fifty men, comprising mounted infantry and dragoons, and a body of volunteer militia under Graham, to the Charlotte town common to organize the militia. They were armed with muskets, in addition to pistols and swords. As Graham and his men "were best acquainted with the country and by-roads," Davie asked him to relieve a skirmishing party who had been two days out near the British lines.[25] That evening Graham's men captured four British stragglers who had been foraging for milk and sent them on to Davie for safekeeping.

Just before sunrise the next day, September 26, Graham "discovered the front of the enemy advancing," and "the whole army in motion ... artillery, baggage, etc., coming on."[26] With the rising sun just over their backs, it must have been a captivating and terrifying spectacle; pickets and skirmishes in the green or blood-red jackets; drums, wagons, noise, amidst the still-dark morning woods.

Graham immediately sent word to Davie that the British, indeed, were coming. Davie remembered that "early in the morning of the 26th [his] patroles were driven in by the enemy's light troops, and in a few minutes the Legion & light infantry were seen advancing towards the town followed by the whole Army."[27]

Graham's men fired off a volley "which the enemy returned briskly, and began to deploy."[28] At first, Tarleton's cavalry was nowhere to be seen, for which Graham's men were grateful, but when the well-known green jackets appeared from the ferry-road to Grahams' right, the Americans kept a "respectful distance."

They were now just two miles from the county courthouse in the village square. The British cavalry pushed Graham at a brisk canter for a mile, then slowed as the outlines of the scattered log cabins and fences of Charlotte came into view. There they halted to close up their rear, while scouts were sent out to reconnoiter what lay ahead in the silent, seemingly deserted village.

The village of Charlotte-Town stood, as the downtown essentially still does, at the corner of two cross streets, set at right angles to one another. The first, called Tryon Street, after the previous Royal Governor, ran north towards Salisbury, the largest neighboring town (and was thus called the Salisbury Road), and meandered south towards Camden, from whence Cornwallis approached. Another muddy street, called the trade street, ran east to west. Various log buildings, twenty or so, set with fenced vegetable gardens fringed the town common.

In the middle of the cross-streets stood the Mecklenburg County Courthouse, "a frame building raised on eight brick pillars ten feet from the ground, which was the most elevated [building] in the place. Between the pillars was erected a wall of rock three feet high," with an open-air space used for market beneath.[29]

This was, of course, the same county courthouse where the various militia officers had angrily debated a series of anti–British resolutions on May 19–20, 1775, later attested to by many (including definitively by Graham himself) to be a declaration of independence. Whether it was or was not, and whatever the text of the resolutions actually said, it was beyond dispute that they were "horrid and treasonable." Royal Governor Josiah Martin, riding that day amidst the British Legion entering Charlotte, had called them such in a letter to the Earl of Dartmouth dated June 30, 1775 ("The Resolves of the Committee of Mecklenburgh … surpass all the horrid and treasonable publications that the inflammatory spirits of this Continent have yet produced"). In that same letter, Governor Martin had warned, "your Lordship may depend its Authors and Abettors will not escape my due notice, whenever my hands are sufficiently strengthened to attempt the recovery of the lost authority of Government."[30]

The *due notice* of the British was now clearly at hand. What was at issue was what if anything Graham, Davie and the hundred or so militiamen staring south down Tryon Street could do about it. Yet despite the overwhelming odds, said Davie, he "was determined to give his Lordship some earnest of what he might expect in North Carolina."[31]

With his main body of troops, Graham established three lines behind the courthouse facing the British advance. The first was just twenty feet from the stone wall, the others behind that. A second body of cavalry under Davie was placed on either side of Graham's flanks, roughly eighty yards away, hidden behind various buildings. A skirmishing party of twenty men under a Major Dickinson was sent out ahead and to the left, "posted behind some houses and gardens," while a small reserve stood farther back down Tryon Street.[32]

Tryon Street rises very slightly as one travels into town from the south, but in such a way that today, even a modern passenger bus standing one hundred yards on the north end of Tryon Street is hidden if approached from the south. Due to this slight swell in the ground, as well as the houses and the brick wall beneath the courthouse, Graham and his men were "nearly masked from the view of the advancing foe."[33] These were classic partisan tactics, of the kind that so enraged the British. George Hanger, in command of the British Legion that day, as Tarleton was ill, wrote that "the enemy planted behind the houses … were impervious to my view," until his men were "considerably advanced into the town."[34]

It took Cornwallis just half an hour to consolidate his forces in front of the village, at which point they advanced. The Legion cavalry led the way, advancing cautiously. They formed up, three hundred yards from the courthouse, the infantry on either flank. When the charge was sounded, they "advanced in full gallop within sixty y[ards] of the Court-house."[35] At this point, said Graham, "our first line moved up to the stone wall and fired."[36] The fire "fell with such effect among the cavalry that they retreated with great precipitation."[37]

After firing one round, the first line was supposed to move away to either side and allow the second line to advance and fire, while the first line reloaded, and so forth. It was a common but hazardous tactic, especially with untrained militia forces, as it forced the first line to get out of the way of the second, and quickly, and the pullback could often encourage the men to keep moving out of harm's way entirely and run for it.

Unless it was quickly executed, the British cavalry could also advance on the men before the second line was formed, attacking the men not yet ready to fire, as well as those with their backs turned. All the British could see, however, was the line of militia emptying from beneath the courthouse; the second and third lines remained hidden by the stone wall.

The British cavalry, Graham said, "supposing that we were retreating, rushed up to the court-house and received a full fire from the companies placed on the cross streets."[38] Surprised by the flanking fire, they "immediately wheeled and retreated down the street to their infantry, halted and fronted." As they fled, the second line under the courthouse "fired at the column of cavalry in retreat, but at rather too great a distance" to be effective.[39] For a second time, Hanger's Legion cavalry was forced to retreat "in the outmost [sic] confusion, in the presence of the whole British army."[40]

Ambush at the Mecklenburg Courthouse in Charlotte-Towne, September 26, 1780, as painted by Dan Nance. The Americans' fire "fell with such effect among the [British] cavalry that they retreated with great precipitation," recalled William R. Davie (painting held at CPCC) (courtesy Dan Nance).

In any event, Cornwallis was unimpressed at the inability to drive off a hundred militiamen, when he had ten times that number facing them. He rode up in person, shouting: "Legion, remember you have everything to lose, but nothing to gain!"[41]

British light infantry then advanced on either side through the fences and small farm lots to get after the Americans.

Hanger had part of the British Legion mounted but "ready to dismount and support the dragoons." These troops dismounted on the British right. "I ordered them to take possession of the houses to the right," Hanger wrote, and the firing increased amidst the log houses.[42] A young militia man named Henry Connelly, from Guilford County who was fighting with Davie's troops noted, "[we] received the first onset from Tarleton's Cavalry, and the firing became general on the left wing."[43]

Graham said the British appeared "in rear of lots" on each flank, where "they opened a cross-fire on each flank of Davie's men, which for a short time was handsomely returned from behind the buildings; but their numbers and firing increasing as they deployed, and the cavalry advancing along the street in a menacing attitude, [thus] General Davie ordered a retreat."[44] The fire from the British advancing under the cover of houses and gardens was "galling," admitted Davie, and with both flanks threatening to be turned, he gave the order to pull off.[45] The Americans on the right were "driven in, although bravely resisting" wrote Lee, so Davie recalled the men on the left and "receded from the unequal contest."[46]

The retreating American troops moving north up the main street "had to sustain the whole fire of the Legion" while the reserve let off two volleys before moving off in order through the woods.[47] Graham's men began a tactical retreat up the Salisbury Road and through the woods east of town, turning to fire periodically at the pursuing British cavalry. At this point, Graham "ordered his men to disperse, as the woods were thick and they all knew the country."[48]

The Americans rallied a few miles away in thick woods near a creek crossing, waiting for the British to arrive. Two men were sent ahead to see if there were cavalry or infantry pursuing, "and if the former, the troops should fire from their saddles."[49] The scouts had "not gone one hundred yards" when they sighted Hanger's men and reported back. Graham and his men remained in the saddle, when:

> The first thing that presented itself to their view in the edge of the bottom beyond the creek, at the distance of ninety steps, was the front of a full platoon of [British] infantry on each side of the road, on whom they instantly fired and retreated. The enemy fired at nearly the same time, and their balls passing directly through the woods where our line was formed, and skinning saplings and making bark and twigs fly, produced more of a panic on the militia then any disaster that which occurred on that day. All the

firing in Charlotte and beyond had generally passed over their heads, but here it appeared to be horizontal.[50]

The British chased Graham and his men north for several miles. They caught a number of militia, including one young private, sixteen-year-old George Locke, who they "literally cut to pieces, in a most barbarous manner."[51]

Not far from Sugar Creek Presbyterian Church, Graham and his men turned to fight their pursuers, face-to-face. According to his grandson's later account:

> As Captain Graham was engaged in a hand-to-hand fight, his horse backed under a limb of a tree which knocked him off. He received three bullets in the thigh, one saber thrust in the side, one cut on the back of the neck and four upon the forehead. And from one of these some of his brains exuded. The cut on the back of the neck must have been given as he fell or fought on foot. It cut a heavy silver buckle which he wore on his stock entirely in two; but for the buckle it would have severed his head from his body.[52]

The remaining Americans fled into the woods. Graham lay in the grass, bleeding profusely from nine wounds. The British cavalrymen gathered their wounded, regrouped, and prepared to head back into the village.

One British soldier saw Graham's bloody body. He approached and aimed a pistol at him intending to finish him off. Hanger stopped him. "[P]ut up your pistol," he said, and "save your ammunition; he has had enough."[53]

The British rode off, leaving Graham in the woods to die. The Mecklenburg militia had been scattered, and Mecklenburg County, like Graham himself, lay prostrate at the feet of Cornwallis.

A Pyrrhic Victory

The next day, Cornwallis summarized the days' events in a letter to Lord Balfour. He said he had been "fatigued" the night before as a result of the day's exertions, and though he had received several communiques from Balfour to which he owed a response, he had "postponed answering them till morning."[54]

"Colonel Davie staid for us here with some mounted riflemen and fired at the Legion from the houses, trusting to the strength of the country behind them and to their knowledge of it," Cornwallis wrote.

He reported that "we *cut up* about 14 of them and had only one man wounded and one horse killed." Hanger and Captain Charles Macdonald, a captain of horse in Tarleton's British Legion, both "had slight contusions," while Captain Patrick Campbell of the 71st Light Infantry "was wounded, but we hope not dangerously." (Lee gave the British losses as a dozen non-commissioned officers and privates killed, with a few officers and many other privates wounded[55]; Graham saw several British dead and thought the British "must have sustained the greatest damage in Charlotte."[56])

Although the British had seized possession of Charlotte, the resistance of volunteer American militia standing to fight the entire oncoming British army was not a good omen. Although they had taken the frontier cross-roads town, the British had not been welcomed with open arms. In fact, nearly everyone had fled into the woods. The townspeople had "totally deserted the town on our approach," said Hanger, and "not three or four men remained in the whole town."[57]

What's more, rather than being "cut up," as Cornwallis had put it, besides Graham, Locke and a handful of casualties, the Americans had in truth escaped nearly Scot-free.

"Perhaps we might have followed up the blow farther," Cornwallis concluded wistfully, "but I did not care to trust the corps too far or risk them much."[58]

But the British were not the only ones to regret their choice of tactics. The Americans had chosen to stand in small numbers and resist the mass of the British army. It was brave, but arguably reckless. But for the fact that the swell in the ground along Tryon Street and the stone wall under the courthouse hid their tiny numbers, they could have been routed, even massacred, as Buford's men had. "The small damage sustained in proportion to the risk appeared providential," Graham later wrote. In fact, "[s]everal of the British officers stated afterwards, if Colonel Tarleton had commanded their van, instead of Major Hanger, it would have been worse for us."[59]

> Had we omitted fighting on this day, kept our men and horses fresh (except a few to reconnoiter and give intelligence of the enemy's movements), and been in readiness to strike the foraging parties, which his new position would soon compel him to send out, and thus endeavored to take him [Cornwallis] by detail, it would have been better than with three or four hundred mounted militiamen, of whom not one-fourth were equipped as cavalry, attacking a regular army completely organized of ten times their number, in an open field, where every person was sure he would be beaten.[60]

For his part, Hanger later dismissed the firefight in Charlotte as "a trifling insignificant skirmish."[61] He was of course correct, in a larger sense. Militarily, the "battle" of Charlotte was really nothing more than a brief delaying action; not even a battle at all, arguably, and inarguably one of no real over-arching strategic significance (although that being said it would have felt *quite significant* to Graham or Locke as they were slashed with British sabers, or to the handful British soldiers who were killed or wounded that morning in this remote frontier town). What's more, the Americans had not prevented the British from moving into town, so in that narrow sense it was surely not an American victory.

However, like other military "defeats" such as Bastogne or the Tet Offensive, the Battle of Charlotte took on a symbolic value which the British were quick to appreciate. Like Hanger, Stedman brushed aside the affair as merely a "slight resistance," although he undercut his own argument by conceding in his memoirs that "the whole of the British army was actually kept at bay, for some minutes, by a few mounted Americans, not exceeding twenty in number."[62]

If it was not a American victory, it is hard to see that it was a British one either. None of Cornwallis' stated objectives in taking Charlotte was achieved. The Loyalists militia did not rally. Despite the preceding defeat of Gates' at Camden, the American militia had not been over-awed. Not only that, they even retained the temerity to stand and fight the British, despite the overwhelming disparity in numbers.

And not only had the townspeople fled, but also hundreds from the surrounding farms and plantations, driving their hogs and cattle ahead of them, carrying their meager possessions on their backs. "[Y]ou cannot conceive the distress and consternation of the inhabitants, who almost universally appeared disposed to fly with the little property they could take with them," one eye-witness wrote that month to a friend. The villagers, he wrote, seemed determined to find "asylum in some other part of the world, rather than be under the domination of Great Britain."[63]

The British had seen this dynamic before. The previous June, when Rawdon's forces had moved into the Waxhaws in a reconnaissance in force, Hanger reported "a total desertion of that settlement by the efficient inhabitants, who joined the American army, leaving behind them only the aged and the women and children."[64] And worse, in that instance, many of the Irish soldiers in Rawdon's army had slunk away from camp to join their Scotch-Irish kin. Rawdon "learned what experience confirmed," wrote Tarleton, "that the Irish were the most adverse of all other settlers to the British government in America."[65]

Now, in the rainy and cold days of October 1780, Charlotte was a ghosttown. The area seemed nearly deserted, except, of course, for the partisans who haunted the nearby woods, using creeks and little-known deer or hunting tracks to watch the British. To the occupying British, it was all quite sinister.

Still, for all that, the British were clearly on the ascendant. They had moved into North Carolina for the first time and paid the rebels the "due attention" Governor Martin had promised Lord Dartmouth they would. With the Continentals defeated and broken, they could regroup in safety and peace and let the friends of the Crown rally to them. It was all, they thought, according to plan.

In reality, as they would soon learn, they were in extremely hostile country, cut off and surrounded.

"More hostile than any other"

In the autumn twilight following the battle, Graham lay in his own blood where Hanger and the British Legion had left him. Using what little strength he had, he crawled to a nearby spring where he drank as much as he could. That night, a young Scots-Irish woman named Susan Alexander found him when she came to fetch water. With the aid of her mother they carried Graham back to their house. His clothes were caked with blood, and he was badly cut up, but he was alive. The Alexanders hung flax sacks around the bed so no prying eyes could see that a wounded patriot officer was there. They kept watch over him for several nights. Graham was so quiet that more than once they thought he had died.

A few days later British foragers arrived near the Alexander's farm, looking for milk. It was not safe for Graham to stay. Despite his condition, he had to be moved further into the countryside somewhere more safe. The Alexanders helped mount Graham on a horse, where he rode four miles to his mother's house. From there, he was placed on a wagon and spirited out of the county.

The British, meanwhile, found their stay in Charlotte just as unpleasant as their arrival had been.

The farms in the area had been drained by the continentals or militia who had passed through over the year, and very little remained. Lee noted that, "[s]o exhausted was the country, that in this well-improved settlement, the British general was straitened for provisions, and obliged to send his light party in every direction."[66]

Consequently, British expeditionary parties were forced to travel farther and farther into the countryside, searching for supplies. Travelling on unknown paths, in hostile territory and far from their colleagues, was a perilous assignment. "The foraging parties were every day harassed by the inhabitants," wrote Tarleton. The local citizens "did not remain at home, to receive payment for the produce of their plantations, but generally fired from covert places, to annoy the British detachments. Ineffectual attempts were made upon convoys coming from Camden, and the intermediate post at Blair's mill; but individuals with expresses were frequently murdered."[67] And in Steadman's words: "So inveterate was their rancour, that the messengers, with expresses for the commander-in-chief, were frequently murdered; and the inhabitants, instead of staying quietly at home to receive payment for the produce of their plantations, made it a practice to way-lay the British foraging parties, fire their rifles from concealed places, and then fly into the woods."[68]

Hanger recalled that, "the foraging parties were attacked by the enemy so frequently, that it became necessary never to send a small detachment on that service. Colonel Tarleton, just then recovered from the yellow fever, judged it necessary to go in person, and with his whole corps, or above two-third [of them], when he had not detachments from the rest of the army."[69]

In one well-known episode on October 4, a large British detachment (one source gives it as 450 infantry, 60 cavalry, and 40 wagons) under Major John Doyle was sent out from Charlotte towards Hopewell Presbyterian Church, a hotbed of radical anti–Anglicanism before the war. A detachment of this force, about 110 wagons, was sent to the farm of Mr. McIntyre on Long Creek. Here they gathered corn, oats, livestock, and, of importance to the later legend, honey from McIntyre's beehives. They were watched from the nearby woods by a small force of approximately a dozen men commanded by Captain Francis Bradley. As the story goes, the British upset a beehive, causing the bees to swarm around the men and leading to a furor. It was at this point that Bradley's men opened fire, killing eight and wounding a dozen others.

The affairs at McIntyre's farm was symbolic of the attritional warfare fought against the British while they camped in Charlotte. Nonstop, galling and relentless guerrilla attacks, none of which were large enough to cause serious damage, but which contributed to a morale-sapping and terrifying sense of encirclement and dread. One militiaman named Moses Hall reconnoitered the area around Charlotte that month. "Our small scouting parties frequently fired at the British as they passed about in large foraging parties," he said. "Our object in this tour was to annoy the enemy and to impress them with our intention to resist them to the last."[70] It worked.

"Notwithstanding the different checks and losses sustained by the militia of the district," as Tarleton put it, "they continued their hostilities with unwearied perseverance."[71]

Isolated and unable to communicate outside the county, "no estimation could be made of the sentiments of half the inhabitants of North Carolina, whilst the Royal army remained at Charlotte town," recalled Tarleton.

> The vigilance and animosity of these surrounding districts checked the exertions of the well affected, and totally destroyed all communication between the King's troops and the loyalists in the other parts of the province.
> No British commander could obtain any information, in that position, which would facilitate his designs, or guide his future conduct. Every report concerning the measures of the governor and assembly would undoubtedly be ambiguous; accounts of the preparations of the militia could only be vague and uncertain; and all intelligence of the real force and movements of the continentals must be totally unattainable.[72]

"It was evident," concluded Tarleton, "and it had been frequently mentioned to the King's officers, that the counties of Mecklenburg and Rohan were more hostile to England than any others in America."[73]

Graham's Recovery

Cornwallis' occupation of Charlotte, the foretaste of a greater invasion of the State, lasted just over two weeks. The annihilation of Patrick Ferguson's army at a small hillock southwest of Charlotte, ironically named Kings Mountain, on October 7, left Cornwallis' flank exposed, and with provisions difficult to come by in the hostile county, the British army retreated the way they had come and made winter quarters in South Carolina.

Graham was two months at home recovering from his wounds. But the war was not through with him yet. In December of that year, he met with Davidson, who was commanding militia in the Mecklenburg region. Davidson told Graham "the enemy would again advance in North Carolina as soon as a reinforcement and some stores on the way from Charleston should arrive."[74] He told Graham that if he "would raise a company or more, he should be entitled to such rank as the numbers would justify," and by way of encouragement the term of service would be just six weeks, not the usual 3 months. Graham quickly "set out among the youth of his acquaintance, and in two or three weeks had upwards of fifty." Their arms and equipment "were not splendid," but were "the best that could be procured at that time" he said.[75] Graham's men served as a mounted infantry company, fighting either on foot or on horse, harassing the British along country roads, killing their sentries or waylaying messengers.

Throughout 1781, the final year of Cornwallis' campaign in the south, Graham's men were engaged in dozens of small skirmishes and actions. They opposed the British crossing of the Catawba River at Cowan's Ford (losing two men, and covering the retreat). A week later, in mid-February 1781, they ambushed a small party of British regulars along the Yadkin River, killing one and taking five prisoner. They fought Loyalists at Clapp's Mill, along the Salisbury Road and a half dozen other obscure backwoods creeks, plantations or mills. "Eight battles or skirmishes" in total that spring, Graham recalled, and lost four killed, three wounded and two taken prisoner, of his volunteers from Mecklenburg.[76]

The Roman

After the war Graham returned to Mecklenburg County and served in a variety of public roles, including commissioner, in charge of buying and selling government property, and Sheriff. He was a delegate to the first state convention to consider the proposed Constitution of the United States, in the summer of 1788, as well as the 1789 state convention which adopted it. He was a member of the North Carolina State Senate from 1788 to 1792 and led in adopting several bills.

In 1788, in order to develop industry, the state enacted a law granting 3,000 acres of land to those willing to establish ironworks. Those granted land had three years to demonstrate that they had manufactured 5,000 pounds of iron and if they had, they were deeded the land and were exempt from taxation for 10 years. Graham, in partnership with two others, purchased some land in Lincoln County and established a foundry which they named "Vesuvius Furnace" (after the Italian volcano near Naples). The works were a success, and in 1792 Graham moved his family across the Catawba River and built a long, two story wooden home, with a large front porch, on the property.

He made wrought iron to be worked into crowbars, wagon wheels, shovels, plows and horseshoes. It was so successful that a few years later he built a second furnace called Spring Hill Forge, on Leeper's Creek, six miles from Lincolnton.

As settlers moved into Western North Carolina, and farther, into Tennessee and Kentucky, business boomed. Graham's products "supplied the country to the west with cooking utensils and all other iron goods, also to the east as far as Hillsborough." Iron was rare and valuable, and because it was fungible, served as a proxy currency for nearly everything. In the backcountry, iron was as valuable as gold, and certainly more useful, and traders from all over made their way to Vesuvius Furnace to barter for it. "The western merchant generally came to the works with his wagons laden with the products of his section, such as cloth, woolen or flax or tow, leather hides, dried beef hams, cheese, etc., etc., which he exchanged for iron goods. Sometimes these wagons would have to wait several days for their load, as there would be some ahead of them and each would be served in turn."[77]

In addition to his business and political duties, he served as a Presbyterian elder in the local church, and also as magistrate (or justice of the peace), in which role he arbitrated complaints, laid off public roads and divided estates. He interpreted the law for neighbors, teaching himself the common law by reading four volumes of the British jurist Blackstone. He even served as the local doctor, setting fractured limbs, sewing up cuts, and, "on one or two occasions by releasing jaws that had been unhinged by yawning."[78] It is said he particularly enjoyed officiating wedding ceremonies, which he did with "a good deal of merriment."

Graham continued in the iron business until 1834 when he transferred it to his sons and moved to a new house a mile or so away, along the same creek that fed the ironworks. The aging "General" (as he was called) ate mush and milk everyday for supper, in the old Scots-Irish manner, and drank ale and peach brandy. For fun, "at log rollings, house raisings, harvest time or other occasions which gathered the neighbors together, [he] would challenge some of the young men for combat with hickory canes instead of swords," and give them permission to strike the old man—if they could.⁷⁹ They could not, and time after time, Graham would swat the wooden sabers from their hands and follow with a smart but friendly tap on their heads.

The old Roman was called to service one last time. In January 1814, President Madison called up troops in North and South Carolina to reinforce Andrew Jackson in a war against the Creek Indians. It was expected to be a brief campaign, and so it turned out, with no major engagements.

North Carolina Governor Hawkins requested Graham to take command of the brigade comprising the two state's regiments. He was reluctant to do so, as it would take focus and time away from his large business interests and family. But like Cincinnatus, Graham accepted the call of duty stoically and left his farm to serve the Republic, once again, without complaint.

8
The Forgotten Charlotteans: African American Slaves

> "However humble an individual may be, we must not forget that he is a part of the whole, and may be known to all the citizens of a small town, especially if respectful and makes himself useful."
> —Dr. John Brevard Alexander, *History of Mecklenburg County from 1740 to 1900*

Many of the stories of Mecklenburg County history revolve around military or political figures, whose names have been celebrated for centuries: Thomas Spratt, Captain James Jack or Joseph Graham. The story of the Scots-Irish Presbyterians and their contribution to the development and growth of Mecklenburg County is well known, well researched and well documented.

Indeed, arguably, too much so. These men were of course part of the cultural and racial elite of their age; by which we mean that they were English-speaking, Protestant (Presbyterian, largely) white men. To decry them as "dead white males" (DWM) is popular in certain historical circles, but also ignorant and facile. Their importance and contribution to history does not diminish because of their ethnic background. Captain Jack did, in fact, carry treasonable resolves to Congress in the summer of 1775 (exactly which ones, the Mecklenburg Declaration, the Mecklenburg Resolves, or both, is the crux of the whole controversy). Joseph Graham did, in fact, stand and fight the British troops as they advanced into the cross-roads town in the autumn of 1780. Those are immutable facts.

But so is this. For every Jack or Graham, there are hundreds, even thousands, whose names we do not know and whose life stories are entirely lost. These are the enslaved African Americans who labored, built and shaped the economy and culture of Mecklenburg County, as surely as did the Scots-Irish. "One fact is undeniable," writes historian Dan Morrill. "Slavery was a fundamental component of the social hierarchy of pre–Civil War Mecklenburg

County."[1] But unlike many of the Scots-Irish heroes, the stories of these African American men and women are not known. They are the forgotten Charlotteans.

And while the early history of Mecklenburg County is often written as the story of the voluntary emigration of the Scots-Irish, it could with equal justice be characterized as the story of the *involuntary* emigration of the West Africans. So-called DWMs constituted, by rough accounts and at any one time, a large part of the population. For example, in 1860, whites composed approximately 60 percent of the local population (10,200 of 17,000); but of the military, civic and political elite they constituted virtually 100 percent. This means that African Americans, some freed men or women, but the vast majority slaves, constituted 40 percent of the overall population, "making Mecklenburg County one of the highest in terms of the number of bondspeople in the North Carolina Piedmont," according to Morrill. In 1860, for example, only 139 freed blacks lived near Charlotte.[2] The rest were slaves, working as farmhands or domestic servants, tending horses, growing crops, or laboring in the goldmines. Ironically, the county that prided itself on declaring itself "free and independent" from Great Britain in May 1775 was the same county of which roughly half of the population was anything but.

And of these thousands of people, of their individual stories, we know almost nothing; not because their lives were without interest, or passion or importance. On the contrary. But because they were slaves, little was written of them during their lives; and since very few were literate, they kept no personal records which have survived, other than by word of mouth. And finally, until the end of the Civil War they were, of course, property. And there are few historians of personal property.

There are also few physical, tangible remains of the slave period in the area, beyond some scattered and barren graveyards. One, known as the McCoy Slave Burial Ground, stands in farmland just off McCoy Road in Huntersville. There is little there, other than a stone marker, erected in the early twentieth century, which contains the following inscription:

> ERECTED BY
> ALBERT McCOY'S
> CHILDREN TO HIS SLAVES
> UNCLE JIM AND HIS WIFE
> LIZZIE
> UNCLE CHARLES & FAMILY

"Lizzy's" real name was Elizabeth McCoy, and she was the nanny to the McCoy children. According to St. Mark's Episcopal Church, which maintains the cemetery: "Lizzie was mammy to Albert McCoy's (1843–1925) twelve children. She and her husband, Jim, had three children of their own who did not survive, but we are uncertain when they died. With so many questions looming, we can be certain of how very beloved she was. Lizzie's stories, rhymes, and proses have been passed down for generations." The church estimates that there are 25–50 bodies in the cemetery, which was in use from 1840 to 1880. But, as is common with these sites, "there are no markers to indicate placement, names, and dates. Individual markers placed were sometimes large rocks, crockery, or crafted from wood which would have disintegrated many decades ago."

Another such spot is the Neely Slave Cemetery in the area of Steele Creek, so named for the Neely family. According to Morrill,

> Thomas Neely, who had arrived in southwestern Mecklenburg in 1754 and who owned fewer than ten slaves at the time of his death in 1795, was a generous, kind-hearted, and compassionate master. He made special provisions in his will for the welfare of his chattel labor. He stipulated that "our negro Joe ... to be taught to read" and wanted his son to give "our negro wench Susy two days every week for the purpose of providing herself in clothing." Neely ordered that the "negro child Dinah ... to be learned to read," and even insisted that "none of my legatees may sell any of my negroes out of the family under penalty of losing their inheritance."[3]

What *kind-hearted* and *generous* means in this context is hard to deduce. Perhaps Neely was "kind-hearted" by the standards of his time, perhaps not.

A handful of scattered slave cemeteries still exist in Mecklenburg County. Here is the McCoy slave cemetery in Huntersville (photograph by the author).

Mecklenburg County had hundreds of Thomas Neelys, and one could multiply this by thousands over the south as a whole. Some were perhaps good Christian men, many surely were not. How they each treated their human property varied greatly.

"Blind Dick"

The father of Dr. Annie Alexander, Dr. John Brevard Alexander (1834–1911), is another such conundrum. He was an unreconstructed Confederate, with racial views which although common at the time, we find deplorable today. But by all accounts he was also a good and moral man; intensely civic minded and a devout churchgoer. No better proof of his quality is needed than the fact that his daughter was Dr. Annie Alexander, who herself was a great woman.

Dr. Alexander was also the first historian of the county, publishing *The History of Mecklenburg County from 1740 to 1900* at the beginning of the twentieth century (1902) and in doing so, giving an authentic and unique glimpse into the small rural community of that time. It is an eclectic and colorful account. Alexander writes of the things that interest him—the Alexander family and their contributions, principally, but also MecDec, the history of local churches and other local curiosities. From time to time he launches into digressions against Yankees, modernity and the decline of the southern civilization which he had grown up in. Mostly his book is a lament for a passing world. As he put it, "Our old civilization is fast disappearing, giving way for the new."[4]

Steam and rail power were making horses obsolete. Trade and commerce were erasing agrarian culture and Protestant traditions. And more dramatically, in Alexander's view, racial equality (at least in principle, if not yet in practice) was shattering the white-dominated hierarchical society which Alexander and other property owners had known. Faith and religion were on the wane, he believed, while secularization and capitalism were spreading like one of the contagions Alexander as a doctor sought to treat. "One of the great changes we see in Charlotte is 'the get up and push' of all the trades people," he wrote. "The mighty push to pick up the floating dollar seems to be the chief aim of life."[5]

We would dispute many of his observations, or at least characterizations, particularly as they relate to African Americans and the legacy of slavery in Mecklenburg, as simplistic and bigoted. For example, his belief that "the affection that existed between master and slave was wonderful indeed" or that African Americans "has more real enjoyment prior to 1865 than they have ever had since."[6]

But Dr. Alexander, in trying to recount, by his lights, the history of the community in which he lived also attempted something grand, and ennobling. He named and thus kept alive in the historical consciousness at least one African American of that time, who otherwise would be lost to us as well.

"If the great events that occurred in the county should be preserved with fidelity, why should those of lesser grade be passed over in silence [?]" he asked. "It is our desire to treat all subjects fairly; even slavery that we not only tolerated, but defended for one hundred and fifty years." And with this spirit in mind, Dr. Alexander included in his *History* a brief portrait of an African American slave named "Blind Dick."

Where this man came from, his age and real name we don't know. He might have been taken as a child from Africa, or perhaps he was born in America, perhaps even in Mecklenburg County. Likewise, we don't know the names of his parents, siblings, or children. In this, the man named "Dick" stands for thousands of others in the area who spent their life in bondage and whose life stories have disappeared.

He was, wrote Alexander, "the most noted negro in the county. He was a slave, the property of Lawyer James Hutchinson."[7]

According to Alexander, Dick "was a noted, landmark in the town for more than twenty years before the great civil war, and lived for several years afterwards. His master gave him his time and protected him from evil-disposed." He must have suffered unimaginable challenges as a blind man and a blind slave at that, in the pre–Civil War period.

He labored "to feed and watered and curry hoses, carry fresh water to a number of rooms or offices, black boots, make fires and do sundry turns. He went about everywhere by himself, feeling his way with his stick. Almost every person in the county knew Blind Dick. He was very polite and respectful to every one, and every one wished to help him along, so he was well cared for."

Dick could also fend for himself, despite his handicap. "Once while carrying a bushel basket of fine apples on his head along the street, a gentleman standing in his door reached up and picked an apple off the basket, which Dick at once perceived, and struck with great force where he supposed the offender was who had taken the fruit that had been entrusted to his care. Dick was regarded as honest, and always bore a good name from white people." Dr. Alexander sought in the sweep of his book to account for the great deeds of the county. But still he found a place for this simple man, and for that we must give him credit. "However humble an individual may be," Alexander wrote, "we must not forget that he is a part of the whole, and may be known to all the citizens of a small town, especially if respectful and makes himself useful."

St. Lloyd Presbyterian Church Cemetery

On busy Colony Road, not far from SouthPark, near the northwestern corner of the intersection of Colony and Sharon Roads, there is an wooded lot. Passersby wonder—without inquiring further—why and how there is an undeveloped piece of property in the heart of Charlotte's high-value commercial and residential SouthPark area. The answer is that the site, maintained and protected by the Grubb Preservation Foundation, is the site of St. Lloyd Presbyterian Church cemetery. The church that once stood here is long gone, perhaps lost in a fire. All that remains is the unmarked remnants of the cemetery, overgrown, hidden in ivy, among the scattered trees and scrub brush.

St. Lloyd Presbyterian Church was established by newly freed-African Americans following the end of the Civil War. They named the church for abolitionist William Lloyd Garrison. Seventy eight graves have been identified at the site, dating from 1868, and the topography testifies to many of their locations. The ground, carpeted with periwinkle, rolls and visibly sinks in many spaces.[8] It is not a "slave cemetery," per se, but surely many of its occupants were slaves at one time.

The black congregants could not afford decorative headstones. Thus they had either wooden crosses (which are now long since disintegrated) or simple, unmarked field stones. Many of these stones now lay scattered throughout the ground. At least one other stone, shaped almost like an arrow-head, remains firmly fixed in the ground. The base of a stacked stone wall, covered in creeping vines, runs in a wide arc around the cemetery, hidden to the naked eye.

The only other visible sign of the cemetery is a single stone marker, the size of a shoebox, jammed beneath a large oak tree. Many years ago a small sapling was planted at the base of the collapsed grave. Now, over a century later, a massive oak has nearly swallowed the grave, pushing the stone at nearly a forty-five degree angle. The bottom of the stone is buried, but the top reads, in primitive, but clear, hand-carved letters:

ANNA ["RAY"? OR "ROY"?]
DIDE
JAN 30
[1868?]

It is not clear what Anna's last name is: possibly "Ray" or "Roy," or even something else. The etching in the stone is worn and unclear. "Died" is misspelled as "dide," which is phonetically correct. In addition, the "N" in "JAN" is transposed. There is a grace and love in the simple forgotten stone.

Who was Anna Ray (or Roy?). And who was the hand that carved her

The remains of the St. Lloyd Presbyterian Church cemetery, near Southpark, founded by freed slaves following the Civil War. The top of the buried headstone reads "ANNA [RAY?], DIDE, JAN 30" (photograph by the author).

gravestone? A father, husband, or someone else? We do not know. Anna also falls in the category of Mecklenburg's forgotten Charlotteans.

The man once known locally as "Blind Dick" is buried in another of these forgotten lots, somewhere in the county, presumably alongside the bodies of dozens of other African American slaves. Both he and "Anna Ray" must stand as proxies for thousands of other African Americans of Mecklenburg County whose stories are forgotten.

9

The Silent Barber: Thaddeus Lincoln Tate

"If I told what I knew—whew!"
—Thad Tate, 1934

Barbers are unusual subjects for stories of heroism and civic achievement, all the more so when the barber in the story is a black man; the son of slaves, living in the ruins of the American South after the Civil War. One would think that the poverty and stifling racial oppression of that period could not, after all, create the necessary preconditions for greatness. But perhaps that is the whole point of this tale.

Thaddeus Lincoln Tate was born in the small, mountain town of Morganton, North Carolina on October 26, 1865.

The day he was born Andrew Johnson was President of the United States, a country that (once again) included the former Confederate State of North Carolina. In fact, the day of Tate's birth, only 172 days had passed since General Robert E. Lee had surrendered the Army of Northern Virginia to Lieutenant General Ulysses S. Grant at the small Virginia hamlet of Appomattox. A few weeks after Lee's surrender, on April 26, at the farm of Joseph Bennett near Durham, North Carolina, Confederate General Joseph E. Johnston surrendered his remaining armies to Major General William T. Sherman. With Johnston's surrender of thirty thousand men, the Civil War, in North Carolina at least, was over. Like much of the south, the state of North Carolina was economically devastated; its infrastructure wrecked; and its future uncertain. It was not an auspicious period to be born, nor a very hopeful one.

The facts around Tate's childhood are unclear, but it seems likely that his parents—Thad Tate, Sr., and Maggie Kinson—named him Thaddeus after Thaddeus Stevens, a Pennsylvania Congressman and one of the leading prewar abolitionist leaders. His middle name was Lincoln, surely for the former president. His parents were recorded as being mulatto; that is of mixed white and black race (usually of a white mother). Tate was small, slight and very fair-skinned, so much so that in later pictures it is difficult to tell that he was of African American descent. He had prominent ears, which made him look youthful, even later in his life. As an adult he wore a moustache, kept his hair in a fashionable wave and dressed quite elegantly. He could almost be mistaken for a wealthy Italian merchant. In photos he didn't smile, but kept a polite, if inscrutable, mien.

Morganton had less than 800 residents in 1865 when Tate was born, and of those, able bodied white men were scarce. Many were interned as prisoners, missing, or buried in places as remote as southern Pennsylvania or coastal South Carolina. When he was twelve, the Tate family moved from Morganton to Charlotte. Charlotte was a sleepy southern town, but as a commercial center and transportation hub, more affluent than Morganton. It was larger too, with a population of around 6,200 in 1877.

Prior to the war, Charlotte had been a small but thriving railroad city. Its population had more than doubled between 1850 and 1860 (from 1,065 to 2,265), making it the sixth-largest city in North Carolina. People and commerce largely passed through town, giving it something of a transient air, but nevertheless it was calm, prosperous and homely. Except, of course, to its enslaved population, which constituted 36 percent of the population at the outbreak of the war. They would have found their circumstances very far from "homely."[1]

The war had impacted Charlotte, but only indirectly. There were no major battles fought in the Piedmont, nor large-scale property damage. The nearest true fighting Charlotte had seen had occurred in April 1865, when federal forces exchanged fire with Confederate cavalry north of town (on Beattie's and Cowan's Ford) and also south at Nation's Ford on the Catawba River.[2] But these were isolated incidents. "Charlotte was spared the destruction inflicted on places like Atlanta, Columbia and Richmond," notes historian Michael Hardy in *Civil War Charlotte*. "Much of the infrastructure remained intact. The rails to the north and south were wrecked, but the line to Greensboro was repaired within days."[3]

Although the physical damage was limited, what was less obvious was the silence of the missing. Many young men were simply no longer there. By one estimate 2,713 men from Mecklenburg had served in the Confederate Army, of which 638 had died, or roughly 23 percent.[4]

The ghosts of the Great War lingered in the cross-roads town. Charlotte was in a sense the "last capital of the Confederacy," writes Hardy. "[T]he papers of various departments were shipped to Charlotte and stored locally; the remnants of the Confederate treasury were deposited in Charlotte's United State Mint building for a time; and official acts, like examining and commissioning officers, took place there."[5] Indeed, the last formal meeting of the

Confederate Cabinet was held on Trade Street on April 26, 1865, in one of the upstairs rooms of William Phifer's home. "After Jefferson Davis left Charlotte, the Confederacy effectively ceased to exist."[6]

With the end of the Confederacy, the antebellum world of North Carolina was shattered forever, although it wasn't clear what was going to replace it. Especially in the sphere of race relations—the *causus belli* for the war just ended—the atmosphere was tense, and the future entirely shrouded.

At Lee's surrender, there were 6,000 newly freed slaves in Mecklenburg County alone. According to one story, a slave owner went into the fields to tell his slaves that they were now freed. They looked at him quizzically. What were they to do now? No one was certain. Some left, but the former master asked the remainder to carry on working through the end of the year. Many of them did so, having no better idea of where to go, or what to do next. Other freed ex-slaves set out to start new lives, as the Tate family did, to a bigger city with perhaps better opportunities, or at least no fewer.

By 1877, the year the Tate family arrived in Charlotte, the city's population had doubled in a little more than a decade. A large proportion of the new arrivals were freed ex-slaves, or "freedmen." Although a federal Freedmen's Bureau had been established to promote the well-being of the ex-slaves and to protect them from injustice, its impact was limited. Nor were the government officials entirely sympathetic. For example, the federal officer in charge of the Freedmen's Bureau for Charlotte complained in June 1865 that "the whole population of Blacks were completely wild,"[7] a rather tactless remark by which he meant that many thousands had left their former plantations, and were now seeking to move, almost anywhere, to escape the site of their former enslavement and terror.

Not that there were many places to go where life was better. A severe depression began in 1873, one of the worst in American history, and continued to grip the country until the 1880s. An ad in Charlotte during what was called the "Long Depression" (1873–1879) by Burgess Nichols & Co., a furniture seller announced, "PRICES REDUCED TO SUIT THE TIMES! Owing to the GREAT DEPRESSION in business, I am enabled to buy many Goods in my line at GREATLY REDUCED RATES."[8]

Although times were difficult, the area was on the cusp of a textile driven boom. "The village [in 1877] was now a bustling small town, but it was not until the next decade that Charlotte was about to move into manufacturing."[9] Cotton manufacturing, specifically. Prior to the 1880s, the south was largely a commodity economy, undiversified and requiring large amounts of unskilled labor. There was cotton to be sure, but only the *production* of cotton, not the manufacturing base to process cotton into clothing and fabrics. Those industries were in New England.

Under the slogan "Bring the Mills to the Cotton," the textile industry slowly began to relocate south towards the end of the nineteenth century. Steam power could now be used in lieu of water power, which had been a northern competitive advantage. Freight and logistics costs were cheaper and of course labor was plentiful. Charlotte also had a competitive advantage over other similarly sized southern cities due to its railroad nexus (five railroads connected in town). And so ironically, it was in part the expansion of the cotton industry with the industrialization and urbanization it brought that sparked the "New South" movement; a movement that powered Charlotte and the area's growth and launched the textile revolution.

Charlotte being Charlotte, most of the civic elite were keen to put the recent unpleasant mess behind them and get on with the business of making money. "Picking up where they had left off in 1861," writes Historian Janette Greenwood of the period "the people of Charlotte lured more railroads to their town and built more banks, iron-front buildings, and fashionable Italianate homes."[10]

By the 1880s a sense of normalcy had returned, albeit one that obscured the fact that black and white societies now existed in their own largely self-contained worlds. Nor were they equal worlds. According to the 1870 census, 86 percent of black Charlotteans were unskilled laborers (comprising half of town's unskilled labor force). African Americans comprised just 5 percent of the skilled craftsmen in the city. Per the 1870 census, there was only a single black grocer, saloonkeeper, boardinghouse proprietor and restaurateur in town. And importantly for Tate's career, there were only two black barbers.[11]

Black society was keen to embrace its new rights and freedoms. White society, or at least some of it, still resented the "Lost Cause," the downfall and oblivion of the Confederate project, and the intrusion of northern rule and law in their lives. "The threats of Yankee Radical papers," announced the *Charlotte Democrat* in June 1877, "that unless the Southern people do so and so, they will be put through another course of 'reconstruction,' is pusillanimous and contemptible."[12] Thus inevitably, the "black and white townspeople of Charlotte clashed repeatedly," writes Greenwood, "as blacks tested the limits of their freedom and whites tried to enforce customary rules of race relations."[13]

One episode from 1875 captures the mood. Six black men took seats in the whites only section of the theater one evening. "No attention was paid them by the audience," noted the local press, but word of the incident "was not long in extending to the streets." A "crowd of young gentlemen" attacked them, dragged them outside and kicked them down the steps of the theater.[14]

In this social reality, personal aspiration among African Americans could be found in religion, in family and social engagements. Economic aspiration, however, had only one route; through working for, or servicing in some way the dominant, white society. Thad Tate's route was to become the leading barber and stylist to the white community.

The Barber

In 1875, Charlotte had three barbers, one of whom was another African American man named Gray Toole. Toole kept a barbershop in the rear of Charlotte's Central Hotel, which the *Charlotte Democrat* reported in June 1877, "keeps the best workmen employed, and guarantees pleasure and satisfaction to customers." By 1880, Tate's father had died and his mother remarried Pethel James, who was also a barber. This was perhaps the link into the profession where Tate would make his name. (The 1880 census lists Tate as a barber; most likely he was working for his step-father.)

When he was seventeen, Tate left for New York City, but returned to Charlotte after just a few months. By one account, "he did not like the life of the big city."[15] When he returned he went to work for Toole and, at age seventeen, about 1882, Tate put up a red, white and blue pole on the west side of South Tryon Street, barely a hundred feet from the Square and "within spitting distance" of three major pharmacies.[16] His shop was below the Garibaldi and Bruns Jewelry Company. The shop had six chairs.

At this time, barbers were a black-only occupation. As such, they occupied a unique bridge role between the African American and white southern worlds (as, for that matter, did bartenders). Their position gave them face-to-face opportunities to speak and interact with whites on a daily basis, and from less of a position of inferiority than in most service jobs. (After all, a man can only be so rude and oppressive when another man has a straight razor at his neck.) Tate's physical appearance, being quite light skinned, allowed him to "pass," meaning that in the rigidly race conscious world, it was not entirely clear to whites if he were truly black at all. This gave him better social standing and opportunities than those with darker skin.

Around 1895, Tate and Toole decided to consolidate their competing businesses. Tate became part owner of the Central Hotel barbershop. By now he had already built a good reputation in the community. Within a few years the name "Thad Tate" became synonymous with the Central Hotel barbershop.

As its names suggests, the "Central" (as it was known) was in the very center of Charlotte, on the south east corner of Tryon Street, near what was called Independence Square (after the location of the famous Mecklenburg Declaration). A hotel and tavern had stood on spot since at least the 1830s when it was known as the "Mansion House." An advertisement in 1843 boasted that the table at the "Mansion House" was "well and plentifully supplied with every thing the country affords, to please and satisfy the palate even of an epicure." The horse stables, it was said, were "attended by faithful and attentive hostlers and supplied with abundant provender." And, of greatest importance, as any business travel will gleefully attest, the hotel bar was "furnished with a choice selection of liquors."[17]

9. The Silent Barber

It was more than a hotel, however, it was the place to meet up; the center of town; and the focus of commerce, with businessmen nearby selling gold, grains, oats (35 cents per bushel in 1837) and other commodities.[18] In the hotel itself or nearby worked clock and watch repairmen ("in the very best manner," said the ads), bakers ("Fresh Bread, Cakes, Pies, &c"), dentists specializing in teeth replacement (including the "much admired MINERAL TEETH, which are considered equal, if not superior, to the Parisian, on account of their beautiful pearly white enamel") and, of course, barbershops.

In 1873 the hotel's name was changed from the "Mansion House" to the "Central Hotel." By now it was a four-story stone building, which fronted both Trade and Tryon Streets, and looked out over the Square, where horse and buggies, men in top coats, commercial wagons and, eventually, black Model Ts clattered past. The local papers that year commended the landlord, H. C. Eccles, as being "as clever a landlord as we ever saw," and had no hesitation in recommending him "to our citizens and the public generally."[19] The hotel had recently been enlarged with 50 additional rooms, each "handsomely fitted up" with new furniture, making it, as it boasted, "the largest Hotel in the State."[20] There was a wine and a billiards room which sold cigars, brandy and "Ole Kentucky Whiskies." In 1887, shortly before Tate began working there, the Central Hotel, newly painted and refurbished, had a modern system of electric bells and lights installed. With a street car passing out front every

Charlotte's Central Hotel, circa 1900. Tate's barbershop was located here (courtesy the Robinson-Spangler Carolina Room, Charlotte Mecklenburg Library).

fifteen minutes, it was, said a page one ad in the Charlotte City Directory, "the headquarters for commercial travelers."

In short, it was the place to be, especially for an enterprising, social climbing and entrepreneurial spirit like Tate. Standing on the main street, in the center of town, heavily trafficked, it was inevitable that as Charlotte grew and prospered, Tate's barbershop would too. "Central Hotel Barber Shop has five of the best barbers in the city," read one of Tate's advertisements. "Come and try them. Thad Tate, Prop."[21]

The Businessman

In 1886, when Tate was twenty-five, he married Mary Lincoln Butler. (Ironically, they shared the same middle name.) They made their home in a quaint, two-story brick Italianate house at 504 East 7th Street. The house had flat rooves, wide eaves, tall windows and decorative, Gothic front-porch spindles. Typically for the style, the banisters and columns were painted a bright and distinctive color (pink, yellow or white) to offset against the brick. Downstairs there was a one-story covered porch covered with numerous flowers and ferns, where the family took the air during the hot and muggy summer months.

Tate's home was in an integrated neighborhood in First Ward, near the south side of the intersection with Caldwell Street. (As with much of Charlotte's historic architecture, the house is now gone; where it stood is now the Charlotte Housing Authority Community; much of the old black neighborhood is an un-quaint succession of grim parking lots.) The residential First Ward area was called a "salt and pepper" neighborhood, meaning it had a mixture of black and white families. The men were largely shopkeepers or blue-collar tradesmen, living side-by-side in Victorian homes intermixed with "shotgun" row homes. In time the Tate Family had ten children: five daughters and five sons, with the attendant noise and rambunctiousness. Friends and neighbors called them the "dozen family."

By the end of the nineteenth century, Tate had become a Charlotte celebrity, loved and respected in both the white and black sections of town. "One of the most thoroughly equipped shaving parlors in this vicinity is that conducted by the well-known and popular barber, Thad L. Tate.," stated the paper. Tate's store, had:

> [A]ll the modern improvements, [and] include[s] six of the latest hydraulic chairs, baths and other conveniences. His parlor is conveniently arranged, and he and five skilled artists are kept constantly busy in the various departments of shaving, haircutting, shampooing, etc, which is done in the most prompt and reliable manner ... his careful and painstaking work has gained for him an enviable reputation in this section of the State.[22]

Thad Tate with his wife and nine children in a photograph taken around 1905. The large Tate family was known as the "dozen family" around town, for obvious reasons (courtesy the Robinson-Spangler Carolina Room, Charlotte Mecklenburg Library).

"Thad is 'one of the finest,'" reported the *Charlotte Observer*, "and his shop will be kept as clean as he looks."[23] It was "a Well-Kept Tonsorial Parlor," the paper said next year, and "a credit to the city." There were porcelain bath tubs and showers, as well as "handsome new chairs, cases and fixtures. Thad is not to be outdone by any artist in his line. He is not only one of the best barbers going, but his shop is as handsome as any to be found in the State."[24]

The type of employees he sought attests to the type of business Tate ran. Per one 1904 ad:

BARBER WANTED—(colored)—Good pay to sober, steady, first-class barber. Thad L. Tate, Central Hotel.[25]

The great and the good visited Tate's shop. His customers included prominent local civic leaders such as Governors Cameron Morrison and Zebulon Vance, business leaders William Henry Belk and J. B. Ivey and the neighborhood developer Edward Dilworth Latta. "[T]his locally famous tonsorial emporium was, for many years, far more than a mere place where gentlemen went to have the waving whiskers whisked away or their troublesome tresses trimmed. Thad Tate's barber shop was, as any old Mecklenburger worthy of his keep will tell you, the social center for the men."[26] It was the place to see and be seen. An 1896 article reported:

> The wealth of the gentlemen who gathered about this famous institution was not measured by the money they had in the bank or the clothes they wore or the size of their daddy's plantations. These gay blades showed the extent of their worldly possessions by the size and magnificence of their shaving cups. These cups were kept in a large cabinet, especially built for the purpose which almost covered one of the walls of the shop. On each cup, emblazoned in gold, appeared the name of its owner. Some of the cups were elaborately decorated in colors of vermillion, blue and gold. And upon these objects of splendor the less prosperous gentlemen used to cast envious glances.[27]

Like all service businesses, sometimes customers were difficult. Col. Wade Hampton Harris, the editor of the *Charlotte Observer*, insisted upon having a haircut that "befits an editor." Once, Tate took off too much of the Colonel's hair, and Harris stormed out, vowing to have his revenge in the gossip papers if his hair didn't grow back within a week. (Fortunately for Tate, it did.)

E. T. Cansler, a law clerk who worked in the law office above Tate's shop, was known to be "old-maidish about his haircuts." At the time, Cansler was courting a young woman named Lily Scott, and from time to time Cansler would slip downstairs to Tate's shop, where he would:

> [S]cribble off a hurried note, and tell Thad to have it delivered at once to Miss Lily. Then he would sneak back up to his work. But in five minutes or less, he would come hurryin' back down-stairs demanding to know whether the boy that took the note had returned. "What's he goin' to do? Take all day?" he would shout. And when the boy would finally return with an answer, young Cansler would read it. It is suited him, he would take out his jew's-harp [an old-fashioned mouth instrument] and play a couple of tunes. If it didn't suit him, he would walk out of the shop shouting: "I'm never going to let that boy delivery another note for me. It takes him a week!"

In another episode, a customer became "mighty sore," recalled Tate, "when his hair wasn't combed just right."[28] Another time, a customer named Dr. Hillary Wilder was charged fifty cents upon conclusion of his haircut, twice the going rate. "Fifty cents!" he exclaimed. Robert Hall, one of Tate's barbers replied, "Yes sir. While I was cutting your hair your ol' greyhound dog, Joe, eat up my supper." Dr. Wilder paid the fifty cents.[29]

As the nineteenth century gave way to the twentieth, Tate began expanding his business ventures beyond the tonsorial. He speculated widely in real estate, leasing, and buying and selling properties across Mecklenburg County. Papers of the period are full of advertisements for rooms to rent, acres of land to be bought or sold, even touring cars for sale. At the end of each ad is the simple two word contact information: Thad Tate. "Thad L. Tate, the well-known colored barber, was the successful bidder on nearly $9,000 worth of real estate sold at the court house yesterday at noon," comprising 155 acres, in one common example.[30]

In 1922 Tate helped build the Mecklenburg Investment Company Building. It was the first building in Charlotte for the purpose of accommodating African American businesses, professional offices, civic and fraternal organizations.[31] It was built at the then-impressive cost of approximately $28,000. On the first floor there was a pharmacy, on the second were offices for African American doctors and lawyers, and on the third a meeting hall for African American Masonic lodges.[32] Tate's grandson later said, "the building was a financial success to the extent that the mortgage was retired in less than ten years, and thus was not a problem when the Great Depression struck."[33]

From real estate, Tate moved into insurance. He was one of the founders of the Afro-American Mutual Insurance Company ("AAMIC") and served on its Board of Directors. AAMIC catered to the black community, which was largely ignored by white-owned companies. Its headquarters were in Charlotte (on 412 East 2nd Street) with a second office in Rock Hill, South Carolina. "Sickness is sure to come," brochures for the AAMIC cheerily pronounced: "Death Follows." Using super-effective scare tactics directed towards its elderly target market, tactics that dominate the industry to this day, the AAMIC asked: "If you were Suddenly Sick to-night and die, WHAT THEN?"

What then indeed? A nickel to twenty five cents a week (when you were well) returned $1–$5 per week during times of illness, and up to $75 upon death. Death, like sex, guns and alcohol, was a recession-proof industry, and in catering exclusively to the African American emerging middle class, AMMIC hit a gold mine. The business strategy and sales pitch was simple, direct and effective, perfectly merging a capitalist sales pitch with the language of liberation from bondage. "An Afro-American policy, by an Afro-American agent, made by Afro-American clerks, on an Afro-American husband, an Afro-American wife, or an Afro-American child, makes an Afro-American *home independent* in the hours of sickness or death." Within three years AAMIC had more than 22,500 members and had paid over $25,000 in benefits, with over two hundred agents throughout the Carolinas.[34]

For the final Christmas of the century, in December 1899, Tate's team of six barbers gave him a handsome watch fob for Christmas. "Thad is deserving of all good that comes to him," stated the local press.[35]

The Philanthropist

If Thad Tate's story was only that of a young African American entrepreneur who made good, it would be interesting, but not much more. Usually in commerce, being the gathering of wealth, the story ends with the death of the entrepreneur. Tate's achievement, however, was in civic engagement, being the spreading of wealth, and those stories go on and on. Through his civic achievements Tate became the foremost African American leader of his time.

Until Tate's era, black civic leaders had largely been preachers, or politically oriented writers or activists, such as Frederick Douglass. There was a white, southern tradition of engaged, wealthy, entrepreneurial men and women who spent their time and money in various charitable causes. Until Tate, the African American community in Charlotte did not have a comparable tradition, for the obvious reason that there had not been a class of wealthy, accomplished African American business leaders. According to historian Greenwood, Charlotte's "black community remained fundamentally a one-class society. Yet the churches and schools of the Reconstruction era spawned a new, self-conscious generation of black teachers, preachers, and businesspeople who would come of age in the 1880s."[36] In this, Tate was in the vanguard.

Through his white contacts Tate pressed for improvements in basic services for the black community; services that were desperately inadequate or had never even existed. He raised money for the Brevard Street branch of the county library, the first free branch of the public library for African Americans in the south, which opened in 1905 and contained 9,000 volumes ("for the sole use of the Negroes"). The building was "artistic in structure and beautifully located being on one of the most prominent streets in the city." It had "two large reading rooms and [a] large lobby which can be converted into one large room affording splendid facilities for social meeting, reading circles, lectures, sewing circles and other meetings."[37] (The library is all the more astonishing when one thinks that at the time of Tate's birth, it was illegal to even teach black children to read.)

He raised money for and helped establish a new, brick building for Grace A. M. E. Zion Church on South Brevard Street, for which he served as a trustee. Grace became a center of the African American community in Charlotte in the last two decades of the nineteenth century. (By the time of Tate's death in 1951, it was known as "Thad Tate's and Silas Washington's church.") He acted as a trustee, chaired committees, endorsed political candidates, lent his name to advisory committees, sat on boards, organized fundraisers, endured organizing meetings, and gave time and money in hundreds of causes. "Thad Tate and other leading colored citizens brought the Jubilee Singers here," announced the paper, as a "benefit of the Colored Reform School."[38] The Jubilee Singers, eight in all, were a nationally known singing group performing "jubilee songs, plantation songs, negro melodies, camp meeting songs, negro lullabys," and so forth.[39] The organizers asked for a "liberal patronage" at the event, even pointing out the "seats will be reserved for white people."⁴⁰ During World War I, Tate and his wife served on the welcome committee for a new club to entertain the 4,000 black soldiers stationed at Camp Greene, who were en route to Europe. On opening night, the club, of which Mrs. Tate served as head of the reception committee, was decorated with flowers and American flags "in compliment to the colored soldiers who will go over to do their bit, and help Uncle Sam lick the Germans."⁴¹

Education for African Americans was bad and inconvenient. So, Tate helped found a branch of the YMCA for African Americans. He also launched the Morrison Training School for African American youths, a boys' reform school. The facility opened in 1924, housing eight boys. (In 1939, its name was changed to Morrison Training School for Governor Cameron Morrison; and changed again in 1969 to Cameron Morrison School).

He did more; in 1913, Tate supported establishment of the first night school for African Americans in the United States.⁴² He helped initiate the appointment of the first black police officers in Charlotte.

High school students from Washington Heights had to travel to Second Ward High School on the other side of downtown, the city's only secondary facility for blacks.⁴³ In the late 1930s, the Mecklenburg County school Superintendent approached Tate with a proposal that he sell or donate ten acres for a new African American school, which would be named "Thad Tate High School." Tate was generous, but was also a businessman. Tate asked for one night to think the proposal over. The next morning he told the Superintendent that he would forego the honor of having his name on the school, but he would, he said, "take the $5,000." It was said of him that he "wanted no honors that he had to buy."⁴⁴ The school was started, ultimately becoming West Charlotte High School (now Northwest School of the Arts).

"Progressive in every respect"

In all his endeavors, Tate sought to better the black community morally, financially and spiritually. He was uniquely placed to do this, through his connections in the white community. As the barber to the leading public citizens, he could lobby them, bend their ears and put a face to the black community, which otherwise white Charlotte might never see.

At the same time, Tate and Charlotte's white business elite had a mutually supporting, symbiotic relationship. The business community could point to Tate as an example of the type of African American leader they liked and would promote; one who was helpful, accommodating and polite, but who ultimately worked within, rather than sought to subvert or overthrow, the existing order. In turn, the community rewarded Tate and supported his projects. It was an unapologetic, practical, business approach to social progress, in a business-oriented town. And, for its period, it is perhaps all that could have been done within the system in any event.

Leaders like Tate were critically important to maintain social stability. "It is delightful to contemplate that, whereas during recent months serious clashes between the races have occurred in many parts of the country," one article noted, "the feeling between the two races in Charlotte is now of warmth and most sympathetic friendship." Despite a number of race related crimes that had occurred, noted the paper, "there has been a spirit among the better classes of both races here to look to the courts to adjudicate wrongs and Charlotte has gone along through the years without any attempt at mob violence." For that the credit went to the "leadership of such broad-minded negroes as Thad Tate," and others, who "are rendering valuable service in the betterment of conditions affecting the negro race and in wielding more securely the ties that bind the white and the colored people together."[45]

Part of this was of course self-serving on the part of the white establishment, but that was perhaps inevitable if not exculpatory. So it was neither cynicism nor ill-will when the *Charlotte News* described Tate in 1909 as "one of the very best citizens in the colored race" who "has always been courteous and obliging to his many white customers. As a result his business met with success and he owns some valuable property in the city. His courtesy should be a model for the colored race. It has won for him the friendship of many of the best white citizens of the state."[46]

Another editorial sounded a similar note when it stated: "Charlotte has been blessed in many ways from the lavish hand of the Giver of every good and every perfect gift. She has been favored in her colored population. As a whole the race in this city is above the average for intelligence and good common sense. Their leaders apart from the preachers have been men of the stamp of Thad Tate…"[47]

Time after time, Tate was cited and lauded as representing the best of the black community—at least according to the standards of white society. "Charlotte is progressive in every respect," the local paper boasted at one point, "even to the extent of her barbering. Thad Tate left this morning for New York to take lessons in dressing and cutting ladies' and children's hair."[48]

Not everyone would call the city, or the region, *progressive* however. While the Charlotte white business and civic elite took to Tate, it would be incorrect to say he was "*one of their own.*" He was not, and never fully would be. He remained a black man in a white dominated society. Even in the laudatory op-eds quoted above, one cannot escape the patronizing subtext.

Even the anecdotes about his customers, such as Cansler, quoted earlier, which are meant to be humorous, carry an ugly, bullying undercurrent that's difficult to ignore. For example, note that one customer storms out when his hair isn't cut correctly; or the young lawyer Cansler demands to have a note delivered and then shouts at the young courier when it isn't done to his satisfaction. And if you read the story about Cansler even closer, you notice that throughout Tate is called "Thad," while the white men are all called by their surnames and the woman being courted is called "Miss Lily." Such was the period.

What did Tate think of his white customers? What belittling remarks did he have to accept, or what injustices did he see, or indeed suffer? What where his thoughts when he cut the hair or trimmed the whiskers of Vance, Cansler and others, as he did, day after day, year after year? Some of them, such as Governor Vance, were former Confederate officers who, had their side won, would have kept Tate, his family and millions of others in bondage. Did Tate think about such things? Or was it just business?

Tate kept his counsel. He was "no talker," his customers would say. "Thad won't admit much," one reported noted. "'If I told what I knew—whew!' was all he would say." Indeed.

A World in Flux

By the mid–1930s, Tate's barbering career was approaching a half century. In 1909 he sold his shop in the Central Hotel (for a "handsome profit"), and moved to East Trade Street. (Thereafter, he moved once more to East Fourth). Late in life, he continued to serve only six long-standing customers, regularly, every day, but only at fixed hours. He was slowing down.

"My sons runs it," he said of the barbershop. "He runs it better than I do. It's a modern shop now—and, well, I like the old shops better. So I can stay at home as much as I can—happy among my treasured memories of the old days."[49] His civic achievements were widely known and respected. Tate had seen an extraordinary amount of change during his lifetime. He was born at the conclusion of the Civil War, lived through two world wars and the Great Depression and witnessed the invention of the airplane and automobile. Change, it seemed to Tate, was constant. Even his barbershop had felt the force of the coming modern world. When he had arrived in Charlotte, in 1878, the town had three barbers. By 1948, there were more than seventy.

In the mid–1920s, women began coming into his shop, which the all-male clientele deeply resented. At least one customer (a Dr. Sidney Johnson) deserted Tate entirely in protest.

"But it wasn't my fault[!]" Tate argued. "I realized the world was changing and I couldn't turn the ladies down. All sorts of things were happening in barbershops." In addition to accommodating women, technology had gotten completely out of control. "Electric clippers had come along," Tate noted, "and the first time I used a Pair on one of my customers he almost jumped out of the chair." Similarly, the new-fangled head massage caused great unease amidst his clients. According to Tate, only one of the old gentlemen—a Mr. Tom Griffith—cared for it. "These things, however, as Thad well know," wrote the *Observer*, "represented progress."[50]

Tate retired from barbering, after 60 years. As the story went, at work that morning, he

> called together Mr. William Johnson and Mr. Ernest Friday, two of his faithful and loyal barbers, who had been with him for over 27 years. He told them he had been in business for 61 YEARS. He felt that his feet were giving away from such a long period of standing. Momentarily he came to definite conclusions. He announced to these two men that he was ending his work that day. As an appreciation for their support, high degree of integrity, and faithfulness, he made his entire business over to them without any compensation.[51]

Tate died in 1951, a respected and well-known public figure, mourned in both the white and black spheres of Charlotte. His wife had died a few years earlier, as had many of his coworkers, including Ed Butler, who had worked with Tate for 18 years. At Tate's birth, Andrew Johnson was President and the nation was devastated. At his death, Harry S Truman was President, much of Europe and Asia lay in ruins, and America was rising as a superpower.

Tate's impact on the city was tremendous, but as with many civic leaders, many of his contributions were made behind the scenes, without pomp or ceremony, but were no less important because they were unglamorous. "Possessed of business acumen, he also was very industrious and thrifty and he had attained much success," read his obituary in the *Charlotte Observer*. "He also was widely recognized as a public-spirited citizen genuinely interested in community betterment."[52] The *News* quoted attorney Francis O. Clarkson, a white friend of Tate's, who described him as "an outstanding Christian citizen who came up after the Civil War under very harsh and averse conditions. He had great vision, foresight and by his kindly spirit, his energy and fine citizenship, made an outstanding record and endeared himself to many of our citizens who knew and had great respect for him."[53]

An earlier (patronizing, if sincerely intended) summary of Tate's life printed in the *Charlotte Observer* in 1934, during the height of the Great Depression, had stated:

> Nearly half a century has passed since Thaddeus Tate, a colored boy from the country, opened his first barber shop in this city. During all these years he has watched the parade go by. He has seen depressions come and go, politicians rise and all, so-called great men spring up like mushrooms soon to crumble away, and the nouveau riche flaunt gains that have since disappeared. Thad, however, with the true hear of a white man, has smiled and gone on.
> Death alone can remove him from the high place he holds in the hearts of those who really know him, and even after death, his memory will linger on.[54]

All true, except for the one jarring and racist line. Tate did not have a black or white heart, but a human one.

10

The Cavalryman: Lt. William Ewen Shipp

> "What a gallant fellow he was!"
> —Theodore Roosevelt in a letter
> to Shipp's widow, May 29, 1902

Tucked away behind a gated fence at the U.S. Federal Courthouse on West Trade Street is what is known as the "Shipp Monument." It is a large monument and quite a stately one. When it was erected the local paper noted it was "finely proportioned," with a white needle of Winnsboro granite soaring thirty feet high over a rough-hewn base.

It is a strange monument, however, as its size and elegance are in exact disproportion to the renown of the person for whom it was erected—Cavalry First Lieutenant William Ewen Shipp. It commemorates a man few people have ever heard of, for a war that almost no one remembers. It was unveiled in May 1902, amidst a surge of patriotic fever associated with American victory in the Spanish American War. Shipp—then only thirty-six years old—was a commander of "Buffalo Soldiers" of the U.S. Tenth Cavalry and was killed in the charge up San Juan Hill in Cuba; the same charge in which another Cavalryman, Theodore Roosevelt, was made nationally famous.

By coincidence, Roosevelt was one of the last to see Shipp alive that day. Shipp had shared breakfast with Roosevelt. Later that day, Shipp brought the order to advance up San Juan hill, and was shot and killed moments later. Roosevelt would repay the favor to his fallen comrade, taking an instrumental lead in having the memorial in Charlotte unveiled. As Roosevelt would put it in a letter to Shipp's widow, Margaret Busbee Shipp, in 1904, "Few things have given me more pleasure than to be able to do what the widow of my comrade in arms desired."[1]

But in fact, paying respect to Shipp was only part of Roosevelt's motivation. Reinstating the still-sullen former *Confederate* States to the *United* States of America, was really what the Shipp Monument was all about.

A Tale of Two Monuments

The Shipp Memorial is one of three memorials, all quite alike in style and character, which were erected around 1900 in Charlotte. A resurgence in history, greater disposable income, and access to local building materials, such as granite from quarries near Winnsboro, South Carolina, or Mount Airy, North Carolina, led to a local boom in monument-erecting.

The first such monument was unveiled on June 30, 1887, in Elmwood Cemetery, near downtown Charlotte. Called the "Confederate Monument," it was a thirty foot obelisk, atop seven-steps of tiered granite. Its purpose, according to its sponsors, was to honor the Confederate Veterans, the United Daughters of the Confederacy, and the four-year lifespan of the Confederate States of America (from 1861–1865). Spread in neat little rows under its shadow lay the graves of various rebel soldiers from the area. Amidst the quiet trees just a short walk from the center of Charlotte, it was (and is) an unapologetic commemoration of the Confederate cause.

Ten years after it was unveiled, on May 10, 1898, an attorney with the extraordinary name of Armistead Burwell, Esq., gave a brief but touching speech to various onlookers on the small, quiet hill just west of the center of town, amid the rows of Confederate dead. "Almost a third of a century has passed since the host that followed Lee and Johnston laid down its arms before that which followed Grant and Sherman," Burwell began, as the crickets buzzed and birds chirped in the warm air, "the one returning to homes made desolate by defeat, the other to a land made joyful by victory."[2]

None of the sons or daughters of the Confederacy listening to Burwell that day had any doubt which side they were on. The losing side. After touching on such "distant scenes" as Gettysburg and Chickamauga, and of Grant and Bragg, all places and people receding each day from memory, Burwell turned to the task at hand: "We come to deck these graves with the flowers of spring, testifying thus again that we who survive here have not forgotten those who 'sleep in fame.'" It was a touching scene.

The public appetite for Romanesque funeral orations at that time must have been great, for just ten days after Burwell's speech, a larger, grander, all-day event took place. This was the unveiling of another granite obelisk.

This second Charlotte monument was to the "Signers of the Mecklenburg Declaration of Independence." MecDec of course was considered *the* principal event for which Charlotte was (or it was argued, should be) nationally and justly famous. The MecDec (or "Signers' Monument") looked very much like the Confederate Monument and was virtually identical in scale. The base was nine feet, two inches, and its white granite needle was 29 and a half feet tall—all in all just under 40 feet in height.

The Signers' Monument was unveiled on May 20, 1898, a day which, according to the local paper, had "dawned auspiciously. Not a cloud was in the sky. The sun shone brightly." And, importantly for the quaint and sleepy town, the "streets were free from dust."[3] Although this was ostensibly a celebration of a local historical curiosity—the Mecklenburg Declaration—that had occurred (if it occurred) 123 years earlier, in reality the celebration that day looked and felt more like a commemoration of the American Civil War, which had ended just forty years earlier.

Before 8:00 am that morning, a "compact mass of Confederate veterans, horsemen, carriages, floats, etc." had begun massing, more than a mile in length, reaching "from the square back as far as Morehead Avenue." The Steel Creek band kept up a looped rendition of "Dixie" on the square. Crowds lined the (non-dusty) avenues and packed the balconies and windows of buildings overlooking Tryon Street. As Dixie played, they "cheered again and again the gay and giddy strains of the old war song," said eye-witnesses.[4]

The first carriage in the parade was the Grande Dame of the Confederacy herself—Mrs. Stonewall Jackson. Behind her carriage, Confederate veterans, such as the Durham Veterans, 123 of them in total, "in gray suits and leather leggings," marched in lockstep. They bore a standard that read, "First at Bethel, Last at Appomattox," and carried canteens and knap-sacks.[5] As Stonewall's widow received the salutes of the marching men, "continued cheering rent the air. Mrs. Jackson waved a Confederate flag, which she held in her hand, constantly, as a response to the reverential affection and regard as expressed by all who passed."[6]

It might have been asked: *what on earth did this have to do with the Mecklenburg Declaration of 1775?*

Nothing, at first glance, but also everything. The Confederacy was dead, but, in the views of the (white) local citizens, the principles it embodied—liberty, resistance to authority, courage—were the principles that animated the "second" rebellion of 1861. Not for nothing, in their view, had North Carolina succeeded from the Union on May 20, 1861. They believed they were doing to the federals what their great-grandparents had done to the British.

Of course, the federals, unlike the British, had won the war in the end and devastatingly so. And just as the British regarded the militant Whigs of 1775 as treasonable rabble, much of northern public opinion still regarded the ex-Confederates the same way; as traitors who had led the nation into unnecessary war and devastation and had done so in service to a deplorable, even unforgivable cause—human slavery.

Still, the war between the states (or, locally, the War of Northern Aggression) was long since over in 1898, and the project of national reconciliation had to continue. And it was with that in mind that projects of historical commemoration—such as the Confederate Monument and the Signers' Monument—were undertaken.

For southerners, these monuments represented a chance to honor and commemorate their past. For northerners, they were a peaceful and non-contentious way to allow the southerners to accept their defeat with good grace. And so, across the south during this period, Confederate monuments of all kinds were erected not necessarily to keep alive southern recidivism and prejudice (although some no doubt saw it that way), but rather to bury these causes amidst tons of cold, dead stone. Not by coincidence, historical monuments and gravestones of the period often have inscribed on them images of clasped hands—northern and southern—evidencing the reconciliation of the states. Historical commemoration, in this period, was less about memory, ironically, than forgetting. After all, if a few monuments would shut the southerners up, what harm was there?

The Shipp Monument was to be the third pillar in this project. And while it ostensibly commemorates First Lieutenant Shipp and the Spanish-American War, like its two predecessors whom aesthetically it bore an uncanny resemblance, in reality it was a monument to national reconciliation and the end of the Civil War.

Geronimo and Cuba

William "Willie" Shipp was born near Asheville on August 23, 1861. His father, Judge William Marcus, was a judge and, according to one historian, "one of the state's most eminent jurists."[7] The family had a distinguished military pedigree in the state. Judge Shipp had recruited a volunteer company from Henderson County to fight in the Confederate Army, where he served as a Captain (Company I, 16th Regiment) and was later elected to the North Carolina Assembly.

Shipp's mother, Catherine (Kate) Cameron Shipp, died when Willie was very young. He was raised by his grandmother, Mrs. Bartlett Shipp, in Lincolnton. According to one who knew her she was a "good and wise woman," and from her Shipp acquired the character traits and virtues that would positively impact his life.[8] In addition to his grandmother, young Willie became "a scholar in the school of Miss Alexander"—incidentally, always and everywhere in Mecklenburg history it seems there is an Alexander—who was "a lady of great culture and refinement. There he was studious and obedient, and soon became a favorite with his accomplished teacher."[9] Clearly Miss Alexander, and his grandmother, together filled the missing mother figure in young Shipp's life.

He was fond of sports, exercise and the outdoors, as children of that era and place were. On one occasion, when he was fourteen, Shipp walked from Charlotte to Asheville to visit some friends, arriving "footsore and weary," according to a family friend.[10]

His father remarried in 1872 to Margaret Iredell, daughter of Governor James Iredell, and the family moved to Charlotte a year or so later (to a house on the corner of North Tryon and 11th Street). Here Judge Shipp kept a law office. The family attended St. Peter's Episcopal Church on South Tryon. Per family tradition, Judge Shipp's was the last funeral held there, in June 1890.[11]

Judge Shipp was a devout Christian, and "especially admired and adhered to the King James version" of the Bible; so much so that he would not allow people to be sworn in as witnesses in his court using it.

In 1874 Willie was enrolled in the Carolina Military Institute, now the location of the Dowd YMCA on Morehead Street. Colonel J. P. Thomas, Commandant of the CMI, recalled Shipp as being "of fine physique, of admirable morals, of marked mental ability, [and] with studious habits, in him I saw the promise of a brave and honorable career in life."[12] Another family friend recalled that Shipp "seemed even then, as those who watched him tell, to have known no feeling of fear, and to have had a high sense of honor."[13] Favorable recollections praising dead soldiers are common, but in the case of Shipp it is striking how the same characteristics—courage, honor, decency—are cited again and again about him by those who knew him.

A military career was ideal for him. Shipp was one of forty applicants for an appointment to West Point in 1879. He graduated in 1883, eleventh in a class of fifty-two and was commissioned as a Second Lieutenant of Cavalry. He was the first southerner to graduate from West Point since the Civil War.

At his own request he was assigned to the Tenth Cavalry, a unit composed entirely of African Americans. They were famously known as the "Buffalo Soldiers," an expression thought coined by the Comanches and Southern Cheyenne, "either out respect for the regiment's fighting ability or because the Indians thought the soldiers' dark curly hair resembled a buffaloes' coat."[14] It was not a glamorous assignment. The U.S. army, like American society broadly,

The Cavalryman William Ewen Shipp in a photograph taken when he was a First Lieutenant, 10th Cavalry U.S. Army (photograph by the North Carolina Museum of History).

was heavily racist, and African American units like the Tenth Cavalry were generally under equipped and disrespected. They were given worse food and gear, more dangerous assignments and no respect by white units.

Black regiments were led by white officers, such as Shipp. "For black recruits, nearly all of whom were illiterate ex-slaves, the army offered both a career and a chance to demonstrate the potential of their race," writes historian Peter Cozzens.[15] Southern officers were particularly thought to be effective, as they were born into and instinctively understood racially hierarchy. "Notwithstanding the racism of the time," writes Cozzens, "the officers and their men commonly developed a deep mutual esteem. Officers whose white units fought alongside black troops could admire their fighting ability and esprit de corps without granting racial equality."[16] But bigotry remained. In one episode, one colonel refused to allows the "nigger troops" of the Tenth Cavalry to form near his white regiment on parade. Ute warriors taunted the Buffalo Soldiers with a song:

> Soldiers with black faces,
> You ride into battle behind the white soldiers;
> But you can't take off your black faces,
> And the white-faced soldiers make you ride behind them.[17]

When Shipp joined as a Second Lieutenant, the Tenth Cavalry was in Arizona. Assignment on the western frontier was usually a mixture of stifling boredom and rare, but terrifying episodes of violence. Shipp's first campaign, against the Apache leader Geronimo in the winter of 1885–1886, would be just that.

For several years, the Apache renegades Geronimo and Naiche had engaged in off-and-on guerrilla warfare against settlers and U.S. military forces in the south-east. On December 11, 1885, an expeditionary force of four officers and a hundred Apache scouts (half of them Chiricahuas) led by Captain Emmet Crawford crossed the Mexican border. Accompanying him were Lieutenant Marion Maus, as well as Shipp, each commanding two Apache scout companies. The only other white men on the expedition were two scouts (Tom Horn and William Harrison) and a mule packer named Henry Daly, with his twenty Indian assistants.

Peter Cozzens in his history of the American Indian wars, *The Earth Is Weeping*, gives a marvelous account of what happened next, which is worth quoting at length as it cannot be bettered.

> At dusk on January 9, 1886, Crawford's lead scouts located Geronimo and Naiche's winter *ranchería* in the remote Espinazo del Diablo (Devil's Spine), an unearthly patchwork of sawtooth mountains and deep canyons about two hundred miles south of the border. The news placed Crawford in a difficult predicament. The command had marched all day without food. Even the Chiricahuas were near exhaustion, and the pack train was far in the rear. Judging the risk of discovery too great to rest, Crawford

pushed on. The night was moonless, and the going slow and treacherous. For twelve hours, the scouts inched forward in blackness. In poor health and utterly exhausted, Captain Crawford hobbled along with his rifle as a walking stick. Lieutenant Maus was convinced that Crawford survived the ordeal by "sheer force of will."

Crawford reached the *ranchería* before daybreak. Not a soul stirred, and no sentinels stood watch. Crawford whispered orders: Lieutenants Maus and Shipp and the scout Tom Horn were to take one detachment each and work their way into position in the hills above the hostiles. A giddy Lieutenant Shipp thought the campaign was all but over. After all, the scouts need only complete the encirclement of the *ranchería*, wait until dawn, and then with a single rush capture the renegades. But Shipp had not accounted for the roughness of the terrain. In the darkness, some of the scouts tripped. Loosened stones trickled downhill alerting the renegades' mules and burros—the "watchdogs of an Indian camp." Three warriors emerged from their wickiups to investigate the braying.

As so often happened, overeager Indian scouts spoiled what would otherwise have been near-certain surprise. In this case, the culprits were White Mountain Apaches who had lost relatives in Ulzana's raid. Understandably vengeful, they ignored orders and opened fire the instant their target came into view. With their positions now compromised, Maus and Shipp urged their Chiricahua scouts to charge. They too ignored orders, seeking cover among the rocks and firing a few halfhearted, poorly aimed volleys. Shipp understood the reluctance of the Chiricahua scouts to push their advantage. All had friends or family members in the *ranchería*. "They wanted peace, but not at the expense of much bloodshed." The White Mountain Apaches, for their part, were too fearful of the renegades to chance close combat.

The scouts' diffidence cost Crawford little. The hostiles scattered, leaving behind their food stock and animals. That afternoon, an old woman appeared bearing a message from Naiche. The renegades were ready to surrender and return to the reservation. Terms might have been negotiated then and there, but Crawford's Apache interpreter had been too tired to make the night march. With nothing to fear from the hostiles, Crawford's command bedded down for the night beside campfires in the high-country cold.

A chill fog rolled over the hills before dawn on January 11. The scouts tended breakfast fires. Shipp and Maus lounged under their blankets and chatted. Then the unthinkable happened. Through the mist, a straggling line of shabbily clad but heavily armed men appeared on a ridge above Crawford's camp and opened fire. The scouts ducked behind rocks and held their fire.

Their assailants drew nearer. The fog lifted, and daybreak revealed their identity—two hundred Mexican Tarahumara Indians out for plunder and Apache scalps. Lieutenant Maus and Captain Crawford dashed forward. In plain sight, Crawford climbed a large rock between the opposing lines and waved a white handkerchief. Tom Horn, standing nearby, yelled his lungs out in fluent Spanish, telling the Tarahumaras that they were firing on American soldiers. The shooting stopped, and the Mexican commander came forward with his officers. Crawford told Lieutenant Maus to go back and make sure the scouts kept quiet while he parleyed.

No sooner had Maus turned his back than a single shot rang out. He whirled around to find Crawford crumpled in the mud, his brains seeping from a gaping hole in the forehead. Enraged Apaches riddled the Mexican officers. "No power could stop the firing," said Maus. The Tarahumaras and the Chiricahuas, bitter adversaries, taunted each other between volleys.... The skirmish ended only after the Taramahuras realized they had come up against more Apaches than they had bargained for.[18]

It became known as the "Crawford Affair" and for a time so enraged the American population that it seemed it would precipitate a general war between the United States and Mexico. In addition to Crawford, four other scouts were wounded. The Mexicans suffered four killed and five wounded. Crawford, mortally wounded, lingered seven days before dying. Shipp carried Crawford's body, slung behind his saddle, back to American lines. Geronimo and Naiche escaped to fight another day.

For his role in carrying out the martyred Captain Crawford, Shipp was promoted to First Lieutenant in 1889. Shortly thereafter, however, he suffered some ill luck, spraining his ankle playing polo. During his recovery, Shipp was assigned to the Davis Military Institute at Winston, N.C., where he served as professor of military tactics and special instructor of the North Carolina State Guard.[19] It was also during this period (1894) that he married Margaret Busbee of Raleigh. The best man at his wedding was William Elliott, a classmate of Shipp's at West Point.

In August 1897, he rejoined the Tenth Cavalry at Fort Assiniboine, in the most northern tracts of Montana. The fort (named for the local Sioux tribe) anchored a military complex near the Milk River. It had been built to guard against attacks by the Sioux Chief Sitting Bull. Comprising nearly a hundred buildings and outbuildings it was to become the largest such fort in North America.

The Indian wars were about to be overshadowed, however, by another "civilizing" mission of the United States government: the liberation of the Spanish province of Cuba. On the evening of February 15, 1898, the USS *Maine* suffered an internal explosion and sank in Havana Harbor. 266 out of 355 American sailors were killed. Although the cause of the explosion remained unclear, the occupying forces of Spain, with whom Cuban freedomfighters had been fighting for many years, were blamed. American sentiment was broadly anti–Spanish in any event, seeing it as a dying and anachronistic occupying power in America's backyard. Enthusiasm to intervene in the ongoing Cuban liberation movement, and expel Spain from Cuba by force, was irresistible. In April 1898, the U.S. government issued a call for 125,000 volunteers to "free" the island of Cuba from its Spanish overlords. The regular army mobilized.

Shipp accepted the post of Brigade-Quartermaster, bound for Cuba.

The Tenth Cavalry stayed for weeks in Port Tampa. It was monotonous. Troops spent hours swimming in the ocean, playing cards or, in the worst cases, getting drunk on rum. Shipp's regiment embarked on the *Leona* on June 7. When the ship left, rumors spread that the Spanish fleet was lying in ambush. Alarmed, they returned to port. Another week passed. On the fourteenth, Sergeant Major E. L. Baker wrote in his diary, they "steamed out of Tampa Bay, amid cheers and music from the thirty odd transports, heavily escorted by naval vessels." The weather, he wrote, was "splendid."[20]

The weather might have been splendid, but the passage from Tampa, into the summer heat of the Caribbean, from thence around the eastern shore of Cuba to the windward passage, would prove a hot and terrible torment for the black troopers below decks. One recalled, "After miles of railroad travel and much hustling we were put on board the transport. I say *on board*, but it is simply because we cannot use the term *under board*. We were huddled together below two other regiments and under the water line, in the dirtiest, closest, most sickening place imaginable. For about fifteen days we were on the water in this dirty hold, but being soldiers we were compelled to accept this without a murmur."[21] Every day they were fed the same meal of corned beef, canned tomatoes and hard bread. The drinking water was muddy and made many ill. To add insult to injury, cooks on board offered to sell the black solders water, bread and tainted meat for $1.

Men grew angry and rebellious, and Shipp and other officers were forced to maintain control. Sergeant Major Baker of the Tenth Cavalry wrote in his diary that the ship "was deliberately stopped around midnight, June 16, and left to roll in the trough of the sea until the morning of the 17th, in consequence of which we were put 20 hours behind the fleet and without escort, almost in sight of the Cuban shores. Men were indignant at having been placed in such a helpless position, and would have thrown the captain of the ship, whom they accused of being a Spanish sympathizer and otherwise disloyal, overboard without ceremony, but for the strong arm of military discipline."[22]

After two weeks at sea, on June 20, land was sighted. They were just off Guantanamo Bay, fifty miles from Santiago. Three days later, seventeen thousand men, plus horses, arms and equipment began unloading on the southern coast of Cuba. At the landing site, Baker wrote in his diary, "flames could be seen reaching almost to the heavens, the town having been fired by the fleeing Spaniards upon the approach of war vessels."[23] The Tenth Cavalry was the last to disembark, landing in rowboats at an abandoned railroad pier. Waves were high, and two troopers were killed, "doubtless crushed to death between the lighters," according to Baker.[24]

Shipp helped wrestle the horses from the transport ships to shore. There he secured mules and a small Cuban donkey cart to carry ammunition for the Hotchkiss guns. Each man was assigned three days rations and minimal equipment. As they moved inland, the Tenth quickly became engaged with Spanish troops, entrenched around the landing beaches, or firing from fortified houses or rifle pits. Lieutenant Webb C. Hayes, of the First Ohio Cavalry, recalled that early on the morning of June 24, two days after they had landed, "we marched past the outpost of the Second Infantry Division, whose troops were the first to be landed at Daiquiri under the orders for landing, and then attached the Spaniards in their intrenched position" at the Battle of Las Guasimas.[25]

> We had but few stretchers with us, so that most of our wounded were carried from the battlefield back to Siboney in rudely constructed stretchers made by soldiers' blankets stretched over carbines or poles. Just at dusk that day our dead were buried in a large pit dug among the ruins of a fine mansion on the wall of which was still partially preserved, an old sun-dial. I well remember how Lieutenant Shipp interested himself in having the dead carefully wrapped in their blankets and properly marked to identify them, and then all the bodies were laid side by side in the graves.... The scene made a deep impression on us as we could not but wonder whether we would be able to care for our dead of subsequent engagements.

Shipp, like the others watching the sunset burial at the destroyed home, must have wondered if he would in turn end up in an unmarked grave in this faraway tropical land.

In the next few days, Spanish fire on the Americans was "almost incessant" in the words of Hayes.

On the afternoon of June 30, 1898:

> The order came for the Cavalry Division to advance to El Poso at 4 p.m., and in the absence of General Young, who was then lying delirious from fever, the brigade marched out, the headquarters officers mounted, in column of two's, Colonel Wood, the acting brigade commander, with Captain Mills, Lieutenant Shipp and I coming next. We bivouaced that night on El Poso Hill and early in the morning prepared for the action of the day. General Young's personal aides of course remained with him, but Lieutenant Shipp, although a brigade quartermaster, voluntarily joined the column, and with Captain Mills accompanied Colonel Wood, assisting him in every way possible, and exposing himself recklessly to the enemy's fire. When the brigade marched across the San Juan River, Colonel Wood was temporarily called away by the division commander, and Captain Mills, as adjutant-general, with Lieutenant Shipp, took charge of the column, of which, it so happened, Lieutenant Colonel [Theodore] Roosevelt's regiment was in the lead.

On the morning of July 1, the Tenth Cavalry—comprised of 22 officers and 507 men—was pinned down by Spanish fire from Kettle Hill, adjacent to the San Juan heights. In a catastrophically bad decision, someone had attempted to raise a reconnaissance balloon in the exposed road. This alerted the Spanish troops on the high ground to the Tenth's location and brought a torrent of fire down on the Americans. "The atmosphere seemed perfectly alive with flying missiles from bursting shells over head, and rifle bullets which seemed to have an explosive effect."[26] The Tenth hunkered down in a sunken road, three feet deep and lined with barbed wire, along the riverbank.

Hayes recalled:

Owing to the attempt to raise a balloon from the road in almost the centre of our brigade, the entire artillery and infantry fire of the Spaniards was drawn to our brigade, which was then marching through the underbrush in column of four's, parallel to the Spanish line of fire. The 1st and 10th Cavalry protected themselves as best they could along the banks of the river until the balloon collapsed, but Lieutenant Colonel Roosevelt's First Volunteer Cavalry, with Captain Mills, Lieutenant Shipp and the rest of the brigade's staff, pushed on through the high grass under orders to join on Lawton's Division, but halted in an slightly sunken road which afforded some protection.

The officers debated what to do next. All options were bad. Either they advanced uphill into the Spanish fire, or they retreated under fire. As they deliberated, "Mauser bullets drove in sheets through the trees and the tall jungle grass making a peculiar whirring or rustling sound," one officer remembered. Spanish snipers hidden in palm trees shot at everyone, including the wounded. Roosevelt was heard to mutter over and over again, "*I wish they'd let us start, I wish they'd let us start.*"[27]

For half an hour the troopers crouched low, awaiting orders, while suffering "considerable loss."[28] Shipp rode on horseback, delivering orders. Seeing him, one officer cattily remarked, "You are having a good time riding around here." Shipp, according to another, replied that "it was no picnic riding among bullets, and that that he would prefer being with his troops."[29]

The decision was made to advance up Kettle Hill. According to Hayes, "[w]hile the regiment was lying in this road Lieutenant Shipp was most busy and efficient in carrying orders to the detached portions of the brigade, until finally Captain Mills received orders from the Division in making an assault on San Juan Hill, whose deadly fire could no longer be endured."

The hill was very steep, and the approach was totally exposed to plunging fire from the Spanish entrenched on top. One solider remembered that, "the ground was entirely open and fenced by wire. From this line it was necessary to storm the hill, upon the top of which is a house, loop-holed for defense."[30] With a roar, the Tenth Cavalry, and Roosevelt's Volunteers, stood and charged the hill. "The slope of the hill is very difficult," one recalled, "but the assault was made with great gallantry and much loss to the enemy."[31]

Sometime after noon on July 1, during the charge that would make "T.R." famous, Lieutenant Shipp was killed. As a member of Wood's staff, Wood had "sent [Shipp] to deliver an order to a regiment of the brigade, ordering it to advance; on his return, it seems, he passed his own regiment, the 10th, which is also a regiment of my brigade, just as it was starting forward to the charge. He joined his troop, and was leading it when killed."[32]

Shipp was shot just feet from his West Point classmate Lt. William Smith who was in command of a troop of the Tenth Cavalry. Shipp's wound according to Hayes, "caused almost instantaneous death" (although surviving soldiers always told that lie to family members back home). Shipp was known to carry a portrait of his wife in a locket around his neck, and "from the position of the body and the arrangement of his clothing, it seemed to us all as though he was engaged in searching for something in the pocket of his blouse, or flannel shirt" when he died; surely the portrait of his wife. He had been in Cuba ten days.

After taking San Juan Hill, the Cavalry kept moving, pressing the retreating Spanish. Shipp and other casualties were buried where they fell, just as he had watched other boys being buried near the ruined mansion but a week earlier.

A few days later, during a pause in the fighting, Hayes returned to find and mark the shallow graves where Shipp and William Smith had been laid. Hayes covered their graves "temporarily with boulders," as he said, "and enclosed the little slip of paper on which the names were marked, in bottles which I drove with mouth downward into the loose earth." "[F]earing that the drenching rains would wash away all marks at the graves," he "secured pieces of zinc, 18 inches wide and some three feet long, from the roof of the San Juan House, and on these traced, in pencil, the names of the dead, in case of Lieutenant Shipp the inscription being, in large letters:

> Wm. E. SHIPP,
> 1st Lieut. 10th Cavalry
> Killed July 1st, 1898[33]"

In the driving rain, Hayes fixed the zinc banner to stout pieces of plank and drove them into the ground to serve as makeshift headstones. "There was absolutely nothing else that I could do that I knew of at the time," he later recalled, "and I felt that it was all that I would have wished for him to do for me had the conditions been reversed." In his recollections, he eulogized Shipp as follows:

> Lieutenant Shipp was one of the most lovable men that it had ever been my good fortune to meet. He was generous, frank, and kind heated. In this campaign he literally shared his blanket, and divided his last piece of hard bread with his comrades. He was an indefatigable worker in his efforts to get us supplies. On the battlefield he was utterly fearless and neither by voice nor action indicated that there was anything to be feared in the bullets which whirled about him. He was a noble, true-hearted soldier.

Roosevelt wrote Shipp's brother a few weeks later from his headquarters near Santiago to describe the circumstances of Shipp's death. "Your most gallant brother was with me in the early part of the fight in which he was killed," he wrote.

> That morning he and Capt. Mills, who had been sleeping within a few feet of me, and had lost their mess kit, breakfasted with me, as I was fortunate enough to have plenty of coffee and hard tack and bacon. They then acted as my aides, and it was your brother

who brought me the word to advance with my regiment. I did not see him again. He had been riding to and fro with absolute coolness and fearlessness, paying no more attention to the bullets than if they were hail-stones, though men were dropping on every side.

A few weeks later, they located the temporary grave where Shipp was buried and exhumed him for reburial in the United Sates. Shipp's body left Cuba aboard the transport *McClellan*. Along with Shipp's remains were the bodies of his West Point roommate and best friend, Lieutenant William Smith, as well as Lieut. Elliot, who had been best man at Shipp's wedding five years before.

General Wood recalled that Shipp's death "was a great shock to all his friends, of whom I have been one for many years. His conduct during the entire action was distinguished by the greatest gallantry and absolute disregard of danger."[34] Roosevelt also testified to the First Lieutenant's courage, many years later writing privately to his widow: "Lieutenant Shipp breakfasted with me the morning of the day he was killed. What a gallant fellow he was!"[35]

Roosevelt and others had also displayed gallantry on San Juan Hill, but they had luck on their side that day, whereas Shipp did not. How might American history have changed if Shipp had lived and his breakfast companion that day, the future twenty-sixth American President, had been killed instead?

The Shipp Monument

In describing what he called "the grand charge on the San Juan fortifications," Hayes would later say: "It was the grandest scene that I will ever witness and the most exhilarating, and to me, enjoyable" of his life. During the charge, Roosevelt himself was reported to have turned to a colleague and said, "Holy Godfrey, what fun!"[36]

It was still a period where wars, or battles at any rate, could still be described in such terms.

A century of world war, devastation, mass murder, holocaust and atomic bombs had yet to unfold. Death in war, because it remained small scale, uncommon and far-away, could still be commemorated and exalted in a way that seems foreign to us today.

In Charlotte, a movement to erect a monument to Shipp gathered pace. In August 1898, the *Charlotte Observer* wrote: "Young Shipp was of those who, foremost fighting, fell. Beautiful to look at; game as became a solider; a gentleman by inheritance and living up to his history; the husband of a young and beautiful wife; the father of two young children—what could have been more pathetic that his death? He well deserves a monument, and the

Observer herewith opens a subscription to a fund for such purpose."³⁷ The newspaper kicked off the fundraising itself with a handsome $100 pledge.

Shipp *did* deserve a monument, but arguably so did the 2,909 other American fatalities of the Spanish-American War (345 from combat, the remainder from disease, accidents or other causes). But Shipp had several advantages that these other unfortunates did not. First, he had had a personal relationship, even friendship, with the man who was now President of the United States, Theodore Roosevelt. And Shipp embodied all the virtues that Roosevelt held highest in man: he was a warrior, masculine and tough.

Second, Shipp's death, while personally of interest to TR, also has a higher symbolic purpose; indeed, a political purpose. The Civil War was only two generations past. Civil War veterans still walked the streets of Charlotte, many of them unrepentant and unreconstructed. The Spanish-American War, brief, uncontentious and victorious, gave the nation a common cause for all Americans to unify around—northerners and southerners alike. It represented a great coming together, a rallying point that the nation had not had for many years.

Willie Shipp, the first southern graduate of West Point since the War Between the States, an unequivocal hero killed in the line of action, was the perfect symbol that united southern martial values with *American* national purpose. He had all of the appeal of a Confederate hero, but without the Confederate baggage.

For these reasons, the movement to erect a monument to Shipp, on a scale as grand as that of the Confederate War dead (just erected in Charlotte), had an irresistible political momentum.

And what was more appropriate than to place a memorial to Shipp, not in a far-away cemetery, or on county or city land, but on U.S. *federal* land? It was a grand gesture of reconciliation by the federal government to the former rebels. Building on federal land required federal approval, however, but when the President was involved this would not be difficult. So on April 21, 1902, a joint resolution of the House and Senate of the Fifty-Seventh United States Congress gave permission for the Shipp Monumental Committee to erect a statue to William E. Shipp on the grounds of the U.S. Mint at 405 West Trade Street. Charlotte had a MecDec monument, and a Confederate monument, but now it was to have an *American* war monument, in the guise of a memorial to Willie Shipp.

The Unveiling

Thus it was that four years to the day after the unveiling of the Signers' Monument, the Shipp Monument—the third such historical memorial of its size and scale within the last several years—was the focus on another public celebration. "Charlotte Celebrates," read the banner headline of the *Charlotte News* on May 20, 1902. "Unveiling of Stately Shaft to Late William Ewen Shipp the Feature of an Eventful Day."[38]

Five thousand spectators crowded the streets around the post office. It was a warm day, and people were anxious to be outdoors. "Long before the exercises began the thoroughfare were crossed for several blocks in every direction from the square," reported the press, "with a good natured multitude that patiently waited for the line of march to appear."[39]

At 9:30 in the morning a military procession began to form ranks. Leading the parade were the mounted police, the marshals and a brass band. Following were the military companies from Charlotte and the surrounding area, most prominent among them the Fayetteville Light Infantry, the Blue Ridge Rifles of Asheville (Shipp's birth place), the Salisbury Overman Guards, and the Kings' Mountain Rifles. Behind them came nine horse-drawn carriages, the first of which carried Shipp's widow and two sons, William and Fabius.

The procession began promptly at 10:00 a.m., proceeding from the county courthouse up Tryon Street to Independence Square, in the center of town. A large crowd followed on foot as they made the 20 minute procession to the location of the Shipp Monument, which remained hidden behind a white cloth. Arriving at the monument, the militia stacked arms and a dirge was played.

Despite the thousands of on-lookers, it was a quiet scene. As a reporter would write, the "odd tone of the surging assembly was quietude; this being, in some way, appropriate to the character of the memorial on which all attention was fastened."[40]

"Around the monument, which is located on the green sward in front of the post office building, an immense concourse had gathered, while vast numbers of spectators blocked the road for a long distance, filled the premises of nearby houses and stood close together in the balconies of the post office and in the large area on the first floor of the building."[41]

The date of the unveiling, May 20, was not a coincidence either. Shipp was to be the next chapter in the story that had begun in 1775, passed through the unfortunate but glorious events of 1861–1865, and continued to the Spanish-American War of 1898.

That Shipp was to be part of this larger narrative was made clear by the remarks. "The twentieth of May," Colonel John Thomas, the keynote speaker began, "heretofore dedicated to the immortal memories of the Mecklenburg Declaration of Independence, is henceforth to be further linked with the gallant career and the touching sacrifice of the lamented solider in honor of whom this monument is reared."[42]

The military procession formed a hollow square around the white-sheet shrouded monument. When the order was given, Shipp's sons drew back two long cords that parted a veil, revealing the granite obelisk. The monument had been contracted to I.W. Durham, who had fabricated and installed it. He was an excellent local craftsman, reported the local paper, and "all who have seen it agree that he has done his work well."[43]

It stood thirty feet above the ground, soaring into the Carolina sun. It was heavy, as the occasion demanded; fifteen tons of "finely proportioned" Winnsboro granite. On the rough base were crossed cavalry sabers and the number "10" for Shipp's Cavalry regiment. On the base of the shaft, the name "SHIPP" was etched. The audience cheered and clapped its approval. Soldiers presented arms and the band played "America."

"It was a sublime scene," reported the Charlotte paper, "one that will be cherished in memory by all who were so fortunate to witness it."[44]

The theme of continuity from 1775 to 1898, of rebellion from British tyranny and liberty from Spanish rule, was not lost on those in attendance that day. "A happy and striking coincidence confronts us," Colonel Thomas pointed out. "On this day, at this hour, a grand drama is enacting on Cuban soil.... Today, in the inauguration of the Government elected by her people, Cuba realizes her aspirations as she takes her place among the Republics of America."[45]

Indeed, at that very moment, 841 miles away, in Havana, Cuba, the last American soldiers who had fought in the Spanish-American War were departing aboard the *Brooklyn*. Throughout Havana, wild celebrations took place. Celebratory arches were erected in plazas, bunting hung across narrow streets and public parks burst with bright tropical flowers. "Above every red tiled roof," reported the Associated Press, "rose a Cuban flag. The whole city seemed suddenly buried beneath a forest of waving banners."[46]

At precisely noon on May 20, 1902, the Stars and Stripes were lowered from the top of Morro Castle and the Lone Star of the Republic of Cuba was raised in its place before the gathered notables, which included American military officers and the new President of the Cuban Republic, Tomás Estrada Palma. Victory arches were erected across the city, reported the *Charlotte News*, and "the city was filled with thousands of happy citizens of the new born Republic."[47] As the Cuban flag flew over the city ramparts, "the streets below fairly shook with the cheer that arose. It was caught up by the people on the roofs, and rolled over the city."[48]

The coincidental alignment of the ceremony in Charlotte and the liberation scenes in Havana could not have been more perfectly scripted. President Roosevelt was delighted at the happenstance. In a cable to the President and Congress of the People of Cuba, T.R. expressed "the sincere friendship and good wishes of the United States and our most earnest hopes for the stability

The Shipp Monument in downtown Charlotte. Unveiled in May 1902, it was 30 feet high, made with 15 tons of Winnsboro granite. On the rough base were crossed cavalry sabers and the number "10" for Shipp's Cavalry regiment. Today it stands behind the Federal Courthouse on Trade Street (photograph by the North Carolina Museum of History).

and success of your government, for the blessings of peace, justice, prosperity and ordered freedom among your people and for enduring friendship between the republic of the United States and the Republic of Cuba."⁴⁹

Cuba was much on the President's mind that week. Just two days earlier, speaking to a standing-room only crowd in Carnegie Hall, the President set forth a typically bullish speech about the conquest of the American West, but which was also of course a veiled defense and praise of the liberation of Cuba.

"To conquer a continent is rough work," he said.

> All really great work is rough in the doing, though it may seem smooth enough to those who look back upon it or gaze upon it from afar. The roughness is an unavoidable part of the doing of the deed. We need display but scant patience with these who, sitting at ease in their own homes, delight to exercise a querulous and censorious spirit of judgement upon their brethren who, whatever their short comings, are doing strong men's work as they bring the light of civilization into the world's dark places.⁵⁰

In the "rough work" of building a free Cuba, the President invariably associated the name of Willie Shipp. "I am very glad of the monument," he wrote to Shipp's widow that same week. In addition, "I am touched and pleased at your little boy's having named his best guinea pig after me," said Roosevelt, "Your husband's memory will ever be bright in my mind."⁵¹

A Forgotten Story

Over the years that followed, the importance, and indeed meaning, of the Shipp Monument receded almost entirely from the memory of the people in Charlotte. The Shipp family was not a well-known and established family, like the Alexanders, Caldwells or Brevards, and there were few local descendants to keep the story alive. (Shipp's widow, by a bizarre coincidence of fate, was living in Riga, Latvia, by the 1930s).

The significance of the Spanish-American War had also been overshadowed entirely by the bloodbath of World War I. Fought just two decades later, the United States suffered over 275,000 casualties in only five months of combat during the First World War, including over 54,000 combat deaths. Of those, North Carolina lost 828 men killed and 3,655 wounded in battle, while an additional 1,542 North Carolinians died of disease (mostly influenza). Roughly one hundred fatalities were from Mecklenburg County alone. The Spanish-America War seemed almost quaint by comparison.

Of course, not every one of these soldiers could receive his own war memorial, as Shipp had. The numbers were too extraordinary and too horrifying. In light of these catastrophic losses, the sufferings of Shipp and his colleagues in the small and short Cuban campaign were entirely forgotten.

Indeed, by October 1933, the *Charlotte News* noted that the monument "seemed almost a mystery" as virtually no Charlotte citizens knew what it was or why it had been erected.[52]

Around that time, local citizens in Lincoln County began a campaign to move the obelisk to Lincolnton, where Shipp was buried, and where at least it would be noticed and remembered. The cost and effort to move it were too high, however, so the Shipp Monument stayed in Charlotte, where it remains to this day; a magnificent if obscure testimony to a forgotten war and hero.

11
Dr. Annie: North Carolina's First Woman Physician

"She'll serve humanity."
—Dr. John Brevard Alexander, circa 1878

Born on January 10, 1864, Annie Lowrie Alexander, North Carolina's first licensed female physician, began life as so many did in her day, in a small rural area near the present town of Cornelius in northern Mecklenburg County. She was the third of six children born to Dr. John Brevard and Ann Wall Lowrie Alexander. Her father had graduated with high honors from Davidson College in 1852 and the Medical College of South Carolina in Charleston in 1855. The year she was born, towards the end of the American Civil War, her father was away from his family serving as a surgeon in Company C of the North Carolina 37th Infantry.

As her surname suggests, she was part of the well-known local Alexander clan, members of whom were involved in commercial and political life of the region and even the state. Indeed, Annie was Mecklenburg aristocracy. Through both of her parent's lines, Annie was related not only to the Alexanders, but the Bain, Craighead, Caldwell and Davidson families as well. Many of her ancestors played instrumental roles in the establishment of Mecklenburg County as well as supportive roles during the American Revolution.

When the war ended in April 1865, Dr. John Brevard returned to his farm and family, and resumed the practice of medicine. For many years after, Dr. Alexander served as one of only a few physicians in rural Mecklenburg County. He saw and diagnosed patients, dispensed pharmaceuticals, attended the Presbyterian church, and, in his spare time, researched and wrote about local history. Later in his life, he published the first history of the county, *The History of Mecklenburg County from 1740 to 1900*.

According to one family tradition, her father had "determined that she should become a doctor after one of his female patients died after refusing medical attention out of fear of being examined by a man." Dr. Alexander considered which one of his three daughters was most suitable for the profession and chose Annie. Her mother resisted the idea, believing it was a waste of money. Once she was of appropriate age, she believed, Annie would abandon any medical career for the "normal" course of marriage and motherhood. Dr. Alexander's response was blunt. "She must never marry," he said. "She'll serve humanity."[1]

Annie herself appeared not to have resisted this predetermination of her fate. Asked once how she went into medicine, she told a friend, "Papa decided that for me."[2] By all accounts her father was a man of his time, an unreconstructed Confederate, even a racist, but, ironically in this respect, something of a radical feminist. To his credit, his desire to improve the quality of medical care for his female patients overcame any ideals he may have had towards a woman's place in society.

To be a *female* doctor in this time and place was no small thing. The first female doctor from the United States, Dr. Elizabeth Blackwell, attended European medical schools and practiced medicine in England. There were only two institutions opened to training women doctors in the United States. It was not considered a respectable occupation for women. Medicine was a man's profession. Many believed women were too emotional and hysterical; they were unable to see blood without fainting, and temperamentally unable to bear the stress and rigors of medical training let alone the daily life of a physician. Nevertheless, the Alexanders, above all else, were stubborn people, and if John Brevard Alexander said that his daughter was going to be doctor, then a doctor she would be.

The Education of a Doctor

Beginning at the age of fourteen, Annie began a rigorous course of education under the stern tutelage of her father (and later also with a private tutor). She studied Roman and European history, American government, Shakespeare, classical Greek and French literature and, of course, the history and philosophy of the American Revolution. But above all else she studied the family business: medicine. She observed her father as he saw patients, dispensed medicines, and read anatomy and chemistry books. She was, quite literally, born to be a doctor.

There were few medical schools opened to women, so at the age of seventeen Annie entered the prominent Women's Medical College in Philadelphia. In a photo of her taken around 1886, her eyes are wide open, inquisitive and gentle. Her hair is pulled back in a crown. She was short, neither plain nor striking in appearance. In truth, she really did not look much like an Alexander at all. The male Alexanders were angular, all edges and lines, and with hard eyes. By squinting at a picture of her grandfather, J. G. M. Ramsey, you could almost imagine a painting by Picasso, with broken and serrated lines. Annie's face, however, is soft and round; not an abstract, more a Watteau.

We have a great deal of insight into Annie's thoughts during this period due to an unpublished short story she wrote, entitled "Doctor Katherine." The story is clearly autobiographical. The heroine is a young and aspiring medical student named "Katherine Caldwell."[3] Katherine is clearly Annie's alter ego. For example, Katherine is described as "the second daughter in a large family of children," just as Annie was. Katherine was "shy and diffident toward strangers, gentle and quiet in manner, and was possessed of that excellent thing in woman, a voice soft and low." Again, a description of Annie herself. And as a physical description, Annie (Katherine) has "light wavy hair, coiled loosely at the back was her one crown of beauty. From her blue eyes shone her steadfast earnest soul."[4] It is the picture of Annie herself.

In one passage in "Doctor Katherine," Katherine and her friends discuss their future plans. "It was the day before commencement at Parkhurst Academy," she writes. "Several members of the graduating class were assembled in the grounds in front of the building talking of the future before them.

"I am going to be a teacher," said one.

"I am going to be an artist," said another.

"And I a professor of languages," said Mary Barry.

"I shall marry," said Nettie Bell.

"What are you going to do Katherine?" asked Mary Barry.

"Study medicine."

"Study medicine! Be a doctor! Who ever heard of such a thing!"

"Are you in earnest or romancing?" asked Mary.

"Yes, I am going to be a doctor. It has been father's desire all my life, that I should be a physician."

"Your father must be a mad-man to allow such a thing or to consider it for a moment," said Nettie Bell. The idea of a daughter in a Southern family doing anything outside of home or the schoolroom was unheard of. And to bring the idea closer home, for Katherine Caldwell the fetted daughter of Dr. and Mrs. Caldwell to study medicine was shocking."

"Yes, I am going to be a doctor," the stubborn Annie-character starchily responds to her friends. "If you have recovered from your shock I'll tell you about it."

But Annie was in for a shock herself. The Philadelphia Women's Medical College was a four story, austere, gothic red brick building. It was imposing and intimidating. The people were unfamiliar and cold, and spoke with weird accents. They were entirely unlike the friendly southerners she had left behind. She was alone in a busy, dirty and at times terrifying Yankee capital.

Nothing in her childhood in the rolling farmlands of Mecklenburg had prepared her for this, or for a "winter in Philadelphia where hard pavements, brick walls and English sparrows abound."

The course of instruction, as the school described itself, was "progressive, and requires three years' attendance upon college lectures" culminating in a final exam. Students were expected to attend, during the first year, chemistry, anatomy, physiology and histology (that is, microscopic anatomy), materia medica (the healing properties of various substances), anatomy and general therapeutics, as well as one other optional course. Practical work included hands-on practice in chemical, pharmaceutical and physiological labs, and attendance at the Woman's Hospital clinic.

The first year of medical school "quickly passed with lectures, clinics and laboratory work." The students attended laboratory class in long sleeved, full length dresses, hair pulled tight in buns. Annie was one of only two students from the south. It was hard slogging, difficult and demoralizing. But it was also exhilarating. As she recalled:

> The first lecture she heard was on "Protoplasm." After listening to the lecture one hour she turned and asked the student behind her, "what is Protoplasm?" What a trial those first six weeks were! Loneliness, and homesickness and tears. She attended the lectures and studied the dictionary. Everything was chaotic. After a while things became clearer and a keen interest took the place of the homesickness. A new world was revealed to her. Sickness and suffering such as she never suspected aroused her deepest interest and sympathy.

Annie (Katherine)'s "greatest trial was the dissecting room," she wrote. "How the shivers ran up and down her spine as she heard the elevator rumbling up from the basement to the top story!"

On one occasion her fellow students teased her, suggesting she did not have the stomach for another dissection. "Oh she is chicken hearted," one said. They recommended she stay behind.

> "Oh I don't mind it," said Katherine faintly, "I'll go of course."
> The sight that greeted her eyes was appalling. Several long marble tables, on each lay a subject carefully covered, but the human outlines were visible. It was horrible. It was the first time she had seen death. She walked over to the window and stood for a few minutes looking over into Girard College grounds, until she could get her nerves under control. By degrees she brought herself to look upon the "subjects." How cruel and wicked it all seemed! Once these poor bodies were a joy and comfort to someone's heart. But now—now—it was too much for her. She quietly left the room unnoticed.
> The worst part was to come. Later in the winter Katherine was assigned a part to dissect. It was awful. It seemed impossible for her to make the first cut. But after it was begun her horror and disgust were gradually absorbed by her interest in the wonderful and beautiful arrangement of muscle, nerve, vein and artery.

She persevered.

Annie was one of twenty-six graduates of the 1884 spring term. Only one other classmate, Ruth McCown, was from the south, the Commonwealth of Virginia to be exact. The other twenty-four graduates that term were from Pennsylvania, New York, Ohio; some even from Canada and England. Annie had written her required thesis on "The Vascular Mechanism." On March 13, 1884, the former trembling student, who had been forced to slip out of the dissecting class a year earlier, received the Degree of Doctor of Medicine, graduating first in her class. She was twenty years old.

She had all the makings of a good doctor, not least of which was determination. One of her instructors predicted that she would have an "honorable & brilliant" medical career, "because besides her mental accomplishment & good observing faculty, she has three other qualities of the good physician, dignity, gentleness, firmness, & a calmness & coolness in emergency which inspires confidence in others."[5]

Medical Practice

In 1885 she obtained her license from the Maryland Board of Medical Examiners. It was, as her instructor had predicted, surely the beginning of an auspicious, indeed unprecedented, medical career.

She accepted a position teaching anatomy at the Woman's Medical College, Baltimore. It did not pay very much, and she continued to receive financial support from her father, with whom she maintained a close relationship. She had chosen to live and work in Baltimore, although it was hardly her first choice. It was too provincial, illiberal and rural. She wanted to live in a big city, where the curiosity of a female doctor would be less obvious. In 1884, before she finished medical school she mused in a letter, "I can't decide where to locate when I leave Philadelphia. I've thought of Baltimore, Atlanta, and Jacksonville, but there will be obstacles wherever I locate. My success will depend on my ability and the liberal views of the people among whom I will be."

In 1885 Mecklenburg County was not, to put it mildly, a hotbed of *liberal views*, so it held little interest to her. In fact, in her own mind she had already crossed Charlotte off her list of possible destinations. According to one writer, Charlotte was "the one southern city she had determined in January 1885 to avoid at all costs." She was afraid the people would not take her seriously. The people in Charlotte, she wrote to a friend, "have more curiosity then sincerity and politeness."[6]

But events were to send Annie's life and career in an unexpected direction. That summer of 1885, she contracted a severe case of pneumonia. She was twenty-two years old and very slight. She became very weak and lost a great deal of weight. In her weakened condition, and probably as a result of exposure to a patient at the Baltimore House, she developed tuberculosis. The latter was the scourge of humanity until the discovery of penicillin. A patient could linger for many years; however by the late nineteenth century, doctors developed a treatment that included extensive convalescence in either an extremely cold or warm environment. Determined not to become an invalid, Annie made the decision to leave Baltimore, and spend the winter of 1886–87 at her Uncle Henry Lowrie's home in Florida. It was there, that Annie received word of the death of her younger brother, Samuel, at Davidson in 1886. (It is likely that she began writing her story "Doctor Katherine" to amuse herself during the long days of inactivity.)

It took more than a year for Annie to make a full recovery and her lungs were permanently scarred. A return to working in a large northeastern hospital, where the chance of recurrence was great, was neither desirable nor recommended. The appeal of practicing medicine with her father may also have been a decisive, for some time around 1887 she returned to Mecklenburg County to relaunch her medical practice.

In the spring of 1887 the following advertisement appeared in the *Charlotte Observer*: "A nice young female physician, Miss Annie Lowrie Alexander, has located in this city ready to practice among women and children and consult about female disorders generally." The article pointed out that Dr. Alexander "has been educated in the best medical schools of the country."[7]

"Mecklenburg now boasts of a female M.D.," another local paper lukewarmly announced, "Miss Annie Alexander, who comes home from Philadelphia with her diploma."[8]

Was she disappointed to have returned to Charlotte? It was, after all, a place she had escaped from, and the appeals of the sleepy southern town, compared to the glamour of Philadelphia or Baltimore, must have been few. Or was it a relief to be home amidst her family?

Initially "Dr. Annie," as she soon became known, boarded with a Mrs. Harvey Wilson and shared office space with another woman (a Mrs. Lathan), on South Tryon Street. Two years later, she purchased a small, one-story home on North Tryon. A year later her parents, who were now aging, left the family farm in northern Mecklenburg County and moved in with her. She would remain in the home on North Tryon for the rest of her life. In 1897, she had the home remodeled and added a second story to accommodate patients who were recuperating from surgeries she performed. Further renovations took place in 1900 and again in 1905. In the latter case, the *Charlotte News* noted approvingly, the renovations were "handsome" and had "tasteful colors."[9]

According to surviving family members, she struggled in her first year in private practice, although surely not as much as she would have had she not had the Alexander name behind her. Beginning in 1890, Dr. Annie began purchasing rental properties to supplement her income. At one time she owned as many as twenty rental houses and commercial offices in Charlotte.

There were only a handful of doctors in the small town in 1890, and, needless to say no other *women* doctors. As Dr. Annie had feared, at first she was a curiosity. For the first six months of her practice, as she later recalled, "the prejudice against a woman physician, was such as to almost discourage her."[10] As a friend confides to Katherine in her novella, "With few exceptions every woman has said, 'I hope she will succeed, *but I could never trust a woman when I and my children are sick*.'"

A large proportion of her patients were women, some of whom must have overcome the novelty of having a female doctor attend them, while others no doubt found it a relief. Much of her case work was gynecological, but she also treated common ailments of the period, including bilious fever, consumption, indigestion and carbuncles. She also had what her biographer James Alsop calls "a sizeable practice in neurology."[11]

Like her father, Dr. Annie also lectured widely and wrote for medical journals. Her first published essay, in January 1889, was entitled "Women Physicians." Women doctors were necessary, Dr. Annie argued, as a "suffering woman naturally turns to [a] woman for sympathy." Women were also instinctively care-givers, she believed, as there was "an instinct in women that gives them an insight into the sufferings of the little ones."[12]

While at first Dr. Annie was a curiosity, over time she became a source of local prestige. Bursting with local pride, Charlotteans boasted that, not only was Dr. Annie the first female doctor *in the county* (which was true), *but* she was also the first female doctor *in North Carolina* (also, true, but not the first to graduate from medical school). Indeed, as the story grew, Dr. Annie was the first female doctor it was said *in the south*

"Doctor Annie" in a photograph taken when she was in her 30s. When she was a child her father had predicted, "She'll serve humanity" (courtesy the Robinson-Spangler Carolina Room, Charlotte Mecklenburg Library).

(according to one expert "demonstrably not true," but a good story and hard to dispute nevertheless).[13]

Regardless, whether or not she was the *first* female doctor in the area, she might as well have been, for the uniqueness of her position and the challenges it presented. Prejudice and old habits died hard. Women doctors simply *didn't do*, and if the bigotry was largely soft and irritating, rather than hard and dangerous, it was bigotry nonetheless.

Ironically, some of Dr. Annie's greatest critics were other women. In "Doctor Katherine," one woman cattily remarked that the only woman doctor *she* has ever heard of "has short hair and dresses like a man." It had to have been a remark Dr. Annie heard many times. Another objects that "I can't conceive of a doctor wearing skirts and feathers," while a third pooh-poohs, "I would have no confidence in a woman as a doctor." When asked "why not?" by Katherine, the woman responds, "because women haven't the brain power necessary to make good doctors, and they are too nervous and scarry [sic]."

One exceptional woman who knew Dr. Annie in Charlotte summed up her achievements well. "Her invasion of the field of medicine, so long held by men, and with the laity slow to accept the woman doctor, required very considerable courage."[14]

Dr. Annie in Charlotte

Dr. Annie's reputation grew and so did her medical practice at her home on North Tryon. Due to her skill and renown, she could have simply been a successful and wealthy physician. But that was not the Alexander way. Instead, she worked tirelessly in charitable and civic affairs, particularly focused on helping other women. As she explained it, as a woman, "she has been able to rescue suffering women who are naturally repugnant to the fullest confidence to male physicians."[15] She confined her practice to treating only women and children. An advertisement of in May 1887 reads:

> Dr. Annie L. Alexander,
> CHARLOTTE, N.C.
> Practice limited to diseases of WOMEN and
> CHILDREN, and attention to Female patients.
> Office, at Mrs. Latham's, 214 South Tryon
> Street, nearly opposite the Post Office.[16]

In addition to Dr. Annie's practice, she had hospital privileges at both St. Peter's and Presbyterian Hospitals. She also served as a physician to the Young Women's Christian Association, the Presbyterian College for Women (later known as Queen's College), and the Florence Crittendon Home for unwed mothers. When the Mecklenburg County Medical Society was founded in 1903, she served as its first Vice President and later as President (1909–10). She was a frequent speaker at its events, and led public health campaigns for health education and children's health, and against tuberculosis and hookworm, or, less laudably now (although not exceptional at the time), in favor of eugenics.

Dr. Annie wrote and published research on topics as diverse as "Pneumonia" (1896) (a subject she knew well from her personal experiences), "The Care of the Premature Infant" (1914) and "Tuluremia" (1928, 1929), a serious infection transferred from live rabbits, then a serious health issue affecting dozens of American states. "Her endeavors for systemic reform found expression in campaigns for compulsory medical inspection of school children and co-operative rural public health nursing," writes Alsop. "Equally important to her as a health reformer was moral improvement, within families and especially among adolescent women."[17]

Although a well-known fixture in the community, Dr. Annie remained something of an oddity. She was considered a rebel (and *not* in the good southern way). She was a single woman with a medical practice who lived her own life and had liberal political views and various friends from around the country. Dr. Annie went where she pleased, driving her own horse and buggy. One young woman recalled, "I can remember Dr. Annie stopping to see us every day, driving her horse and buggy, she would always check to see if we were all right, so no wonder that my first spoken words were 'Annie's buggy.'"[18] She travelled widely, sending postcards to her friends back in Charlotte from "many foreign lands."[19] She visited Alaska, Niagara Falls, Canada, the 1904 St. Louis World's Fair and the mammoth caves in Kentucky. Once, in a visit to the Grand Canyon, she rode a donkey wearing bloomers, which, a friend recalled, "was considered very risqué attire at the time!"[20] Despite being a local celebrity, ultimately the locals didn't know what to think of this Yankee-educated free-thinker, notwithstanding her *Alexander* pedigree.

After her father's death in 1911, and no longer obliged to his promise not to do so, Dr. Annie purchased a motorcar. She hired an attendant to escort her to crank the car to start because of her damaged lungs. Rules of the road were still being established for automobiles and driving was a bit of an adventure in those days. In May of 1914, she collided with a street car at the intersection of Long Street and Elizabeth Avenue, and Dr. Annie was slightly injured, but took the time to see to the other driver as well as set the arm of her young assistant. The car, according to the *Charlotte Observer*, was demolished, wrecked into a "shapeless mass" and "had to be carried to the garage on a truck."[21] A year later, she was charged with failing to stop in passing a street car which had stopped to discharge passengers.[22] It seemed she was always in a hurry.

During the First World War, Dr. Annie was appointed medical director of Charlotte's public schools and given the title "acting assistant surgeon" for responsibility for a five-mile sanitary zone around the army's Camp Greene (named for Nathanael Greene), just west of town. The responsibility and title were usually reserved for men-only. Her responsibilities were numerous, and she worked herself to exhaustion. So much so that in December of 1917, suffering a severe cold and grip, she could not leave her home for a month.

A member of the First Presbyterian Church, Dr. Annie was extremely devout, and never lost the stern, no-nonsense Scots-Irish attitude of an Alexander. Although empathetic, she demanded accountability, responsibility and morality from her patients. "Cultivate & insist upon orderliness in all things," she said: "Fitness, self control, & orderliness are the most important." She would also have added chastity to the list. Once she told the young daughter of a friend, "don't you ever let a man touch you unless you are engaged to be married." (The young woman later recalled, "[t]o this day, I haven't decided whether this advice was good or bad."[23])

As Dr. John Brevard had predicted when she was just a teenager, she never married. One friend recalled that Dr. Annie once "confided in me by saying that while she enjoyed the company of men friends, she would never marry." Except for two male friends with whom she corresponded from time to time, she did not have much male companionship, or seem to desire it. As a result though, Dr. Annie never had children of her own, which was a source of sorrow and regret to her. "I believe no woman[']s life is complete until she is a wife and mother," she once wrote. "Some of us never attain to that completeness...."

In 1919 she adopted a three-year-old orphaned boy whom she named Robert. Dr. Annie also helped raise the seven children of her brother after his death. She was a member of what was called the "Mother's Club" (later it became the Charlotte Women's Club), a civic club for prominent Charlotte women. At one meeting, she was asked why she was a member, as she was unmarried and had no children. "I answered that we had helped rear more children than any other member. [...] In heart and soul we [women] are all mothers."[24]

There was at least one romance, but only shadows of it remain. Among Dr. Annie's surviving papers from the period of her illness, in the winter of 1888–89, is a letter from a "male admirer." He proposes marriage. For whatever reason, she said no. The young would-be novelist had predicted these outcomes, or perhaps subconsciously chosen them, many years before. In "Doctor Katherine," she tells the story this way:

> Her gentlemen friends have been slow in calling, fearing to find her changed from a gentle girl into a masculine woman. One evening a few days before her going to college for the last year, a party of young people called to bid her "Good bye." The evening

passed all too quickly. It seemed like old times before Katherine went to College. The last good bys were said, but Will Herndon lingered.

"Good by Katherine. I don't suppose I will ever see you again," said Will dolefully.

"What's the matter," said Katherine, "you're not ill? Don't feel like dying do you? Let me feel your pulse."

"I'd rather you would listen to my heart," said Will with a poor attempt to smile.

"Katherine, will nothing induce you to give up this mad idea of ruining your life?"

"If you call a noble useful life, which a woman doctor's life is, a ruined life, mine will be ruined. I have seen the necessity for women physicians and you must have seen the same in your college and hospital work."

"It seems well enough for others to study and practice medicine but for you—I wish I could persuade you that your happiness lies in another place. Katherine—"

"Will it is useless," said Katherine quickly. "There is a niche for each of us and I must fill mine."

Will is heart-broken, not only for himself, but also for Katherine/Annie. He begs her, "Katherine, don't tell me you will never marry.… The happiest lives are married lives."

"That may be true Will," she replies, "being an old maid I may miss a few joys but I shall escape many sorrows." Will leaves her. In the scene, Katherine sits for a while, "gazing into the heavens through her open window. She neither saw the stars nor the silver crescent that hung in the west. She saw Will's earnest pleading face. She thought of the happiness she might have had as his wife and wondered if the happiness would compensate for all the suffering and sorrow and heartache and tears that might come with it. Her heart answered 'yes'; her head said 'no.'"

As it happens, "Doctor Katherine" is not the only work of fiction which Annie Alexander wrote.

A second, fragmentary story, dates from around 1911, when she was forty-seven; coincidentally also the year her father died. By then, Doctor Annie had made her success as a doctor, and was well known, loved and admired. She had overcome many obstacles. She had also given up much, including a husband, companionship, and love.

Alsop describes the sketches of her novel, as "a love story told from a young heroine's perspective, of her devotion to and cherishing of a man. The text breaks off abruptly. Immediately after these two pages, a large number of leaves have been ripped out of the volume, and destroyed. This story is written in the unused portion of her father's last medical casebook."[25] What she wrote, and why she destroyed it, is unknown. Was the fact that it was written in her father's casebook meaningful or just coincidence? Was this a rebellion against the fate that her father had decreed she follow, the path that she "serve humanity," and the sacrifices she was forced to make in doing so, at the expense of her own happiness?

As her father had prophesied, she had indeed "served humanity," but not without personal cost to herself.

Her Legacy

Dr. Annie died at her home on October 15, 1929, after a brief bout of pneumonia (which by some accounts she contracted from a patient.) The local chapter of the United Daughters of the Confederacy, and many others, fellow doctors, patients, and well-wishers, turned out for her funeral in Elmwood Cemetery. The *Charlotte News* wrote of her:

> More than the mere novelty of having been the first woman South of the Potomac River to enter the ranks of medicine for a professional career attached to the life and achievements of Dr. Anne Alexander whose passing here is so widely mourned. She brought into that profession such high resolutions and nobility of character, such proficiency in maintaining that warmth of relationship between practitioner and patient, that she became outstanding. There was a demureness about her and a humility, a seeking of not her own that glorified her in the esteem of her people. Long has she wrought her good works.
>
> For more than 40 years she has practiced her profession in the homes of the people here, moving among them with a majestic dignity and a proficient touch which enthroned her not only as a medical expert of superb order, but as a woman doing a great work in a womanly way—with tenderness, with soulfulness, and with love for her work no more dominant than love for those she served.[26]

The *Charlotte Observer* recalled what was obvious to all, that "she was recognized as a leader in the civic, social and business life of this city."[27] One of her close friends, Susie Van Landingham, said that Dr. Annie had "won for herself […] an honored place among the [medical] fraternity and a practice that is both lucrative and successful."[28] By all accounts, throughout what were surely at times physically and emotionally challenging work, she remained a model of grace, modesty and commitment.

Her biographer Alsop sums up her remarkable career of self service to Charlotte as follows: "What stands out in Alexander's life is not sacrifice, *but duty*: the dutiful daughter; the dutiful mainstay of societies, charities, and hospitals; the conscientious physician."[29]

A Final Story…

A final story about Dr. Annie, about the first baby she delivered, told in the guise of Katherine, from "Doctor Katherine."

One afternoon she receives a note addressed to "Doctor Caldwell." The note reads: "Dear Doctor = Please call to see my wife as soon as possible.

Yours, J. D. Blake.'" Is the letter addressed to her or her father? It isn't clear. Her father is not in. What to do? She hesitates, then thinks, "I'll risk it and go."

> She hurried on her hat and gloves, picked up her little black satchel which had been filled with all things needful anticipating this call and in twenty minutes rapped at Mrs. Blake's door.
> "I wish to see Mrs. Blake," she said to an old lady who opened the door.
> "My daughter is sick, bad off, and we've sent for the doctor, whom I expect every minute."
> "I am here madam, I am Doctor Katherine Caldwell."
> "You—Doctor Caldwell?" said the old lady in open eyed astonishment. "Why I supposed Miss Doctor Caldwell was—was—."
> "That's all right madam, I received Mr. Blake's note asking me to call. Will you show me to Mrs. Blake's room?" Dr. Katherine followed the old lady into the sick room.
> "Mary this is Miss Caldwell, Miss Doctor Katherine Caldwell." Mrs. Blake turned her head to look at the woman doctor.
> "Mother," she said, "where is the doctor?"
> "I am the doctor," said Katherine, quickly drawing off her gloves and going to the bedside.
> "Oh! O—O—Oh—!! Why didn't your father come? Mother sent for Doctor Caldwell."
> "Dr. Caldwell is not at home," said Dr. Katherine. "If I have made a mistake and am not wanted, I will bid you good morning," picking up her little black satchel to go. The mother quickly laid her hand on the doctor's arm and said, "Don't go Miss Doctor, excuse Mary's talk, she is suffering so she does not know what she is saying, please stay and do something for her." Reluctantly Doctor Katherine stayed, fearing that if all did not go well that it would hazard her success in that most historic of Southern towns where such an innovation as a woman doctor was not looked upon with much favor. Oh! The mental agony and physical anguish of doctor and patient during the next half hour. It seemed hours to both.

After many hours, the "anxiety and pain are at last ended with a heartfelt "Thank God," and a feeble infant cry in a peculiar minor key. Dr. Katherine left the house an hour later, the patient happy with her little pink baby on her arm, and the new grandmother blessing and praising women doctors in general and "Miss Doctor Katherine" in particular.

And that, she wrote, was "the beginning of a successful career."

12

H. Douglas Crotts and the Greatest Generation

> "I just did what I had to do. I would have done it again. Some of the things anybody would have done—and did do."
> —Doug Crotts, on actions at Tarawa

In the autumn of 1960, a young man named Earl Gulledge entered Harry P. Harding High School as a sophomore. Earl was 16 years old. He had been born in a working class family and lived on the city's west side during his entire public school years in Mecklenburg County. His father was an Army Air Forces veteran.

In Earl's junior year, 1961, his high school moved from its old building (which dated to 1935), to its present location on Alleghany Street—now known as Harding University High School. The "old Harding" was a classic school facade of the pre-war period. Ensconced in 1910/20s leafy neighborhoods, surrounded by tall oaks and hickories, adjacent to Elmwood Cemetery and only a few hundred yards from the Seaboard railroad tracks, it was a serene and quiet environment in the sleepy southern town of Charlotte.

Earl's first period class that year was American History, a required course. The class began at 9:00 a.m. and was taught by a man named H. Douglas Crotts ("Doug" to his friends). Professor Crotts was a big, affable, teddy-bear of a fellow, with a large head, dark hair and a broad smile.

Earl recalls seeing Crotts each morning, just before first period. American history class was held in the satellite dining room on the east side of "B" building. The teachers' lounge was located a few steps away from Class Room A. Teachers were permitted to smoke within their lounges, and Crotts would have a cigarette before class and walk to the dining room door about the time Earl would arrive.

"New Harding" was a unique and cutting edge school. It was the first in Charlotte-Mecklenburg's school system to have full air-conditioning. In terms of its design, unlike its classic predecessor, it had multiple buildings set around a quadrangle, reflecting the then-popular "George Jetson" trend in modern architecture. At the new school, there was a good chance one might have one or more walks between buildings with no shelter from cold or wind-blown rain.

Crotts' first period American History class was also unique and cutting edge for its time. For the first thirty minutes students viewed a televised program from UNC-Chapel Hill—apparently an attempt to introduce consistency into the curriculum. After the show ended, Crotts began leading class discussion. Earl recalled that Crotts "spoke in a dispassionate and clear manner to instill in his students an appreciation of who they were and why, and how studying the past can have implications for the future." Crotts was: "A large man with slightly bent shoulders. His coat was draped over his left arm and with his right he carried an old style—uncommon even for 1961—large leather satchel that would expand at the bottom. He would often show slight evidence of perspiration around the arms of his shirts which I presumed to be from smoking in the close confines of the lounge. He was soft spoken and perhaps understated although he did seem to have a good sense of humor."[1]

Crotts was a competent teacher, although some of his former students recall him as being withdrawn and not overly communicative. He was definitely not known for his flair. Most of his students just considered him the same way teenagers at all times think of their high school teachers: old, uncool and uninteresting. He was, after, all a high school history teacher, and what could be more *boring* than that?

Although his students spent an hour each day with Crotts, answering questions, turning in assignments, trying (or failing as the case may be) to pay attention, they knew nothing about Crotts' past. And why would they? Crotts didn't speak of it, and in the pre-internet age, personal information was not easily accessible.

In particular, they knew nothing about Crotts' military service in World War II. "I have no recollection of any mention of his WWII service," recalled Earl. "In fact, I know of no classmate who does. At that time it was assumed that almost any male in their forties had some part in the WWII effort." As it happens, seventeen years earlier, the year many of his students were born, the non-descript and stoop shouldered history teacher was fighting in an obscure and blood-drenched island in the Pacific named Tarawa; an action for which he would receive (in addition to other later medals) the Navy Cross and the British Distinguished Service Medal.

But to Crotts this part of his past wasn't worth talking about. It was simply history.

The Greatest Generation

Tom Brokaw, the well-known anchor of NBC News coined the term, "The Greatest Generation," to describe, as he put it, "the American men and women who went to war against the madness of Nazi Germany and imperial Japan and saved the world with their selfless and heroic actions on the home front as on distant battlefields."[2] The historian William Manchester, who served in the Marine corps in World War II, including at the bloodbath at Okinawa, wrote movingly of this generation:

> To fight World War II you had to have been tempered and strengthened by a struggle for survival—in 1940 two out of every five draftees had been rejected, most of them victims of malnutrition.... You also need nationalism, the absolute conviction that the United States was the envy of all other nations, a country which had never done anything infamous, in which nothing was insuperable, whose ingenuity could solve anything by inventing something. You felt sure that all lands, given our democracy and our know-how, could shine as radiantly as we did. Esteem was personal, too; you assumed that if you came through this ordeal, you would age with dignity, respected as well as adored by your children. Wickedness was attributed to flaws in individual characters, not to society's shortcomings. To accept unemployment compensation, had it existed, would have been considered humiliating. So would committing a senile aunt to a state mental hospital. Instead, she was kept in the back bedroom, still a member of the family.
>
> Debt was ignoble. Courage was a virtue. Mothers were beloved, fathers obeyed. Marriage was a sacrament. Divorce was disgraceful....
>
> All these and "God Bless America" and Christmas or Hanukkah and the certitude that victory in the war would assure their continuance into perpetuity—all this led you into battle, and sustained you as you fought, and comforted you if you fell, and, if it came to that, justified your death to all who loved you as you had loved them.[3]

Manchester's is without doubt the best summary of the worldview of the Greatest Generation, who would find themselves confronted by the tragedy and challenge of the Second World War. Crotts was one of many who personified this generation.

Like Crotts, many of this generation grew up in hardscrabble, rural America. Like Crotts, many of them came from small towns that few had heard of. Like Crotts, they were patriotic, religious and hard-working. Like Crotts, they would go on to fight and destroy fascism in Europe and Asia, and return home to rebuild the United States from the ruins of war and the Great Depression. And like Crotts, upon their return they did not seek individual glory or recognition for their service. While they had given much, others had given everything. They had survived the war when so many of their comrades did not, and that grim reality made them humble.

Crotts was born in Siler City, North Carolina, on February 3, 1921, to Charles Anderson and Clara Allred Crotts (or, as his USMC service record would later botch it, *Silver* City.). He was one of seven children. His father was a candy salesman. Crotts was a big lad, roughly two hundred and fifty pounds, and played on the high school football team. He had grey eyes, brown hair and a ruddy complexion. His teammates called him "Big Toar" after a larger than life, albeit somewhat bumbling, comic book hero called "The Mighty TOAR." (Catchphrase: *"Oh you big fathead Toar!"*)

He was educated in the public schools in Chatham County. During high school he worked in various construction jobs. After high school he went to work in the local textile industry, which was a large employer in the area. For a year and a half he worked at Burlington Mills, Inc. as a dye-can operator. In this role he dyed yarn in a machine to furnish specific colors. He worked there for a year and a half, until May 1941, when he either quit or was let go. Either way, this may have influenced his decision to enlist.

Crotts joined the Marine Corps on July 7, 1941, roughly six months before the attack on Pearl Harbor. Many were voluntarily enlisting in the Marines during this period, to avoid being drafted in the army. In October 1941 he was assigned to the Marine base in San Diego. He was initially assigned to the fire department, which was not a great assignment, and one he wanted to get out of. He then tried to get assigned to the engineers, but his commanding officer dissuaded him. He told Crotts if he joined the engineers, Crotts would be sent to China, and "he never known anybody to come out of China without VD." That was enough to put Crotts off the engineers.[4]

Instead he joined the tanks. In January 1943, he attended tank school at Camp Elliott, California. Four months later he was assigned to C Company, 1st Corp Tank Battalion at Camp Pendleton. He later said his captain gave him the transfer to tank school in lieu of payment of a five-dollar bet Crotts had won on the Rose Bowl.

Crotts' C Company was the first Marines to use new medium tanks. They trained at a place called "Jacques Farm." Tactics and training were primitive. There was no coordination with infantry, nor with artillery. The radios were unreliable and communication was poor. Within a tank, it often involved the tank commander kicking the driver when he wanted him to do something. Tanks were still new weapons, and had never been used in an amphibious assault. No one was sure what role they should play in an engagement, what tactics they should employ, or even how much water they could ford.[5] The latter was especially important, given that the Marines were shipping out to the Pacific.

In the autumn of 1943, Admiral Nimitz initiated a campaign in the central Pacific driving across the scattered island chains—the Gilberts, Marshalls and Marianas—towards the far-away but ultimate target: Japan. "Island hopping" was a tactic whereby the Marines would establish forward bases closer and closer to Japan by attacking and seizing strategic assets, principally islands with airfields, via amphibious assaults. It was a novel doctrine and many questions were unanswered. Could an attacking force from the sea take a heavily defended island? How would air, infantry and armor interact effectively? The Japanese, in turn, had a defensive strategy called *yogaki*.[6] Per this doctrine, the object of the defending force was not necessarily to resist an American invasion. Rather, like baiting a trap, the heavily fortified island fortresses in far-flung Pacific islands and atolls, would draw in the invading American forces and pin them down long enough for a counter-attack by Japanese naval and air forces. Therefore the purpose of defense was to resist invasion by the Americans, where possible, but more importantly to delay them down long enough for the inevitable counterstroke, using the *bushido* warrior spirit. The first clash of these two military doctrines—American amphibious assault vs. Japanese *yogaki*—would come at a remote spit of land in the central Pacific known as Tarawa.

Tarawa

Tarawa (pronounced *TAR-uh-wuh*) atoll is a series of thirty-something tiny sand and coral islands, quite literally in the middle of the Pacific Ocean. At low tide, the chain of islands are strung-together like a pearl necklace. They comprise two edges of a shark's tooth-shaped atoll, ninety miles from the equator, and roughly equidistant from the United States and Japan. The center of the shark's tooth is a large tropical lagoon—nearly two hundred square miles—filed with brilliant, aquamarine-blue sea-water. Within the lagoon, is a hard, sharp, coral reef, which lies submerged at low tide.

At the bottom, left corner of the Tarawa atoll is the island of Betio (pronounced *BAY-she-oh*). The island is quite small, less than two miles from end to end and shaped like a thin bird lying on its back, with its beak to the left, facing upwards, and its tail to the right. The island is dotted with palm trees and scrub brush but otherwise is entirely flat and featureless, just coral and sand. As Manchester puts it, Betio is "less than half the size of Manhattan's Central Park. No part of it is more than three hundred yard from the water. A good golfer can drive a ball across it at almost any point."[7]

Tarawa atoll had no natural resources of any significance; it was isolated and extremely difficult to reach; its climate was hot and miserable. It was this otherwise insignificant speck of land, which in November 1943 would be the crucible of the war in the Pacific. For the island of Betio did have one extremely valuable strategic asset—a 4,000 foot runway. From here, at the farthest outpost of the Japanese empire, the Japanese could provide early warning of an American invasion of the Gilbert or Marshall Islands in the Central Pacific.

Prior to December 1941, Tarawa had been a British protectorate, although there was very little to protect. There were a handful of native islanders, little trade and some buildings. The Japanese seized the Gilberts from the British in the weeks following Pearl Harbor. Another token Japanese force took Makin, an atoll one hundred and twenty miles away. In 1942, these outposts represented the farthest western reach of Japanese military power in the Pacific. In August 1942, a hit-and-run raid by Carlson's 2nd Marine Raiders on Makin destroyed the sea-place facilities and wiped out the Japanese garrison. Although strategically insignificant, Carlson's raid sent a warning to the Japanese of the fragile nature of their defense of the Gilbert Islands. In response, they began turning Betio, in the words of historian Martin Russ, "into nothing less than the most formidable island fortress, acre for acre, in the world."[8]

The beach, as Manchester describes it, "bristled with huge guns, concrete obstacles, and barbed-wire concertinas designed to force invaders into the fire zone of cannon and machine guns."[9] The reef was heavily mined and laced with barbed wire fences to hold up any invaders. The Japanese installed dozens of concrete blockhouses and pillboxes, reinforced with steel rebar, some twenty feet deep, and others as high as seventeen feet. "The strength of the blockhouses was impressive by any standard," writes Russ, "five-foot-thick concrete walls, superimposed with coconut palm logs of extraordinary resilience, reinforced with angle irons and railroad ties. Several feet of coral detritus and sand had been poured on top; from a distance the blockhouses resembled giant anthills."[10]

The pillboxes and bunkers were heavily camouflaged with sand and rock, making many of them nearly impossible to see until one was nearly on top of them. A series of trenches and underground tunnels connected them. A sea wall made of coconut logs made leaving the beach, assuming one could even reach it, difficult. Behind the sea wall were antitank pits, tank traps, revetments, more barbed wire, more coconut log pillboxes and dozens of firing pits. By one some estimates there were over 500 such reinforced positions on the one square mile island. Seven light tanks (type 95 *Ha-Go*) also lay in wait. Snipers were lashed high into palm trees, concealed by the fronds.

Defending Tarawa were 4,836 Japanese, most of them members of the Japanese Special Landing Forces—Japanese Marines. Also unhappily on the island were a number of Korean laborers, effectively Japanese slaves. They had twenty massive coastal defense guns, according to lore some eight-inch cannons captured by the Japanese at the fall of Singapore; 10 75-mm mountain guns; 6 70-mm cannon, and 9 37-mm field pieces.[11] There were anti-aircraft guns (which could of course be turned on infantry) and a hundred machine-gun emplacements. Its commander had once boasted that "a million men cannot take Tarawa in a hundred years." Their spirits were high, and they intended to fight to the death. As it happens, all but 17 did.

It was in this Pacific Stalingrad that Hubert Crotts of Siler City and the other members of Charlie Company, First Corps Medium Tank Battalion, were to land on the morning of November 20, 1943.

"I knew I was going to die"

Following their training at Jacques Farm, C Company shipped out to New Caledonia, and thence to the New Hebrides. The fourteen tanks of C Company, including Crotts, embarked on the USS *Ashland* on November 13, arriving off the Tarawa atoll on the 19th. Despite the massive Japanese fortification of the island, there was little visible indications of it to American reconnaissance. In fact, B-24 aircraft doing pre-invasion bombing over Tarawa saw few signs of life. They reported weak anti-aircraft fire, which was surprising. Some believed the bulk of the Japanese forces had pulled out weeks before.

The night before D-Day was hot, with hundreds of men crammed into sweltering bunks below deck. One Chaplain told the *Time* war correspondent Robert Sherrod that some of the men "have heard that there may not be any Japs on Tarawa and you know what their reaction is? They hope there are at least *some* Japs left there. They say they would hate to come all this was for nothing."[12] The Marines were not going to be disappointed.

To make sure that whatever Japanese remained would be in no position to fight, Navy bombers pounded the island for days. And in the pre-dawn darkness on D-Day, at 5:05 a.m., Sherrod heard "a great thud in the southwest. We knew what that meant. The first battleship had fired the first shot. We all rushed out on deck. The great show had begun."[13] Battleships began shelling the island, as men scrambled down cargo nets into their transports. The Higgins boats and amphibious tractors began assembling and moving in waves towards the lagoon, and towards the reef. For hundreds of the young Americans, it would be their last day on earth.

A successful landing depended on hitting the reef at high tide, for in order to reach the lagoon-side invasion beaches, on the north of the island, the Marines amphibious tractors (or "amphtracs") and Higgins boats would have to clear the fringing coral reef. Both vehicles were slow moving, which would make them easy targets for enemy gunners. The amphtracs could crawl over the reef with any tide, but the Higgins boats could not. They required four or five feet of water to clear the reef. Naval intelligence, relying on 1841 tidal charts, assumed a passable high tide for D-Day. But if they were wrong about the tides, the Higgins boats, full of Marines, would grind to a halt hundreds of yards from the beach. The amphtracs could ferry Marines back and forth to the beach, assuming there were enough vehicles and that no amphtracs were destroyed. Otherwise the Marines would have to wade in.

From the get-go, it was clear that the planners were wrong, both about the level of Japanese resistance and the level of the tides. While the pre-invasion bombardment had temporarily stunned the defenders and destroyed Japanese communications, it had not obliterated the island defenses, as the Navy had promised it would. The fire on the approaching landing craft was immense. Japanese guns opened up on the landing vehicles at 3,000 yards, and as the boats got closer, they were shredded by heavy machine gun fire. The first waves of boats were riddled with fire and decimated, although the amphtracs could clear the reef. However, an unusual "dodging" autumn tide meant that the tide was low and going out. The first waves of assault vehicles could find ways through the reef. But by the fourth wave, the Higgins boats could not and ground to a halt. Amphtracs tried to ferry Marines in, but there were not enough vehicles, and quickly they were engaged in simply carrying wounded out. The only way in was to walk.

In many cases the Marines were hundreds of yards from shore, visible,

Marines on a Higgins Boats approaching the island of Betio, Tarawa atoll, November 20, 1943. This was the first test of Marine amphibious assault tactics in the Second World War (Marine Corps photograph).

slow-moving and obvious targets in the bright blue water. Landing craft in the surf took direct artillery hits and simply disintegrated. Men leapt from burning amphtracs like torches. Waves of Marines, wading in, holding their rifles overhead, were mowed down in scenes reminiscent of World War I.

The water was deep and they were carrying fifty-plus pounds of equipment. "It was painfully slow, wading in such deep water," recalled Sherrod. "And we had seven hundred yards to walk slowly into this machine-gun fire, looming into larger targets as we rose onto high ground."[14] Not only machine-gun fire, but snipers in the trees, plunging mortar fire and other enemy artillery rained down on the slow-moving, exhausted and weighed-down Marines.

One private recalled:

> We had to hold our rifles over our heads as we started to that beach. This was the moment that we had trained for. The "Japs" had machine guns all along the beach pointing at us. There was a sunken ship to the right of us with "Jap" snipers shooting at us from it also [this was the *Saidu Maru*, which an American airstrike had crippled months earlier, and which the Japanese had grounded on the reef to use as a steel emplacement]. I heard the sound of a bullet, then another, and another. Then a Marine in front of me got it in the head and went under; then to my right, and then to my left. Marines were dropping like flies all around me. The water turned blood red.... Marines were floating back and forth like birch wood wrapped in barbed wire, purple, bloated and unrecognizable. These were Marines from the first assault. I knew I was going to die.[15]

The pre-invasion naval bombardment had also created massive underwater shell craters which both men and tanks could pitch into and drown. In order to protect the tanks, special Marine recon units went ahead of the tanks, standing chest high in the water, unprotected and entirely visible, and signaled to the tanks where hidden obstacles lay and marking them (or trying to) with floating buoys. It was a suicide mission, as the spotters, waving to the tanks, were shot down by the dozens from machine guns on the shore.

As he rode in, Crotts would have seen dozens of Marine and Naval planes flying a thousand feet overhead, pounding the island with machine gun fire and bombs; felt the cold sea water pouring over the prow and drenching the thirty or so men hunkering inside; heard the *ratatatat* of Japanese machine gun fire from the beach or the *whoosh* of shells landing nearby, throwing up massive geysers. Then, sickeningly, the grinding *crunch* of steel on coral and rock as the boat ground to halt on the reef, coupled with the dismaying knowledge that it was time to go over the side, or out the ramp.

In Crotts' case, he found himself in neck-deep water, nearly a thousand yards from the beach. The situation, he said, was "very confused." Tracer bullets soared overhead. All around him marines were falling and disappearing;

shells were exploding; and smoke and fire belched from stricken landing craft. Dead fish floated everywhere, some as large as several feet, killed in the concussion blasts. It was time to trudge to shore—if he made it that far.

Crotts landed about the same time as the four tanks of the Third Platoon, in the fourth wave, near the center of the beach code-named "RED-3." One recalled, "gunfire hitting the boats. Men being killed and blown into the water." And everywhere the acrid stench of gunpowder.[16] Another Marine described the hellish wade in to Betio as "like being in the middle of a pool table without any pockets."[17] Crott's assignment was to serve as a replacement for tank crew casualties, but also to act as a tank recon guide (on foot) as the situation demanded. As he remembered: "The thing we were supposed to do there was go ahead of the tanks and look for any shell craters that would disable a tank. We got to that reef just about as the tanks did, and nothing went according to schedule for the next six to eight hours. Actually, the tanks, I saw some ahead of me, saw some completely dilapidated and rendered unusable."[18]

RED-3 was the widest of the landing beaches on Betio and closest to the Japanese buildings. To the west—to the right of the men wading ashore—projecting five hundred feet from the beach—was what Manchester describes as, "a ramshackle, cribwork pier, long and narrow, jutting out from the beach. As shelters the piers coconut stanchions were pitifully inadequate, but they were better than nothing, and those who reached them unwounded thought themselves lucky."[19] Crotts was one of those lucky ones. "I took about three of my close friends, and we went over to the end of the pier," he recalled. "We went down the pier, and we got in. I think it must have taken us four hours."

The "pier at Tarawa" was to become a hallowed geographic feature, like the Peach Orchard at Gettysburg or the Sunken Road at Antietam. That afternoon, it was crowded with men huddling in its defilade, heads peaking above the waves, inching their way on their toes, towards the sea-wall.

"The water was just about up to our chins," Crotts said. "I suppose we would have drowned, with the equipment we had if it had been even two or three inches deeper.... We were getting shot at almost constantly. I remember one of my buddies said 'Looky here,' and he had a spent shell in his hand he had caught kind of as it came into the water."[20]

Creeping beneath the cover of the pier-works, Crotts and the other Marines sprinted the last dozen yards on dry land and huddled behind the four-foot high coconut log sea-wall. There they were (largely) safe from direct machine-gun fire coming from the beach emplacements, although shells from Japanese 89 knee mortars plunged among the clustered groups. By the time he made it ashore his rifle had rusted from hours in the sea water; as Crotts put it, it "wasn't really rusty, just brown. I remember throwing it away and picking up one from a dead Marine."²¹ Crotts and the other marines were on Tarawa, but they owned twenty yards of beach, and even that was heavily contested.

They had to get off of the beach. But to raise one's head over the seawall was surely death. Only a few marines were able to get over or through the sea-wall, but could advance no further, and were in any event subject to the eventual Japanese counter-attack. Clearly more firepower was going to be required. Moving inland through sweeping machine gun fire would have to be done by armor. And only the heavy 75-mm cannon of the medium tanks, applied at point-blank range, had the firepower to reduce the pillboxes. Naval artillery and air support was impossible, given that the Marines and Japanese were nearly on top of one another. Many of the Marine engineers, responsible for blowing the sea-wall and thereafter for dynamiting the emplacements, lay dead in the surf. Only tanks, supporting the infantry as they moved off the beach, could do the job.

Fourteen medium tanks of C Company had landed for the attack with the fourth wave. Each tank had been given a name beginning with "C" to identify them as parts of "Charlie" company. On D-Day, four tanks of the third platoon (*Cannonball, Condor, Charlie* and *Colorado*) were launched from LCTs on the reef east of the main pier, on RED-3. Each tank had a distinctive emblem of the 1st Corps Medium Tank Battalion painted above its name: an elephant with one front foot upraised, firing a cannonball with a puff of smoke from his trunk, and a red blanket draped over the elephant's back.²²

All four tanks of Third Platoon on RED-3 had made it to the beach and rendezvoused at the base of the pier. As the hot afternoon sun rose, they prepared to move inland through an exit they had found in the sea-wall. Incredibly, in retrospect, they had no real plan for what to do next, other than traverse the island and return. "Instructions were to push across the island as quickly as possible and return, firing only as necessary, turn around and come back," one tanker recalled.²³ The orders and tactics were insane and would lead shortly to the near massacre of all four tanks of Third Platoon.

Pushing through the sea-wall gap, the tanks formed line abreast and reached the taxiway of the airstrip. Once there, Japanese 75-mm type 88 anti-aircraft guns, just over 350 yards away—point blank range for these guns—opened up all around them. Maneuvering to avoid the fire, *Cannonball*, tipped over into a fuel-dump trench and was a sitting-duck for the 88s. A second tank, *Charlie*, moved to shield the immobile *Cannonball* from Japanese fire and was also knocked out. Having made it to the center of the narrow island, in the middle of the airstrip, the third tank, *Condor*, was then hit. The crew began bailing out, with several being shot and killed in the attempt. The fourth and only remaining tank, *Colorado*, hammered by Japanese rounds and set aflame, retreated to the beach. Avoiding wounded Marines on the beach, she spent the afternoon moving back and forth in shallow water, firing inland.[24] Within an hour, three of the four Marine medium tanks on RED-3 had been destroyed while accomplishing very little.

Elsewhere on Betio, the story was the same; unable to communicate with one another and only by shouting to communicate with the infantry, the tanks had little positive impact on the battle and were overwhelmed by Japanese firepower and put out of commission. By late afternoon on D-Day, there were no functioning tanks left at all on RED-1.[25] On RED-2, just as on RED-3, only one tank survived. Thus of the fourteen medium tanks that landed on Tarawa, only three were left, and none could communicate with the other due to a breakdown in communications. It was, in short, a complete debacle.[26]

But the destruction of the tanks was not the only problem. The marines had suffered massive, appalling casualties getting ashore. They were out of food, drinking water, plasma and medical supplies, and, more worryingly, ammunition. Although they were on the beach, that's all they held, and as night fell on D-Day most assumed that the anticipated night-time Japanese *Banzai* counter-attack would wipe out the landing force entirely. Marine General Smith radioed to Holland "Howling Mad" Smith aboard the *Pennsylvania*, "Issue in doubt."[27]

The Tank Spotter

D-Day on Betio was bad, but the night was little better. Five thousand exhausted marines "held a shallow, box-like perimeter at the base of the pier," writes Manchester.[28] The beach and surf was littered with destroyed landing craft, boxes, bodies and the scattered detritus of the battle. The flames of burning vehicles and ammunition case an unreal, sinister glow. On RED-3, *Colorado* sat in shallow water, its gun pointing inland. A loud Japanese bomber nick-named "Washing Machine Charlie" flew over and dropped bombs, which was largely ineffective other than keeping the marines awake and alarmed. More sinisterly, Japanese infiltrators swam out to the destroyed American amphibious tractors and Higgins boats, and poured fire from behind into the marines on the beach. Orders were given to the Marines not to fire their weapons in the event of a counter-attack as the risk of shooting marines in the dark was too great. Instead, K-bar knives were unsheathed and held tightly. Japanese shouts were heard in the dark over the crashing waves. But the dreaded counter-attack against the Marines' small beachhead never came.

It was clear that if the Marines were going to get off the beach, the tanks would have to clear a path. And if the tanks were going to function, they would need ammo. That night, Crotts and a small group of marines, acting on their own initiative, began to scavenge ammunition and fuel from the shattered tanks of Third Platoon that lay behind enemy lines. "We went in and got some ammunition two or three times in some rather precarious situations," as he put it.[29] Moving from tank to tank during the late evening, crawling to avoid being seen by the Japanese, they grabbed fifty-caliber ammunition and lugged it back to the beachhead by the pier.

At day break, in a sandy foxhole near the pier, Sherrod wrote in his journal: "The coral flats in front of us present a sad sight at low tide. A half dozen Marines lie exposed, now that the water has receded. They are hunched over, rifles in hand, just as they fell. They are already one-quarter covered by sand that the high tide left. Further out on the flats and to the left I can see at least fifty other bodies."

Moments later, at day break on D+1, Marines commenced landing again with the same results: mass slaughter in the waves. By 7:30 a.m., wrote Sherrod,

Marines at the seawall on Tarawa. The firepower of the medium tanks, like *Colorado*, was necessary to break through (Marine Corps photograph).

"I can count at least a hundred Marines lying on the flats.... This is worse, far worse than it was yesterday."[30]

At some point during the night, the commander of *Colorado*, Johnny Marn, had exited the tank and was shot by a sniper through the shoulder. As the invasion recommenced, Second Lieutenant Louis Largey relieved the wounded Marn, and took over command of the *Colorado*. The first thing Largey needed was a spotter for the tank.

Due to its design, visibility on the model M4A2 Medium Tank, such as the *Colorado*, was limited. Directly in front, there was a six-foot blind spot. Inside the tank, the driver sat to the left and the assistant driver to the right, each on a metal-framed, canvas seat. For better vision, the driver and assistant would raise the seats to put their heads outside the hatch to see where they were going. The tank commander also had a 360 degree periscope, but it too contained a blind spot roughly 33–40 feet in all directions around the tank. During non-combat conditions a ground guide walked in front of the tank and directed the driver with hand signals to avoid obstacles.[31] Obviously, during combat visibility was even more restricted as the hatches were closed, with smoke, fire and natural obstacles on every side, in addition to the deafening noise, there was the physical shock of firing weapons (or receiving fire), stress and terror.

In short, *Colorado* was operating effectively blind. Lt. Largey enlisted Crotts to help him guide the tank. But first, he had to show him what he—Largey—was seeing inside. "Doug, you've got to get in the tank and go with me," he said to Crotts. "I've got to show you what we're looking at here, so when you give me signals you'll know what I can see, what I can't see, and what happenstance will enable me to see."

Crotts got in *Colorado*. The interior was stifling and hot, and for anyone prone to claustrophobia, entirely intolerable. On Tarawa, amidst the equatorial heat, the constant shaking, diesel stench and deafening *vroom vroom vroom* of its twin-engines was terrifying and disorienting.

"Is this our lines straight ahead?" Crotts asked. No, said Largey: Japanese. "Well, there's Japanese soldiers going over a little mound, one after another," replied Crotts. A line of Japanese marines was crawling on their bellies towards the American lines. Largey turned his machine gun on them. As they crawled forward, said Crotts, the *Colorado's* machine gun, would "just roll them over. After they quit coming he just threw a seventy-five [shell] into the group."

Crotts thought "boy, I'd rather be outside than in this thing.... I think I had claustrophobia, to tell you the truth. I never did relax inside. I felt better outside."

The interior of the *Colorado* must have been bad indeed to have preferred fighting, unprotected by its steel shell, outside the tank. Crott's mission was to guide the tank towards pillboxes and bunkers, to point out targets, and to move wounded dead or Marines out of the tank's path; what experts on the battle called "a near-suicidal endeavor."[32]

That morning on Day+1 Crotts led *Colorado* forward, identifying targets by hand signals. "When we could spot anything we thought they ought to see, I would lay my rifle down as if I was sighting," he recalled. "He could look at my rifle, and I would hold up fingers for how many yards out there it was."[33] Crotts would also race back to the tank, bang on the pistol port (a small hatch on the rear of the turret) and shout directions to Largey. The tank was an obvious and visible target, as was its unprotected guide out front. On another occasion, he recalled, "I took a seventy-five millimeter shell [casing] and beat on that tank until they acknowledged that they saw us. That was very risky. Those Japs saw you out there and they knew damn well what you were telling them."[34]

With *Colorado* back in action, the reduction of the fortified emplacements began. It was slow work. One eye-witness recalled the Colorado approaching "this giant pillbox, [where it] fired [a] half-dozen rounds. All they did was fall off."[35] Such was the depth and strength of the pillboxes that *Colorado's* 75-mm cannon would have to fire twenty, thirty or even forty rounds, sometimes at nearly point-blank range to destroy a position. The lighter 37-mm shell of the light tanks "bounced off" the Japanese positions entirely, one tanker said, and without repeated fire, the 75-mm shell that the medium tanks such as *Colorado* fired, did the same.[36] Only when "continuous fire from the 75s was directed at the same spot eventually could you blow away the sand and concrete and penetrate the steel. The ammunition expenditure for this kind of pillbox treatment is prohibitive. In one case it was reported to me that they had used 112 rounds of 75s to do this kind of job."[37] For the long day on D+1, *Colorado* cracked open Japanese pillboxes or provided covering fire for marines on foot to blast them with TNT, drop grenades in ventilation systems, or spray them with liquid napalm from flamethrowers. It was grueling, terrifying work.

The greatest of the Japanese defenses, the tallest on the island, at something like twenty feet high, was the headquarters of Japanese Admiral Shibaski, a bombproof sand and concrete blockhouse known to the marines as "Bonnyman's Hill" (so named after Alexander Bonnyman, a Marine engineer who had charged to the top, and stood there firing on the charging Japanese, until he was shot down). Bonnyman's Hill was the symbolic center of the Tarawa battle. Over two days it had resisted attack after attack. On the morning of Day+2, *Colorado*, led by Crotts, moved in place and began to shell the bunker. Despite Crotts' targeting, round after round of the tank's shells were absorbed harmlessly by the piled sand. Different tactics were required. Crotts guided covering machine gun fire into the portals and loopholes, while infantry raced to the top where they dropped grenades and TNT into ventilation shafts. When the grisly business was done, two hundred charred Japanese corpses were found inside. The fall of Bonnyman's Hill was not the end of the battle, however, although the outcome was no longer in doubt.

Another day was required to sweep and secure the island. On D+3 *Colorado* cleared out the remaining Japanese hold-outs on the eastern, tapering end of Betio, firing high-explosive (HE) rounds at the Japanese, who charged forward waving swords in a final, doomed, *banzai* charge against the advancing Marine tanks. According to Largey, one single HE shell killed between fifty and seventy-five attacking Japanese marines. By now, however, the end was not in doubt, and the Japanese knew it. Across the eastern end of the island, Marines discovered Japanese who had committed suicide, either by holding a grenade to their chest or firing a rifle into their mouth.

Later that day, at 1:10 p.m. on D+3, Tuesday, November 23, seventy-six hours after the invasion started, the Marine corps declared the battle of

Colorado on Tarawa, probably the afternoon of November 23, 1943 (D+3), after the conclusion of the battle. Crotts may be one of the men in foreground (courtesy Romain Cansiere).

Tarawa officially over. The Americans had suffered 1,009 dead and 2,101 wounded. Of the 4,836 defenders on Tarawa alive four days earlier, seventeen Japanese prisoners, and 139 Korean forced laborers remained alive.

After the war, a ferocious debate began over whether the Battle of Tarawa was necessary (a similar debate occurred over the invasion of Pelilieu, an even worse battle, which occurred in September 1944). After all, an area just slightly bigger than Dilworth had claimed several thousand American casualties. Was it necessary? Would a longer bombardment (Holland Smith said ten days was required, not three) have destroyed the Japanese without the bloody invasion? Could the island have been bypassed entirely? And even if it were necessary, was it well-executed? Without question, the mistakes and errors, the misreading of the tides, too few landing craft, lack of Naval and Marine coordination, the ineffective pre-invasion bombardment, and so forth, had led to the deaths of hundreds of Americans, which, with a more thoughtful battle plan, could have been avoided. Monday morning quarterbacking was easy, of course. But still, doubts over Tarawa, at least over its cost, linger to this day. For what it is worth, in his post-war memoirs, Marine General Holland Smith, wrote, "If Tarawa had to be fought, its only justification was the information was gained that saved lives and increased the efficiency of our landing technique in subsequent operations." This was a pretty slender reed to hang a thousand dead on, which even "Howling Mad" begrudgingly conceded. He concluded, bitterly: "Tarawa was a mistake."[38]

Wounded at Saipan

It was for the historians and officers to make this judgment after the fact however. Marines like Doug Crotts were left with a bad job and had to do what they were told. For his gallantry and heroism on Tarawa, Crotts was awarded the Navy Cross and British Distinguished Service Medal. His Navy Cross commendation noted, in part, his:

> extraordinary heroism and devotion to duty while serving as a member of the Second Tank Battalion, Second Marine Division, in action against enemy Japanese forces at Betio Island, Tarawa Atoll, Gilbert Islands, from 20 to 24 November 1943. Arriving on a reef after the tanks had landed ashore and realizing that these vehicles would require trained reconnaissance personnel, Corporal Crotts obtained permission to call for volunteers and, leading a group of five men a distance of a thousand yards under heavy enemy fire, joined the tanks on the beach. On four occasions, he guided a tank over the most suitable terrain through our infantry lines to previously located positions behind the Japanese lines, courageously defying intense machine-gun and mortar fire. During the first night, he salvaged urgently needed ammunition and fuel from wrecked tanks and, consistently exercising splendid initiative and expert technical skill throughout this vital period, was largely responsible for keeping the one remaining tank in the

area [*Colorado*] in operation. Corporal Crotts' inspiring conduct, aggressive determination and fearless devotion to duty in the face of grave peril reflect great credit upon himself and the United States Naval Service.

The British awarded the "big 250-pound Marine" the Distinguished Service Medal, noting, "'Big Toar' served as a link in a human chain to guide the much-needed tanks through the surf to the beach. Corp. Crotts further distinguished himself by securing ammunition and fuel for the 'Colorado' and led the tank on four successful raids far into the Japanese lines."

Tarawa was not the end of "Big Toar's" service in World War II, however. He went on to land and fight at Saipan, acting in a similar role as he had on Tarawa, in performing recon and targeting for tanks. Again, it was very dangerous work. Or as he laconically put it, "it wasn't a good situation." On July 2, 1944, Crotts was carrying a side arm in lieu of a rifle and directing tank fire near an open field. Japanese snipers targeted officers by looked for those naïve enough to wear distinguishing insignia, or officer uniforms, or carrying pistols. Crotts was doing the latter, and his luck finally ran out. As he put it, "damned if they didn't pick me out. Guy took a shot at me. ... We were drawing fire across a big open field. I had my rifle down showing them [the tank] where the fire was coming from, and dadgum if I didn't forget the sonofgun [the sniper] could shoot. All of a sudden the guy tore my legs up. Went through one leg and seared the other one." Another tank pulled "right over me so I got some protection."

Shot through both legs, Crotts was evacuated from the jungle in a jeep ambulance, passing through several aid posts. "They would take me and say 'We can't work on you here, and put me back on that jeep. Every little bounce just tore me up. Then they would take me somewhere else and say 'Can't do it here.' Finally I burst into tears. I said 'You sonofaB, don't you put me back on that jeep! I have had it with the on and off of jeeps!' I just couldn't stand that vibration any more."[39] Delirious, Crotts thought he was being taken back into combat, but instead he was flown to Eniwetok, then Hawaii, then a Naval hospital in Oakland. His war was over.

For actions on Saipan, Crotts received a Bronze Star and a Purple Heart.

The History Teacher

Crotts was honorably discharged from the corps in San Diego, on October 6, 1945. He had served one year, two months and twelve days. He indicated in his discharge interview that he "desires training in political science." That same year, he married Eugenia Farrell in Siler City. Following the war he received his B.A. in History and English at Lenoir-Rhyne College (where he was listed as "pre-law" in the 1948 class yearbook, proudly posing in a heavy wool blazer, black tie and pocket square, smiling broadly). Thereafter he received his Master's Degree in History from UNC Chapel Hill. In 1952, the family moved to Charlotte, where Crotts became a high school history teacher, first at Harry P. Harding (1954–1967), then at Myers Park High for two years and finally at Garinger High, until his retirement. All in all, he had taught in the public high school system in Charlotte for thirty-two years.

Crotts, according to Earl Gulledge's recollection, "was understated in temperament and consistently soft spoken. He would sometimes offer some humor with a twinkle in his eyes; at a time when stern discipline was still in play he seemed to have a light handed touch." None recalled that he ever spoke of Tarawa. Another student (Harding class of 1963) said simply of him, "He was my history teacher. I liked him. I never heard him raise his voice. He was a quiet man."[40]

Crotts and Eugenia raised a family in Charlotte (a son and daughter). He was an active member of Dilworth United Methodist Church. Built in 1925, the church was (and is) a beautiful and austere stone building, in the Gothic revival style, standing along the broad, oak-lined East boulevard. When Crotts attended, street cars passed in front, and well-dressed men and women ascended the nineteen stone steps towards the three sets of wooden double doors at the main entrance. Calm, civilized and serene, the stone church in leafy Dilworth must have seemed a million miles from the heat and blood of Tarawa.

Doug Crotts, top right, in the 1948 Lenoir-Rhyne class yearbook (courtesy Earl Gulledge).

The "Big Toar" died on Wednesday, February 9, 2011. His ashes reside in the columbarium at the stately church. As befits a member of the Greatest Generation, Crotts remained reserved and unboasting about his war-deeds, in part because he knew that he was lucky to have survived, when so many of his generation had not. Speaking of the medals he had won on Tarawa he said, "I don't even know that I deserve it, and I'm a little bit uncomfortable even talking about it. The only thing I'll tell you, I just did what I had to do. I would have done it again. Some of the things anybody would have done—and did do."[41]

Chapter Notes

In citing works in the notes, short titles have exclusively been used except with respect to magazines, newspapers or periodicals. Works frequently cited have been identified by the following abbreviations:

CP—*The Cornwallis Papers: The Campaigns of 1780 and 1781 in The Southern Theatre of the American Revolutionary War,* edited and commented on by Ian Saberton, November 10, 2010. Reference is first made to the volume number and the corresponding pages. Where possible I have included the title of the work and the date. Where the commentary is that of the editor, Saberton, I have tried to make that clear in the text or footnote.

CR—*The Colonial and State Records of North Carolina,* digital edition. Reference is first made to the volume number and the corresponding pages as shown in the digital edition maintained online by the University of North Carolina at Chapel Hill. Where possible I have included the title of the work and the date. These are easily found in the on-line category either by searching a quote within the text or the reference itself. A hard copy of the CR can also be found at the Carolina Room of the CML.

CML—The Carolina Room at the Charlotte-Mecklenburg Public Library in uptown Charlotte, NC contains a wealth of information about many of the figures described here, as well as local genealogical work.

Governor's Report—*The Declaration of Independence by the Citizens of Mecklenburg County,* published by the Governor under the authority and direction of the General Assembly of the State of North Carolina. Raleigh. Lawrence & Lemay. 1831. An online version is maintained by the Charlotte Mecklenburg Public Library at www.cmstory.org in document index in "All About the Declaration" section. Page references in the notes refer to the copy in the online version.

SCARPS—Southern Campaign of the American Revolution Pension Statements. http://revwarapps.org/. This is an excellent (searchable) website for the posting of transcriptions of pension applications filed by veterans of the Southern Campaigns of the Revolution and their widows, created by C. Leon Harris and Will Graves. In each case, I give the name of the applicant, and where possible other identifying information (such as file number).

SHC—Mecklenburg Declaration of Independence Papers in the Southern Historical Collection at the University of North Carolina, Chapel Hill. This historical collection is maintained at Wilson Library, the University of North Carolina at Chapel

Hill. The SHC includes the original papers of John McKnitt Alexander, including the "rough notes," and the Davie Copy. It also includes the Copy in Unknown Handwriting, as well as the original certificates and papers cited in the Governor's Report. Original letters and papers of Dr. Joseph Alexander are also contained in the SHC.

Preface and Acknowledgments

1. Churchill, *Great Contemporaries*, 165.
2. *Ibid.*, 29.

Chapter 1

1. *11 CR,* "Report by James Glen Concerning the North Carolina/South Carolina Boundary" [Extract], July 1749, 113–114.
2. *5 CR,* "Letter from Arthur Dobbs to the Board of Trade of Great Britain," August 24, 1755, 360.
3. Blumer, *Catawba Nation*, 33. The eminent artist and sculptor Chas Fagan was raised in Ligonier, in the western part of Pennsylvania. In the woods behind his house there was an old trail which was called "The Catawba Path," and according to the stories of his childhood, it was along this pass that the "bloodthirsty" Catawba Indians from down south came up to murder the "peace loving" Indians who lived nearby. Private correspondence with the author.
4. Lawson, *Voyage*, 204.
5. *Governor James Glen to the Board of Trade*, Dec. 23, 1749; summary of meeting from Isenbarger, *Native Americans*, 76–78.
6. Lee, *Indian Wars*, 53.
7. *5 CR,* "Report concerning the number of Native Americans in North Carolina," [date unknown], 320–321.
8. *Catawba River Companion*, 17.
9. James Adair, *A History of the North-America Indians*, in Isenbarger, *Native Americans*, 1.
10. Merrell, *Indians' New World*, 110.
11. Adair, *History*, in Isenbarger, *Native Americans*, 3.
12. *Ibid.*, 10.
13. Isenbarger, *Native Americans*, 31.
14. *Ibid.*
15. *Ibid.*
16. *Ibid.*, 33.
17. Adair, "History," in *Native Americans* by Isenbarger, 35–36.
18. Isenbarger, *Native Americans*, 11.
19. "James Glen to the Board of Trade," December 1757, in *Native Americans* by Isenbarger, 9.
20. Isenbarger, *Native Americans*, 5.
21. Adair, "History," in *Native Americans* by Isenbarger, 7.
22. Lawson, *Voyage*, 201.
23. Isenbarger, *Native Americans*, 7.
24. John Brickell, "Natural History of North Carolina," in *Native Americans* by Isenbarger, 8.
25. Isenbarger, *Native Americans*, 73.
26. Adair's summary of the smallpox among the Cherokee, in *Native Americans* by Isenbarger, 74–75.
27. Isenbarger, *Native Americans*, 79.
28. See Adair, in *Native Americans* by Isenbarger, 74.
29. *Ibid.*, 75.
30. *Ibid.*
31. *6 CR,* "Report by Arthur Dobbs concerning general conditions in North Carolina," 1761, 616.
32. Isenbarger, *Native Americans*, 79.
33. *6 CR,* "Report by Arthur Dobbs Concerning General Conditions in North Carolina," 1761, 616.
34. Isenbarger, *Native Americans*, 73.
35. *Ibid.*, 118.
36. *Ibid.*
37. *Ibid.*, 119.
38. *Ibid.*
39. *Ibid.*, 111.
40. *Ibid.*, 131.
41. *5 CR,* "Journal of August Gottlieb Spangenberg's Voyage to North Carolina to Establish a Moravian Settlement," 1.
42. www.nchistoricsites.org/bath/tuscarora.htm. Passage edited and adapted from Herbert R. Paschal Jr., *A History of Colonial Bath* (Raleigh, N.C.: Edwards & Broughton, 1955).
43. *Ibid.* Also see Lee, *Indians Wars*, 36.
44. Lee, *Indians Wars*, 36.
45. Lawson, *Voyage*, 208–209.
46. Blumer, *Catawba Nation*, 30.
47. *Ibid.*, 34.
48. *Ibid.*
49. *Ibid.*
50. *6 CR,* "Minutes of the North Carolina Governor's Council," Dec. 4, 1762–Dec. 31, 1762, 794–795.
51. *4 CR,* "Minutes of the North Carolina Governor's Council," Oct. 2, 1749–Oct. 18, 1749, 971.

52. *5 CR,* "Letter from Arthur Dobbs to Hugh Waddell, [Alexander Osborne], and Colonel Alexander Dobbs, Arthur," July 18, 1756, 604.
53. *4 CR,* "Diary of August Gottlieb Spangenberg During His Journey to North Carolina, September 1752," 1313.
54. "Haigler to Glen," Nov. 21, 1752, *Native Americans* by Isenbarger, 157.
55. *5 CR,* "Letter from Arthur Dobbs to Hugh Waddell, [Alexander Osborne], and Colonel Alexander," July 18, 1756, 605.
56. "Glen to Rowan," Mar. 13, 1754, in *Native Americans* by Isenbarger, 157.
57. Passage and quotes following from *5 CR,* "Treaty between North Carolina and King Hagler and the Catawba Indians," Aug. 29, 1754, 141–144.
58. Foregoing passages, *Ibid.*
59. Passage and quotes following from *5 CR,* "Report by Peter Henley concerning his conference with King Hagler and the Catawba Nation," May 26, 1756—May 28, 1756, 579–584.
60. *6 CR,* "Letter from Arthur Dobbs to the Board of Trade of Great Britain," Sep. 11, 1759, 58.
61. *Ibid.*
62. *6 CR,* "Minutes of the North Carolina Governor's Council," Dec. 4, 1762—Dec. 31, 1762, 772–799.
63. Powell, *Dictionary, Vo. III,* 2.
64. Blumer, *Catawba Nation,* 35.
65. *Ibid.*

Chapter 2

1. *7 CR,* "List of Taxables in North Carolina for the Year 1767 and Report on Church of England Parishes," 540–541.
2. Kratt, *Spirit of the New South,* 16.
3. Blethen and Wood, *From Ulster to Carolina,* 17–18.
4. *Ibid.,* 19.
5. *Ibid.,* 23.
6. *Ibid.,* 23–24.
7. *Ibid.,* 30.
8. *5 CR,* "Letter from Arthur Dobbs to the Board of Trade of Great Britain," Aug. 24, 1755, 355.
9. *1 CP,* 33–34.
10. *6 CR,* "Minutes of the North Carolina Governor's Council North Carolina," Dec. 4, 1762—Dec. 31, 1762, 795.
11. Tarleton, *History,* 86.
12. Woodmason, *Carolina Backcountry,* 50.
13. *Ibid.,* 60.
14. *Ibid.,* 33.
15. *1 CP,* 33.
16. Woodmason, *Carolina Backcountry,* 52.
17. *1 CP,* 33.
18. *Ibid.,* 34.
19. *Ibid.,* 33.
20. *Ibid.,* 34.
21. *Ibid.*
22. Jim Williams, *Thomas "Kanawha" Spratt, Early Settler and Friend of the Catawba.* Charlotte 240 online series of essays, by the Charlotte History Museum. "There is a persistent legend that Thomas Spratt was the first person to bring a wheeled cart across the Yadkin River and that his daughter was the first European child born between the Yadkin and the Catawba Rivers. However, these stories are probably baseless since settlers were there many years before the Spratts arrived." In his 1757 will Thomas Spratt's name is given as "Sprot," but ever since they've been known as the Spratts.
23. Tompkins, *History of Mecklenburg,* 16. The Spratt Land Grant was for 443 acres on the North side of 12 mile creek in Anson County on 6 April 1753. His only other land grant was dated Mar. 31, 1753.
24. *5 CR,* "Letter from Matthew Rowan to the Board of Trade of Great Britain," June 28, 1753, 24.
25. *5 CR,* "Journal of August Gottlieb Spangenberg's Voyage to North Carolina to Establish a Moravian Settlement," Sep. 13, 1752–Jan. 8, 1753, 6.
26. *Ibid.,* 7.
27. *4 CR,* "Diary of August Gottlieb Spangenberg during his journey to North Carolina" [Translation] [Extracts], Sep. 1752, 1312.
28. *5 CR,* "Journal of August Gottlieb Spangenberg's Voyage to North Carolina to Establish a Moravian Settlement," Sep. 13, 1752–Jan. 8, 1753, 3.
29. *4 CR,* "Diary of August Gottlieb Spangenberg During His Journey to North Carolina" [Translation] [Extracts], Sep. 1752, 1312.
30. *6 CR,* "Minutes of the North Carolina Governor's Council North Carolina," Dec. 4, 1762–Dec. 31, 1762, 795.
31. *Ibid.,* 796.
32. Spangenberg quoted in Lee, *Indian Wars,* 52.
33. Spratt, *Recollections,* 43.
34. *Ibid.,* 44.
35. Patterson, *Image,* 272.
36. *Ibid.*
37. *Ibid.*
38. *7 CR,* "Report by Charles Woodmason Concerning Religion in North Carolina, Including a List of Taxable," 1765, 288.
39. Dan Morrill, *A History of Charlotte and Mecklenburg County,* online edition, chapter 1.
40. *23 CR,* "Acts of the North Carolina General Assembly," Mar. 2, 1774–Mar. 25, 1774, 966.

41. *Ibid.*, 49.
42. *1 CP*, 34.
43. Patterson, *Image*, 298.
44. *Ibid.*
45. *Ibid.*
46. Spratt, *Recollections*, 46.
47. *Ibid.*, 50–51.
48. *Ibid.*, 53.
49. *1 CP*, 43.
50. Sherman, *Calendar*, 258.
51. Sometimes given as "Wacab," "Wauchope," "Walkup" or other spellings. The correct name, though rarely used, is Walkup.
52. Lee, *Memoirs*, 195.
53. *Ibid.*, 195–196. "The particulars of this affair are well described by Lee," says Graham, "who, I understand, got the account of that and other affairs from General Davie himself." Graham, *Papers*, 249.
54. Spratt, *Recollections*, 60–61.
55. The following account was given by Susanna Smart to D. G. Stimson in the 1850s in "A Carolina Woman of the Revolution: Susannah Smart," *Godey's Lady's Book and Magazine*, September 1856, 213–217.
56. "A Carolina Woman of the Revolution: Susannah Smart," *Godey's Lady's Book and Magazine*, September 1856, 213–217.
57. Johnson, *Traditions*, 348. "A private soldier [also] died whilst they were there on the plantation. The brutal officers ordered his grave to be made in the yard and he was buried there. My mother [Spratt's daughter] told me that she recollected hearing the lamentations of the soldier's wife, that she had no means of getting her husband out of purgatory, until she could meet with a Catholic priest." *Ibid.*
58. Johnson, *Traditions*, 347.
59. *Ibid.* "[T]he place is yet pointed out, in the pine underwood near the first toll house, where black Bill Alexander often crept up and with his unerring rifle shot down the British sentinels." "Sketch of Mecklenburg County," in *The Land We Love*, Vol. 2 (Charlotte: Hill, Erwin & Co., 1866), 137.
60. *Ibid.*, 349–350.
61. *2 CP*, "Rawdon to Balfour," Oct. 21, 1780, 126.
62. *2 CP*, "Cornwallis to Balfour," Oct. 3, 1780, 106.
63. Much of the details of the life of Harris from Louis Pettus, "Peter Harris, Catawba Indian," ancestry.com.
64. See Scoggins, *Relentless Fury*, 41–42.
65. SCARPS, General Richard Winn's Notes, 1780.
66. Pettus, "Peter Harris."
67. SCARPS, "Peter Harris," SC18, 1822.
68. Pettus, "Peter Harris."
69. *Ibid.*
70. On Peter Harris' gravestone Thomas Spratt is referred to as "Senior." Kanawha and his father, also named Thomas Spratt, are sometime confusedly each referred to as "Senior." The reference therefore on Harris' grave must surely be an error (?).

Chapter 3

1. Woodmason, Carolina Backcountry, 55.
2. Hodge, *Constitutional History*, 484.
3. Drymon, *Scotch Irish*, 43.
4. Woodmason, Carolina Backcountry, 55.
5. Great Britain, *Report of the Royal Commission*, 147–148.
6. Howie, *Faithful Contendings Displayed*, 303.
7. *5 CR*, "William Henry Foote, History of the Presbyterians in North Carolina" [Extracts], 1846, 1220.
8. Craighead, *Craighead Family*, 39. For an excellent summary of Craighead's life see Lila McGeachy Ray Master's Thesis entitled, "Alexander Craighead: With Drawn Sword" submitted in 2001.
9. Bolton, *Scotch Irish Pioneers*, 87.
10. Ray, *Craighead*, 25.
11. *Ibid.*, 56.
12. *Ibid.*, 3.
13. Original copies of Craighead's writings are difficult to find. Excerpts from his writings (if not taken from Ray, see note 7) have been taken entirely from an online source for the *Renewal of the Covenants*. http://www.truecovenanter.com/kirkgovt/creaghead_reasons_of_receding_1743.html.
14. *Ibid.* Sedgwick, *Bowels of Tender*, 403.
15. Ray, *Craighead*, 59–60.
16. McClintock, *Cyclopaedia of Biblical*, 525.
17. *Renewal of the Covenants*, Editor's Introduction, online at "true covenanter." http://www.truecovenanter.com/kirkgovt/creaghead_reasons_of_receding_1743.html
18. Hanna, *Scotch-Irish*, 41.
19. *Ibid.*
20. Armstrong, *Presbyterian Enterprise*, 59.
21. Presbyterian Church, *Records of the Presbyterians*, 163.
22. Ward, *Britain and the American South*, 17.
23. Smylie, *History*, 49.
24. Benjamin F. Owen, "Letters of Rev. Richard Locke and Rev. George Craig," in *Pennsylvania Magazine of History & Biography*, Vol. 24 (Philadelphia: Historical Society, 1900), 474.
25. Gallay, *Voices*, 190.
26. *Ibid.*
27. Ray, *Craighead*, 67.
28. "Renewal of the Covenants," Editor's In-

troduction, *True Covenanter*. http://www.truecovenanter.com/covenants/octorara_covenant_renewal.html.
29. Baldwin, *Sowers of Sedition*, 67.
30. Waddell, *Annals of Augusta*, 79.
31. White, *Southern Presbyterian Leaders*, 67.
32. 5 CR, "William Henry Foote, History of the Presbyterians in North Carolina" [Extracts], 1846, 1221.
33. *Ibid*.
34. 6 CR, "Letter from Arthur Dobbs to Daniel Burton," Mar. 29, 1764, 1041.
35. 7 CR, "Letter from James Reed to Daniel Burton," July 20, 1766, 241.
36. 7 CR, "Letter from Andrew Morton to Daniel Burton," Aug. 25, 1766, 252–253.
37. 10 CR, "Petition from Inhabitants of Mecklenburg County Concerning North Carolina Church Laws," 1769, 1015–1017.
38. McGeachy, *History of the Sugaw Creek*, 31.
39. *Ibid*., 36. "The immediate successor of Mr. Craighead was Joseph Alexander, a connexion of the McKnitt branch of Alexanders, a man of education and talents, of small stature, and exceedingly animated in his pulpit exercises." 5 CR, "William Foote, History of the Presbyterians in North Carolina," 1846, 1224.
40. Hanna, *Scotch-Irish*, 40.
41. Morrill, *History of Charlotte*, 9.

Chapter 4

1. Norton, Spirit of Charlotte, 15.
2. *23 CR*, 772–773.
3. *Ibid*.
4. *13 CR*, "Letter from Thomas Polk to George Washington," June 26, 1778, 451.
5. See E. Thomson Shields, Jr., "'A Modern Poem,' by the Mecklenburg Censor: Politics and Satire in Revolutionary North Carolina," Early American Literature, Vol. 29, No. 3 (1994).
6. *Ibid*.
7. Johnson, *Traditions*, 82.
8. For an excellent summary of the Sugar Creek episode see Jim Williams, *The Sugar Creek War*, a private paper prepared in connection with the Mecklenburg Historical Association. Copy may be obtained by contacting the MHA.
9. Kars, *Breaking Loose Together*, 43.
10. Except where otherwise noted, the Sugar Creek War account is from McCulloh's testimony in *7 CR*, William Tryon, "Minutes of the North Carolina Governor's Council," May 7, 1765–May 9, 1765, 10–31.
11. 7 CR, "Minutes of North Carolina," 37–39.
12. *7 CR*, "Letter from Henry Eustace McCulloh," May 9, 1765, 32–34.
13. *Ibid*.
14. *Ibid*.
15. Kars, *Breaking Loose Together*, 46–47.
16. 7 CR, "Minutes of North Carolina Council," 37–39.
17. As I have written elsewhere: "In copying a new draft, Dr. Alexander (or perhaps the editors of the *Raleigh Register*) had made some minor and essentially immaterial changes: the old English "thro" had been changed to "through"; "awfull" to "awful"; "desolve" to "dissolve"; "S^d." to "said"; and so forth. In addition, the word "*Resolved*" was added before each of the five resolutions; in the first clause, the phrase "Great Britain is an enemy to this County" became "to this *Country*"; in the second clause, the word "innocent" was not included before the clause "blood of American patriots"; the words "civil and religious" were dropped from clause three which read in the original, "independence *civil and religious*"; and one concluding sentence dealing with procedural matters ("a selection from the members present shall constitute a Committee of public safety for sd. County") was not included at all. Other than this handful of changes, however, none of which substantively affected the text, narrative or structure, the text in the *Raleigh Register* was indeed a "true copy." See McNitt, *Chain of Error*, 39–40.
18. SHC.
19. Salley, "Present Status of the Question," 38.
20. *15 CR*, "Johnson, Joseph, Biographical sketch of Thomas Polk [From Johnson's Traditions of the Revolution]," 1776, 82–83, 178–179.
21. Per local historian Jim Williams, "Like so many things in our history, the fame of 'The Liberty Bell' rests solely on an abolitionist poem from 1837 and a popular short story (complete fiction) from 1847. The source for Thomas Polk and the Liberty Bell is *Polk Family and Kinsmen*, by William Harrison Polk, 1912—a fairly good secondary source." Whether Tom Polk saved the Liberty Bell is true or not is not clear, but if the story isn't true it should be.
22. *13 CR*, "Letter from Thomas Polk to George Washington," June 26, 1778, 451.
23. *14 CR*, "Letter from Thomas Polk to Thomas Pinckney," Aug. 6, 1780, 535–536.
24. *Ibid*.
25. *14 CR*, "Letter from Thomas Polk to Horatio Gates," Sep. 10, 1780, 606.
26. *14 CR*, "Letter from Thomas Polk to Horatio Gates," Sep. 11, 1780, 608–609.
27. *14 CR*, "Letter from Thomas Polk to Horatio Gates," Oct. 10, 1780, 684–685.

28. *15 CR*, "Letter from Thomas Polk to the North Carolina Board of War," Oct. 11, 1780, 414.
29. *14 CR*, "Letter from William Smallwood to the North Carolina Board of War," Oct. 31, 1730, 737.
30. *14 CR*, "Letter from William Smallwood to Horatio Gates [Extract]," Oct. 31, 1780, 737.
31. *14 CR*, "Memorandum from Horatio Gates et al. Concerning the Actions of Thomas Polk," Nov. 12, 1780, 736.
32. *15 CR*, "Letter from Horatio Gates to the North Carolina Board of War," Nov. 17, 1780, 416.
33. *15 CR*, "Johnson, Joseph, Biographical sketch of Thomas Polk [From Johnson's Traditions of the Revolution," 1776, 82–83, 178–179.
34. *2 CP*, "Balfour to Cornwallis," Oct. 1, 1780, 115.
35. *1 CP*, "Balfour to Cornwallis," July 12, 1780; 248–250; see also *2 CP*, 115, footnote 115.
36. *2 CP*, 115, note 115.

Chapter 5

1. 9 CR, "Letter from William Legge, Earl of Dartmouth to Josiah Martin," May 3, 1775, 1240–1242.
2. Alexander, *Rough Notes*, SHC.
3. *Governor's Report*, 19.
4. Alexander, *Rough Notes*, SHC.
5. *Governor's Report*, 19.
6. *Ibid.*, 26.
7. *Ibid.*, 19–20.
8. George Will, "America's Self-Validating Tradition," *Charlotte Observer*, July 3, 2008.
9. In Blethen and Wood, *From Ulster to Carolina*, 30.
10. Woodmason, *Carolina Backcountry*, 60.
11. Powell, *Dictionary*, 262.
12. Hunter, *Sketches*, 61–62.
13. Powell, *Dictionary*, 262.
14. McNitt, *Chain of Error*, 23.
15. Washington, *Diary*, 197.
16. Alexander, *Rough Notes*, SHC.
17. *Ibid.*
18. *Governor's Report*, 16.
19. *Ibid.*, 24.
20. *Ibid.*, 16.
21. N.C. Historical Commission, *Records of the Moravians*, 874–875.
22. *Governor's Report*, 16.
23. Hunter, *Sketches*, 67.
24. *10 CR*, "Letter from Josiah Martin to William Legge, Earl of Dartmouth," June 30, 1775, 48.
25. *Governor's Report*, 17.
26. N.C. Historical Commission, *Records of the Moravians*, 876 [emphasis in the original].
27. *Ibid.*, 876, fn. 13.
28. *Governor's Report*, 16.
29. *Ibid.*
30. Alexander, *Rough Notes*, SHC.
31. Hunter, *Sketches*, 68–69.
32. Alexander, *Rough Notes*, SHC [emphasis in the original].
33. *Ibid.*
34. Adams letter to William Bentley, dated July 15, 1819, in Adams, *Works*, 381.
35. *Adams-Jefferson letters*, 543–544.

Chapter 6

1. Danforth, *Boyhood*, 157.
2. Nell, *Colored Patriots*, 215.
3. Danforth, *Boyhood*, 157.
4. For section and quotes on White Oaks see Burns, *Williamstown*, 406–408.
5. SCARPS, Will Graves, "Pension Acts: An Overview of Revolutionary War Pension and Bounty Land Legislation and the Southern Campaigns Pension Transcription Project."
6. Nell, *Colored Patriots*, 214–215.
7. SCARPS, *Pension application of Ishmael Titus R10n623*, Transcribed by Will Graves. Any quotes from Titus unless otherwise attributed are from this source.
8. Crow, *Black Experience*, 6.
9. *Mecklenburg County Court Minutes*, 68.
10. *Ibid.*, 70, 77.
11. See Jeffrey J. Crow, "African Americans and the Revolution," Originally published as "'Liberty to Slaves': The Black Response" at NCPedia (here, "Crow"). See also generally, Crow, *Black* Experience. http://ncpedia.org/history/usrevolution/african-americans.
12. In Crow, note 12.
13. Crow, *Black Experience*, 69.
14. *10 CR*, "Letter from Joseph Hewes to Samuel Johnston," July 8, 1775, 86.
15. Crow, *Black Experience*, 56.
16. *Ibid.*, 69.
17. *Ibid.*, 12.
18. *Ibid.*, 13.
19. Nell, *Colored Patriots*, 214–215. Also Glasco, *WPA History*, 36.
20. For history of the Troublesome Iron Works see the N.C. State Historical Marker website which has a good summary.
21. Graham, *Papers*, 241.
22. SCARPS, *Pension application of William Armstrong S30831 f32NC*.
23. Lee, *Memoirs*, 194.
24. *Ibid.*
25. Dunkerly, *Battle*, 20.
26. See http://www.overmountainvictory.org/blacks.htm.
27. Nell, *Colored Patriots*, 214–215.

28. Crow, *Black Experience*, 69.
29. Nell, *Colored Patriots*, 215.

Chapter 7

1. See Graham, *Papers*, 14, for a copy of James Graham's will.
2. *Ibid.*, 36.
3. *Ibid.*, 37.
4. *Ibid.*, 19.
5. *Ibid.*, 19–20.
6. *Ibid.*, 46.
7. *Ibid.*, 46–47.
8. *Ibid.*, 47.
9. *Ibid.*, 48.
10. Stedman, *The History of the Origin, Progress, and Termination of the American War*, Vol. II, 213.
11. Lee, *Memoirs*, 194.
12. *Ibid.*
13. *2 CP*, "Cornwallis to Clinton," Sep. 22–23, 1780, 46.
14. *2 CP*, "Cornwallis to Wemyss," Oct. 7, 1780, 222.
15. *Ibid.*
16. Stedman, *The History of the Origin, Progress, and Termination of the American War*, Vol. II, 215.
17. Graham, *Papers*, 241.
18. *9 CR*, "Memorandum from the Board of Trade of Great Britain to George III, King of Great Britain Concerning Acts of the North Carolina General Assembly," February 26, 1772, 250.
19. Graham, *Papers*, 241.
20. *Ibid.*, 244.
21. *Ibid.*, 245.
22. *Ibid.*
23. *2 CP*, "Rawdon to Cornwallis," June 11, 1780, 129.
24. Sherman, *Calendar*, 258.
25. Graham, *Papers*, 250.
26. *Ibid.*
27. Davie, *Sketches*, 24.
28. Graham, *Papers*, 250.
29. *Ibid.*, 251.
30. *10 CR*, "Letter from Governor Martin to the Earl of Dartmouth," June 30, 1775, 47–48.
31. Davie, *Sketches*, 24.
32. *Ibid.*
33. Graham, *Papers*, 252.
34. Hanger, *Address*, 55.
35. Davie, *Sketches*, 24.
36. Graham, *Papers*, 252.
37. Davie, *Sketches*, 24–25.
38. Graham, *Papers*, 252.
39. *Ibid.*
40. Davie, *Sketches*, 24.
41. Stedman, *The History of the Origin, Progress, and Termination of the American War*, Vol. II, 216.
42. Hanger, *Address*, 56–57.
43. Sherman, 262.
44. Graham, *Papers*, 252.
45. Davie, *Sketches*, 25.
46. Lee, *Memoirs*, 197.
47. Graham, *Papers*, 253.
48. *Ibid.*
49. *Ibid.*
50. *Ibid.*, 253–254.
51. *Ibid.*, 255.
52. *Ibid.*, 64.
53. *Ibid.*
54. *2 CP*, "Cornwallis to Balfour," Sep. 27, 1780, 99.
55. Lee, *Memoirs*, 197.
56. Graham, *Papers*, 256.
57. Hanger, *Address*, 70.
58. *2 CP*, "Cornwallis to Balfour," Sep. 27, 1780, 99. Cornwallis had cautioned Hanger not to rashly send his cavalry into the settlement before understanding the forces opposing him. "Earl Cornwallis ordered me to be very cautious how I advanced," wrote Hanger, "as he expected a very large body of militia to be either in the neighborhood, or town of Charlotte." Hanger, *Address*, 55. After the war, Hanger admitted he had made a tactical mistake making the cavalry charge in Charlotte. "I acknowledge that I was guilty of an error in judgment, in entering the town [of Charlotte] at all with the cavalry, before I had previously searched it well with infantry," he wrote, and especially "after the precaution Earl Cornwallis had given me." *Ibid.* However, Hanger argued, "when I risked so few lives in drawing the fire from the enemy, I trust *that*, in some measure, [that may] palliate the fault." *Ibid.*
59. Graham, *Papers*, 256–257.
60. *Ibid.*, 256.
61. Hanger, *Address*, 58.
62. Stedman, *The History of the Origin, Progress, and Termination of the American War*, Vol. II, 216.
63. *Pennsylvania Packet*, Jan. 9, 1781, 3.
64. Hanger, *Address*, 64.
65. Tarleton, *History*, 86.
66. Lee, *Memoirs*, 195.
67. Tarleton, *History*, 160.
68. Steadman, *The History of the Origin, Progress, and Termination of the American War*, Vol. II, 216.
69. Hanger, *Address*, 68.
70. SCARPS, *Moses Hall*, W10105.
71. Tarleton, *History*, 160–161.
72. *Ibid.*, 160.
73. *Ibid.*
74. Graham, *Papers*, 49.
75. *Ibid.*, 50.

76. *Ibid.*, 54.
77. *Ibid.*, 138–139.
78. *Ibid.*, 162.
79. *Ibid.*, 161–162.

Chapter 8

1. Dan Morrill, A History of Charlotte and Mecklenburg County, online edition, Chapter 3.
2. Hope Murphy, Charlotte-Mecklenburg Historic Landmarks Commission, "Historical Overview, Survey and Research Report On the St. Lloyd Presbyterian Church Cemetery," April 8, 2004, online ("Murphy").
3. Dan Morrill, *A History of Charlotte and Mecklenburg County,* online edition, Chapter 3.
4. Alexander, *History,* 5–6.
5. *Ibid.,* 208.
6. *Ibid.,* 125–126.
7. *Ibid.,* 123. Quotes and story of Blind Dick that follows all from Alexander, *History,* 123–126.
8. For information on St. Lloyd Presbyterian Church Cemetery see Murphy. Anna's gravestone was found during the author's research in the area, it was not mentioned (and perhaps not known) in Murphy's report.

Chapter 9

1. Hardy, Civil War, 11.
2. *Ibid.,* 63–64.
3. *Ibid.,* 67.
4. *Ibid.*
5. *Ibid.,* 7.
6. *Ibid.*
7. *Ibid.,* 85.
8. *Charlotte Observer,* July 13, 1876.
9. Gaston, *New South,* 41.
10. Greenwood, *Bittersweet,* 37.
11. *Ibid.,* 70.
12. *Charlotte Democrat,* June 8, 1877.
13. Greenwood, *Bittersweet,* 38.
14. *Ibid.,* "Civil Rights in the Theater," *Charlotte Daily Observer,* May 15, 1875, 69–70.
15. Eugene Stitt, "Mr. Thad Lincoln Tate," *An Appreciation of Twenty-One Men Who Have Rendered Long and Faithful Service in One Job,* 8, at CML.
16. Y. D. Kemp, Jr., "Thad Tate Has Lively Recollections of Gay Blades of Charlotte in 90's," *Charlotte Observer,* Nov. 7, 1934, 59 ("Kemp").
17. *Charlotte Journal,* Nov. 24, 1843.
18. *Charlotte Journal,* Dec. 12, 1837.
19. *Charlotte Democrat,* Jan. 7, 1873.
20. *Southern Home,* Jan. 6, 1873.
21. *Charlotte News,* Jan. 18, 1900.
22. "Thad L. Tate," *Mecklenburg Times,* July 8, 1897.
23. *Charlotte Observer,* Mar. 5, 1895.
24. "A Well Kept Tonsorial Parlor," *Charlotte Observer,* Mar. 20, 1896.
25. *Charlotte Observer,* Sep. 18, 1904.
26. Kemp, "Recollections."
27. *Ibid.*
28. *Ibid.*
29. "Twenty-Five Cents for a Dog's Supper," *Charlotte Observer,* Oct. 21, 1903.
30. "Thad Tate Invests in Real Estate," *Charlotte Observer,* Nov. 13, 1906.
31. *Ibid.*
32. See summary on Mecklenburg County website, http://charmeck.org/mecklenburg/county/ParkandRec/TrailOfHistory/Pages/ThadTate.aspx.
33. See "Negro Tenants Will Have Home," *Charlotte News,* April 30, 1922. For quote: http://landmarkscommission.org/Properties%20Foundation%20Reports/meckinv.html
34. "Afro-American Mutual Insurance Company Elects Directors to fill Vacancies," *Charlotte Observer,* July 26, 1908.
35. *Charlotte Observer,* Dec. 28, 1899.
36. Greenwood, *Bittersweet,* 76.
37. "Colored Charlotte," pamphlet printed in 1915 by AME Zion Church, Charlotte, NC, in the CML.
38. "Williams Jubilee Singers at Auditorium To-morrow Night," *Charlotte News,* Feb. 25, 1915.
39. "Williams Jubilee Singers at College Auditorium To-night," *Charlotte News,* Mar. 6, 1916.
40. "Williams Jubilee Singers at Auditorium To-morrow Night," *Charlotte News,* Feb. 25, 1915.
41. "Formally Open Club for Negro Soldiers Tonight," *Charlotte Observer,* Aug. 14, 1918.
42. "Night School for Colored People to Be Opened Here," *Charlotte News,* Oct. 15, 1913.
43. Charlotte Historic Landmark Commission, "Washington Heights," http://cmhpf.org/educationneighhistwash.htm.
44. *Ibid.*
45. "Negroes of Charlotte," *Charlotte Observer,* Oct. 14, 1919.
46. "Thad Tate Sells His Barber Shop," *Charlotte News,* June 14, 1909.
47. *Charlotte News,* Mar. 9, 1907.
48. *Charlotte Observer,* July 5, 1892.
49. Kemp, "Recollections."
50. *Ibid.*
51. Stitt, "Mr. Thad Lincoln Tate," 9.
52. "Thad L. Tate, Prominent Charlotte

Negro, Dies," *Charlotte Observer*, Mar. 30, 1951, 22A.
53. "Thad Tate, Prominent Negro Citizen, Dies," *Charlotte News*, Mar. 30, 1951, 9A.
54. *Charlotte Observer*, Nov. 7, 1934.

Chapter 10

1. "Letter from Theodore Roosevelt to Margaret Busbee Shipp. February 13, 1904," Theodore Roosevelt Paper, Library of Congress Manuscript Division, http://www.theodorerooseveltcenter.org/en/Research/Digital-Library/Record.aspx?libID=o187398. Theodore Roosevelt Digital Library. Dickinson State University.
2. Address of Armistead Burwell, Esq., May 10, 1898, Confederate Memorial Services Elmwood Cemetery, UNC Library. Per SHC: "Armistead Burwell (1839–1913) was a lawyer of Charlotte, N.C., State Senator, and North Carolina Supreme Court Judge."
3. Mecklenburg Monument Association, *Unveiling*, 3.
4. *Ibid.*, 5.
5. *Ibid.*, 4–5.
6. *Ibid.*, 7.
7. "Lieutenant William Ewen Shipp," *North Carolina Journal of Education* III, no. 9–10 (1900): 25 (hereafter, "NCJE").
8. Armistead Burwell, "The Boyhood of William Ewen Shipp," *NCJE*, 26.
9. *Ibid.*
10. "Shipp," *NCJE*, 25.
11. For the life of Judge Shipp see *Forest City Courier*, Nov. 20, 1930, 6.
12. Armistead Burwell, "The Boyhood of William Ewen Shipp," *NCJE*, 26.
13. *Ibid.*
14. Cozzens, *Earth*, 61.
15. *Ibid.*, 60.
16. *Ibid.*
17. *Ibid.*, 61.
18. *Ibid.*, 400–402.
19. Powell, *Dictionary of NC Biography*, Vol. V, 336.
20. Steward, *Buffalo Soldiers*, 254.
21. *Ibid.*, 110.
22. *Ibid.*, 254–55.
23. *Ibid.*, 255.
24. *Ibid.*
25. Lt. Hayes' account of the campaign and Shipp's death which follows, including quotes from Roosevelt, are from "Charlotte Celebrates: Unveiling of Stately Shaft to Late William Ewen Shipp the Feature of an Eventful Day," *Charlotte News*, May 20, 1902, 2–3 unless otherwise noted. Hayes' letter and account on page 2.
26. Steward, *Buffalo Soldiers*, 262.

27. Gardner, *Roosevelt*, 153.
28. Steward, *Buffalo Soldiers*, 192.
29. *Ibid.*, 261.
30. Gardner, *Roosevelt*, 192.
31. *Ibid.*
32. *NCJE*, 25.
33. "Charlotte Celebrates: Unveiling of Stately Shaft to Late William Ewen Shipp the Feature of an Eventful Day," *Charlotte News*, May 20, 1902, 2–3.
34. *NCJE*, 25.
35. "Letter from Theodore Roosevelt to Silas McBee." *May 29, 1902 Theodore Roosevelt Papers, Library of Congress Manuscript Division*, http://www.theodorerooseveltcenter.org/Research/Digital-Library/Record.aspx?libID=o182365. Theodore Roosevelt Digital Library.
36. Gardner, *Roosevelt*, 166.
37. "A Memorial to Shipp," *The News and Observer*, Aug. 24, 1898, 4. A Roosevelt-era tour guide of North Carolina (published by the Works Progress Administration), noted that the significance of the Shipp monument was that it "memorializes the military reinstatement of the Southern States after the war between the States."
38. "Charlotte Celebrates: Unveiling of Stately Shaft to Late William Ewen Shipp the Feature of an Eventful Day," *Charlotte News*, May 20, 1902, 1.
39. "Ship Monument Unveiled," *The People's Paper*, May 21, 1902, 2 (at CR).
40. *Ibid.*
41. *Ibid.*
42. *Ibid.*
43. "The Unveiling Ceremonies," *Charlotte Daily Observer*, May 18, 1902, 5.
44. "Charlotte Celebrates: Unveiling of Stately Shaft to Late William Ewen Shipp the Feature of an Eventful Day," *Charlotte News*, May 20, 1902, 1.
45. *Ibid.*
46. "Up Goes the Flag of the Republic of Cuba," *The North Carolinian*, May 22, 1902, 1.
47. "New Republic Born To-Day," *Charlotte News*, May 20, 1902, 1.
48. "Up Goes the Flag of the Republic of Cuba," *The North Carolinian*, May 22, 1902, 1.
49. *Ibid.*
50. "President Roosevelt Speaks," *The North Carolinian*, May 22, 1902, 1.
51. "Letter from Theodore Roosevelt to Margaret Busbee Shipp." *May 31, 1902. Theodore Roosevelt Papers, Library of Congress Manuscript Division*, http://www.theodorerooseveltcenter.org/Research/Digital-Library/Record.aspx?libID=o182400. Theodore Roosevelt Digital Library. Dickinson State University.
52. "Clear Up Story To Lt. Shipp to Monument," *Charlotte News*, October 26, 1933, 9. An

urban legend began that local school children, inspired by Shipp's life and sacrifice, had started a fund-raising campaign to fund the memorial. According to this account, Shipp's former school—the Old South Graded School (later known as the D.H. Military Academy)—"raised the money for the monument with contributions of pennies, nickels and dimes." *Ibid.* The school children at Shipp's alma mater had "become particularly interested in the life and career of Lieutenant Shipp, not only because he was educated in the school building that they were then using, but because he was a Charlotte man, to them, a glamorous hero." *Ibid.* The source of this story, first cited in 1933, is not clear.

Chapter 11

1. "Annie Alexander," in North Carolina online History Project, at http://northcarolinahistory.org/encyclopedia/annie-lowrie-alexander-1864-1929/. Special thanks goes to Shelia Bumgarner of the Carolina Room, Main Branch of the Charlotte Public Library for her comments and suggestions on Dr. Annie.
2. "An Appreciation of 'Dr. Annie,'" in the CML.
3. Text and quotes from undated manuscript by Annie Alexander entitled "Doctor Katherine" are taken from James Alsop's article "Narratives of Class, Gender and Medicine in the American South: The Dr. Annie Alexander Story" which was published in the online journal *Gender Forum. An Internet Journal for Gender Studies,* Literature and Medicine I: Women in the Medical Profession, Issue 25 (2009) (hereafter, "Alsop"). "Doctor Katherine" begins at note 10. Alsop is the leading authority on Dr. Annie, and has two excellent articles, the first in the internet journal noted above, and the longer account in his chapter "Annie Lowrie Alexander: A Woman Doing Great Work in a Womanly Way," in *North Carolina Women: Their Lives and Times, Volume I.* This chapter is heavily indebted to his research, and many of the quotes and references cited or otherwise are taken from these sources.
4. Alsop, note 10.
5. *Ibid.,* note 11.
6. *Ibid.,* note 3.
7. *Ibid.,* note 3, quoting Kratt, *Women,* 12.
8. *Charlotte Observer,* Mar. 16, 1884.
9. *Charlotte News,* May 15, 1905.
10. "A Female Physician," *Charlotte Observer,* Jan. 22, 1889.
11. Alsop., note 4.
12. *Ibid.,* note 13.
13. Alexander is widely regarded as the first female doctor to practice in North Carolina, she was not the first medical graduate; that was Susan Dimrock. Alsop points out that, "In the standard biography (by Dudley) it is, for example, demonstrably not true that Alexander upon her return to North Carolina in 1887 'became the first woman to practice medicine in the South.' She had been preceded by numerous non-graduate and/or unlicensed practitioners, as well as by several graduate, licensed women physicians who had not been born in the South." (The Dudley he references is Harold J. Dudley who wrote Dr. Annie's entry in Powell's *Dictionary of North Carolina Biography.*)
14. W. R. Stowe, "Dr. Annie Lowrie Alexander," *Transactions of the Medical Society of the State of North Carolina* (Raleigh: Medical Society, 1931), 164.
15. "A Female Physician," *Charlotte Observer,* Jan. 22, 1889.
16. CR, "Charlotte Home Democrat," May 27, 1887.
17. Alsop, introductory paragraph.
18. *Ibid.,* 1.
19. CR, "An Appreciation," 2.
20. *Ibid.,* 3.
21. "Motor of Dr. Annie Alexander Crushed," *Charlotte Observer,* May 24, 1914.
22. *Charlotte Observer,* Oct. 26, 1915.
23. CR, "An Appreciation," 2.
24. Alsop, note 12.
25. *Ibid.,* note 16.
26. *Ibid.,* note 11.
27. *Ibid.,* note 8.
28. *Ibid.,* note 6.
29. *Ibid.,* note 17 [emphasis added].

Chapter 12

1. Earl Gulledge brought the story of Doug Crotts to my attention and prepared an excellent summary of his life and actions, in connection for bringing recognition to Crotts in the Charlotte-Mecklenburg School System. His quotes are taken from this presentation, and private correspondence with Mr. Gulledge.
2. Tom Brokaw, "Pearl Harbor is the birthplace of 'Greatest Generation,'" *USA Today,* December 7, 2016, digital edition. This chapter is indebted to the excellent account of the tanks engaged at Tarawa by Oscar Gilbert and Romain Cansiere, called *Tanks in Hell: A Marine Corps Tank Company on Tarawa.* The moment-by-moment account of the Third Platoon tanks at Tarawa, and Crotts role on the night of D-Day and D+1 are taken from this account. The general story of the battle is told, vividly, in *Goodbye, Darkness,* by William Manchester, as

Notes. Chapter 12

well as Sherrod's eye-witness account and Russ' history of the battle.

3. Manchester, *Goodbye*, 393–395.
4. Interview with Doug Crotts, provided by Ed Gilbert to the author.
5. See the excellent website maintained by Romain Cansiere and Philip Wright called "Tanks on Tarawa" (http://www.tanksontarawa.com/) for extensive information on C Company and its role at Tarawa. Romain provided helpful insight and guidance on Crotts and the battle.
6. Gilbert & Cansiere, *Tanks*, 24–25.
7. Manchester, *Goodbye*, 215.
8. Russ, *Tarawa*, 5.
9. Manchester, *Goodbye*, 218.
10. Russ, *Tarawa*, 6.
11. *Ibid.*
12. Sherrod, *Tarawa*, 54–55.
13. *Ibid.*, 60.
14. Manchester, *Goodbye*, 224.
15. Gilbert & Cansiere, *Tanks*, 111.
16. *Ibid.*, 120.
17. Manchester, *Goodbye*, 228.
18. Gilbert & Cansiere, *Tanks*, 120.
19. Manchester, *Goodbye*, 225.
20. Gilbert & Cansiere, *Tanks*, 120.
21. *Ibid.*, 120.
22. Gilbert & Cansiere, *Tanks*, 74.
23. *Ibid.*, 124.
24. *Ibid.*, 128–129.
25. *Ibid.*, 151.
26. *Ibid.*
27. Manchester, *Goodbye*, 231.
28. *Ibid.*
29. Gilbert & Cansiere, *Tanks*, 154.
30. Sherrod, *Tarawa*, 88–89.
31. *Ibid.*, 226.
32. *Ibid.*, 169.
33. *Ibid.*, 170.
34. *Ibid.*
35. *Ibid.*, 166.
36. *Ibid.*, 168.
37. *Ibid.*
38. Smith, *Coral*, 132, 134.
39. The foregoing regarding Crotts on Saipan from Gilbert, *Marine Tank Battles*, 154–155.
40. From summary of the life of Hubert Crotts compiled by Earl Gulledge.
41. Gilbert & Cansiere, *Tanks*, 154.

Bibliography

Adams, John. *The Works of John Adams*, Vol. 10. Boston: Little, Brown, 1856.
Alexander, J.B. *The History of Mecklenburg County from 1740 to 1900*. Charlotte: Observer Printing House, 1902.
Alexander, Julia McGehee. *Charlotte in Picture and Prose*. New York: Blanchard Press, 1906.
Alsop, James Douglas. "Annie Lowrie Alexander: A Woman Doing Great Work in a Womanly Way." *North Carolina Women: Their Lives and Times*, Vol. I, edited by Michelle Gillespie and Sally McMillen. Athens: University of Georgia Press, 2014.
Alsop, James Douglas. "Narratives of Class, Gender and Medicine in the American South: The Dr. Annie Alexander Story." *Gender Forum: An Internet Journal for Gender Studies* 25 (2009). http://www.genderforum.org/issues/literature-and-medicine-i/narratives-of-class-gender-and-medicine-in-the-american-south/.
Armstrong, Maurice Whitman. *The Presbyterian Enterprise: Sources of American Presbyterian History*. Eugene, OR: Wipf & Stock, 2001.
Baldwin, Alice M. "Sowers of Sedition: The Political Theories of Some of the New Light Presbyterian Clergy of Virginia and North Carolina." *The William and Mary Quarterly* 5, no. 1 (1948): 52–76.
Blethen, H. Tyler, and Curtis W. Wood, Jr. *From Ulster to Carolina: The Migration of the Scotch-Irish to Southwestern North Carolina*. Raleigh: North Carolina Division of Archives and History, 2005.
Blumer, Thomas J. *Catawba Nation*. Charleston, SC: The History Press, 2007.
Bolton, Charles Knowles. *Scotch Irish Pioneers in Ulster and America*. Boston: Bacon & Brown, 1910.
Burns, Deborah, ed. *Williamstown: The First 250 Years, 1753–2003*. Williamstown: Williamstown House of Local History, 2005.
Burwell, Armistead. Address of Armistead Burwell, Esq., May 10, 1898. Confederate Memorial Services Elmwood Cemetery, UNC Library.
Cappon, Lester J., ed. *The Adam-Jefferson Letters: The Complete Correspondence Between Thomas Jefferson and Abigail and John Adams*. Chapel Hill: University of North Carolina Press, 1988.
"A Carolina Woman of the Revolution: Susannah Smart." *Godey's Lady's Book and Magazine*, September 1856, 213–217.
Churchill, Winston. *Great Contemporaries*. London: Macmillan, 1943.
Cozzens, Peter. *The Earth Is Weeping*. New York: Alfred A. Knopf, 2016.
Craighead, James Geddes. *The Craighead Family: A Genealogical Memoir of the Descendants of Rev. Thomas and Margaret Craighead, 1658–1876*. Philadelphia: Sherman & Company, Printers, 1876.
Creaghead, Alexander. *Reasons of Receding from Present Judicatures & Constitution*. Philadelphia: B. Franklin, 1743.

Creaghead, Alexander. *Renewal of the Covenants*. Beaver Falls, PA: Globe Printing, 1748.
Danforth, Keyes. *Boyhood Reminiscences: Pictures of New England Life in the Olden Times in Williamstown*. New York: Gazlay Brothers, 1895.
Drymon, M. M. *Scotch Irish Foodways in America*. South Portland, ME: Wythe Avenue Press, 2009.
Dudley, Harold J. "Alexander, Annie Lowrie." *Dictionary of North Carolina Biography*, edited by William S. Powell. Chapel Hill: University of North Carolina, 1979.
Federal Writers' Project. *WPA Guide to North Carolina*. San Antonio: Trinity University Press, 1939.
Foote, William Henry. *Sketches of North Carolina*. New York: Robert Carter, 1846.
Frey, Sylvia. *Water from the Rock: Black Resistance in a Revolutionary Age*. Princeton: Princeton University Press, 1999.
Gallay, Alan, ed. *Voices of the Old South: Eyewitness Accounts, 1528–1861*. Athens: University of Georgia Press, 1994.
Gardner, Mark Lee Gardner. *Rough Riders: Theodore Roosevelt, His Cowboy Regiment, and the Immortal Charge of San Juan Hill*. New York: William Morrow, 2016.
Gilbert, Oscar. *Marine Tank Battles in the Pacific*. New York: Da Capo Press, 2001.
Gilbert, Oscar, and Romain Cansiere. *Tanks in Hell: A Marine Corps Tank Company on Tarawa*. Philadelphia: Casemate, 2015.
Glasco, Laurence A., ed. *The WPA History of the Negro in Pittsburgh*. Pittsburgh: University of Pittsburg Press, 2004.
Graham, William Alexander. *General Joseph Graham and His Papers on North Carolina Revolutionary History: with Appendix: an Epitome of North Carolina's Military Services in the Revolutionary War and of the Laws Enacted for Raising Troops*. Raleigh: Edwards & Broughton, 1904.
Greenwood, Janette. *Bittersweet Legacy: The Black and White "Better Classes" in Charlotte, 1850–1910*. Chapel Hill: University of North Carolina Press, 1994.
Hanna, Charles Augustus. *The Scotch-Irish: Or, the Scot in North Britain, North Ireland, and North America*. New York: G.P. Putnam's Sons, 1902.
Hardy, Michael. *Civil War Charlotte*. Charleston, SC: The History Press, 2012.
Henderson, Archibald. *Washington's Southern Tour 1791*. Boston: Houghton Mifflin, 1923.
Hodge, Charles. *The Constitutional History of the Presbyterian Church in the United States of America*. Philadelphia: W.S. Martien, 1839.
Howie, John. *Faithful Contendings Displayed*. Glasgow: John Bryce, 1780.
Hunter, C.L. *Sketches of Western North Carolina*. Raleigh: Raleigh News Stream, 1877.
Isenbarger, Dennis, ed. *Native Americans in Early North Carolina: A Documentary History*. Raleigh: Office of Archives and History, North Carolina Department of Cultural Resources, 2013.
Johnson, Joseph. *Traditions and Reminiscences, Chiefly of the American Revolution in the South*. Charleston, SC: Walker & James, 1851.
Kars, Marjoleine. *Breaking Loose Together: The Regulator Rebellion in Pre-Revolutionary North Carolina*. Chapel Hill: University of North Carolina Press, 2002.
Kratt, Mary. *Charlotte: Spirit of the New South*. Winston-Salem: John F. Blair, 1992.
Kratt, Mary. *New South Women: Twentieth-Century Women of Charlotte, North Carolina*. Charlotte: Public Library of Charlotte and Mecklenburg County, 2001.
The Land We Love, Vol. 2, November–April 1866–1867. Charlotte: Hill, Erwin & Co., 1866.
Landrum, John. *Colonial and Revolutionary History of Upper South Carolina*. Greenville, SC: Shannon & Co., 1897.
Lawson, John, and Hugh Talmage Lefler, ed. *A New Voyage to Carolina*. Chapel Hill: University of North Carolina Press, 1967.
Lee, E. Lawrence. *Indian Wars in North Carolina: 1663–1763*. Raleigh: Office of Archives and History, North Carolina Department of Cultural Resources, 2011.
Manchester, William. *Goodbye, Darkness*. New York: Back Bay Books, 2002.
Martin, Russ. *Line of Departure: Tarawa*. New York: Doubleday, 1975.

McClintock, John, and James Strong. *Cyclopaedia of Biblical, Theological, and Ecclesiastical Literature.* New York: Harper, 1894.
McCulloh, Henry Eustace. *Letter from Henry Eustace McCulloh to Edmund Fanning*, Vol. 7, 1765. Colonial and State Records of North Carolina.
McGeachy, Neill Roderick. *A History of the Sugaw Creek Presbyterian Church.* Rock Hill, SC: Record Print Company, 1954.
McNitt, V.V. *Chain of Error and the Mecklenburg Declaration of Independence.* Palmer, MA: Hampden Hills Press, 1960.
Mecklenburg County, North Carolina Court Minutes Docket Book 1, 1774–1780. Greenville, SC: Southern Historical Press, 1996.
Mecklenburg Monument Association. *Unveiling of the Monument to the Signers of the Mecklenburg Declaration of Independence at Charlotte, N.C., May 20, 1898.* Charlotte: Observer Printing and Publishing House, 1898.
Merrell, James H. *The Indians' New World: Catawbas and Their Neighbors from European Contact Through the Era of Removal.* New York: W.W. Norton, 1989.
Meyer, Duane. *The Highland Scots of North Carolina 1732–1776.* Chapel Hill: University of North Carolina Press, 1987.
Milks, Diane, Yon Lambert, and Louise Pettus. *The Catawba River Companion.* Spartanburg, SC: Palmetto Conservation Foundation/PCF Press, 2003.
Miller, S. Millington, M.D. "The True Cradle of American Liberty; Independence Bell Rang a Year Earlier in Charlotte than in Philadelphia." *Collier's The National Weekly*, July 1, 1905.
Morrill, Dan L. *Historic Charlotte, An Illustrated History of Charlotte & Mecklenburg County.* San Antonio: Historical Publishing Network, 2009.
Murphy, Hope, and Charlotte-Mecklenburg Historic Landmarks Commission. "Historical Overview, Survey and Research Report on the St. Lloyd Presbyterian Church Cemetery." April 8, 2004.
Nell, William Cooper. *The Colored Patriots of the American Revolution, With Sketches of Several Distinguished Colored Persons: To Which Is Added a Brief Survey of the Condition And Prospects of Colored Americans.* Boston: Robert Wallcutt, 1855.
Patterson, Daniel. *The True Image: Gravestone Art and the Culture of Scotch Irish Settlers in the Pennsylvania and Carolina Backcountry.* Chapel Hill: University of North Carolina Press, 2012.
Polk, William Mecklenburg. *Leonidas Polk, Bishop and General.* 1778.
Powell, William S, ed. *Dictionary of North Carolina Biography.* Chapel Hill: University of North Carolina Press Chapel Hill, 1996.
Powell, William S. *North Carolina, A History.* Chapel Hill: University of North Carolina Press, 1977.
Preyer, Norris W. *Hezekiah Alexander and the Revolution in the Backcountry.* Charlotte: Heritage Printers, 1987.
Publications of the North Carolina Historical Commission, *Records of the Moravians in North Carolina, Volume II (1752–1775).* Raleigh: Edwards & Broughton, 1925.
Quarles, Benjamin. *The Negro in the American Revolution.* Chapel Hill: University of North Carolina Press, 1961.
Ray, Lila McGeachy, and John P. Burgess. "Alexander Craighead: with Drawn Sword." Master's thesis, Pittsburgh Theological Seminary, 2001.
Salley, A.S., Jr. "The Mecklenburg Declaration: The Present Status of the Question." *The American Historical Revi*ew 13, no. 1 (1908): 16–43.
Scoggins, Michael. *Relentless Fury: The Revolutionary War in the Southern Piedmont.* Rock Hill, SC: Culture & Heritage Museums, 2006.
Scotch-Irish Society of America. *The Scotch-Irish in America: Proceedings and Addresses of the Seventh Congress at Lexington, VA., June 20–23, 1895.* Nashville: Barbee & Smith, 1895.
Sherrod, Robert. *Tarawa.* New York: Skyhorse Publishing, 2013.

Smith, Holland. *Coral & Brass*. New York: Scribner's, 1949.
Smylie, James Hutchinson. *A Brief History of the Presbyterians*. Louisville, KY: Geneva Press, 1996.
Southern, Ed, ed. *Voices of the American Revolution in the Carolinas*. Winston-Salem, NC: John F. Blair, 2009.
Spratt, Thomas Dryden. *Thomas Dryden Spratt's Recollections of His Family* [typed manuscript]. July 1875. CML.
Steward, T. G. *Buffalo Soldiers: The Colored Regulars in the United States Arm*. Mineola, NY: Dover, 2014.
Stowe, W. R. "Dr. Annie Lowrie Alexander." *Transactions of the Medical Society of the State of North Carolina*. Raleigh: Medical Society, 1931.
Tarleton, Lieut. Col. Banastre. *A History of the Campaigns of 1780 and 1781 in the Southern Provinces of North America*. North Stratford, NH: Ayer Company Publishers, 2007.
Tompkins, D.A. *History of Mecklenburg County and the City of Charlotte*, Vol. 1. Charlotte: Observer Printing House, 1903.
Waddell, Joseph Addison. *Annals of Augusta County, Virginia: With Reminiscences Illustrative of the Vicissitudes of Its Pioneer Settlers; Biographical Sketches of Citizens Locally Prominent, and of Those Who Have Founded Families in the Southern and Western States; a Diary of the War, 1861–'5, and a Chapter on Reconstruction*. Richmond: Wm. Ellis Jones, 1886.
Ward, Joseph P. *Britain and the American South: From Colonialism to Rock and Roll*. Jackson: University Press of Mississippi, 2009.
Washington, George. *The Diary of George Washington, from 1789 to 1791*. New York: Charles Richardson & Co., 1860.
Wheeler, John Hill. *Historical Sketches of North Carolina*, Vol. 1. Elibron Classics, 2007.
Wheeler, John Hill. *Reminiscences and Memoirs of North Carolina and Eminent North Carolinians*. Washington: Henkle, 1885.
White, Henry Alexander, A.M., PH.D., D.D., LL.D. *Southern Presbyterian Leaders*. New York: The Neale Publishing Company, 1911.
Williams, James. "The Sugar Creek War." Unpublished manuscript. Courtesy of the Mecklenburg Historical Association, Mecklenburg, North Carolina.
Woodmason, Charles, and Richard J. Hooker, ed. *The Carolina Backcountry on the Eve of the Revolution: The Journal and Other Writings of Charles Woodmason, Anglican Itinerant*. Chapel Hill: University of North Carolina Press, 1953.

Index

Numbers in **bold italics** indicate pages with illustrations

Adair, James 12, 13, 14
Adams, John 69, 78
Afro-American Mutual Insurance Company 129
Airds Moss, Scotland 43
Albany, New York 19
alcohol 9, 16, 17, 20, 29, 34, 54
Alexander, Abraham 55, 68
Alexander, Adam 59
Alexander, Ann Wall Lowrie 154
Alexander, Dr. Annie 4, 116, 154–166, ***160***
Alexander, Hezekiah 51
Alexander, Isaac 68
Alexander, Jimmy 56
Alexander, Dr. John Brevard 113, 116, 117, 154, 155
Alexander, John McKnitt 57–59, 68–69, 71, 75, 77
Alexander, Dr. Joseph 57, 58, 191*ch*4*n*17
Alexander, Robert (adopted son of Dr. Annie Alexander) 163
Alexander, Susan 108
Alexander, William 73, 74
Alexander, William "Black Bill" 37, 190*ch*2*n*59
Alexanders 37, 53, 138, 152, 155, 156, 160, 162, 163, 191*ch*3*n*39
Alsop, James Douglas 164, 165, 196*ch*11*n*3, 196*ch*11*n*13
Amelia County, Virginia 81, 87
American Revolution 25, 38, 41, 51–53, 58, 59, 67, 68, 78, 80–86, 88, 91, 92, 95, 154, 155, 187; *see also* Graham, James; Jack, Captain James; Polk, Thomas; Spratt, Thomas; Titus, Ishmael
amphtracs 173–175
Anglican Book of Common Prayer 43
Anglican Church 26–28, 31, 41–43, 45, 47, 49, 50, 68, 70, 93, 109; *see also* Church of England

Anna ["Ray" or "Roy"] (name unknown) 118, ***119***; *see also* St. Lloyd's Presbyterian Church
Anson County, North Carolina 29, 32, 189*ch*2*n*23
Apache Indians 140–142
Appomattox, Virginia 137
Arataswa 10; *see also* King Haigler
Arizona 140; *see also* Crawford Expedition
Armstrong, William 89
Army of Northern Virginia 120
Asheville, North Carolina 138, 149
USS *Ashland* 173
Atlanta, Georgia 121, 158
Attucks, Crispus 84
Augusta, Georgia 16, 24
Avery, Waightstill 82

Bagge, Traugott 74
Baker, E.L. 143
Balfour, Nisbet 37, 64, 65, 105
Ballston, New York 91
Ballykelly, Ireland 70
Baltimore, Maryland 158, 159
Baptists 49, 70
Barnwell, Colonel John 18, 19
Beattie's Ford 52, 121
Belfast, Ireland 47
Belk, William Henry 127
Bennett, Joseph 120
Bennington, Vermont 91
Bethabara, North Carolina 73
Bethania, North Carolina 73
Betio Island 171, 172, ***174***, 176, 178, 182, 183; *see also* Tarawa, battle of
Bigger, Elizabeth 33
Bigger's Ferry 100
Bissell, Israel 67
The Black Experience in Revolutionary North Carolina 86
Blackstone, Sir William 111

203

Bladensburgh, Maryland 96
"Blind Dick" 116–119
Bluford, Harry 87
Blunt, King of the Tuscarora Indians 14
Board of Trade, Great Britain 11, 14, 98
Bonnyman, Alexander 181
Bonnyman's Hill (Tarawa) 181; *see also* Tarawa, battle of
Boston, Massachusetts 25, 84, 94
Boston Massacre 84
Boston's Bucks of America 84
Bowman, Essius 90
Braddock, Edward 48, 87
Bradley, Francis 109
Bragg, Braxton 136
Brandywine, battle of 60, 84
Brevard, Dr. Ephraim 68, 94
British Distinguished Service Medal 168, 183
British Legion 102, 104, 105, 108
Brodday, John 90
Brokaw, Tom 169
Bronze Star (medal) 184
Brooklyn 150
Brunswick County, North Carolina 49
Buffalo Soldiers *see* Tenth U.S. Cavalry
Buffington, Joseph 87
Buford, Abraham 96, 97, 106
Buford's Defeat (battle of Waxhaws) 96, 97, 106
Buford's Massacre *see* Buford's Defeat
Bunker Hill, battle of 84
Burlington Mills, Inc. 170
Burwell, Armistead 136, 195*ch*10*n*2
Butler, Mary Lincoln 126, **127**, 131

Caldwell, Katherine 156–166; *see also* Alexander, Dr. Annie
Caldwells 152
Camden, South Carolina, battle of 35, 61–63, 82, 88, 89, 97, 98, 107; *see also* Gates' Defeat
Cameron, Richard 43, 45, 46
Camp Elliott, California 170; *see also* Jacques Farm
Camp Greene, Charlotte 131, 163
Campbell, Patrick 105
Campbell, Robert 89
Cane brake, battle of 60
Cane Creek, South Carolina 33; *see also* Fort Mill, South Carolina
Cannonball 177; *see also* Tarawa, battle of
Cansiere, Romain 4, 182, 196*ch*12*n*2, 197*ch*12*n*5
Cansler, E.T. 128, 132, 133
Cape Fear River 128, 132, 133
Carlson's 2nd Marine Raiders 172
Carolina Military Institute 139
Caswell, Richard 71, 74–78
Catawba Indians 7, 9–24, 29, 33, 35, 37–39, 52, 188*ch*1*n*3; American Revolution 38; appearance and dress 14; foodways 13; language 12; origin of name 12; pottery 13; smallpox 15–16; Spratt's relationship with 33; Catawba River 12–16, 34, 35, 41, 52, 100, 110, 111, 121, 189*ch*2*n*22; *see also* Harris, Peter; King Haigler
Catholicism 43, 46, 190*ch*2*n*57
cemeteries 25, 38, 39, 51, 65, 70, 114, **115**, 118, **119**, 136, 148, 165
Central Hotel (formerly Mansion House) 124–127, **125**, 133
Central Piedmont Community College 3, 79
Centre Presbyterian Church 25
Charles I, King of England 42
Charles II, King of England 42, 43
Charleston, South Carolina (Charles Town) 10, 11, 16, 19, 25, 31, 35, 61, 88, 93, 96, 100, 154
Charlie 177; *see also* Tarawa, battle of
Charlotte, North Carolina 2, 5, **30**, 33–37, 52, 53, 56, 60, 62–68, **64**, 70–79, **72**, **77**, 88–90, 92, 94, 96–107, **103**, 108–110, 114, 116, 118, 119, 121–139, **125**, 147–153, **151**, 158–163, 165, 168, 185, 103*ch*7*n*58; appearance in 1775 70; as "trifling" 70, 71; *see also* Charlotte, battle of; Mecklenburg Declaration of Independence (MDI)
Charlotte, battle of 97–107, **103**
Charlotte Liberty Walk 92
Charlotte News 132, 153, 165
Charlotte Observer 127, 128, 134, 147, 162, 165
Charlotte Women's Club 163
Chatham County, North Carolina 170
Chavis, John 84
Cheraw (*Charàh*) Indians 12
Cherokee Indians 12, 15, 16, 18, 88
Chester County, Pennsylvania 93
Chickamauga, battle of 136
Chiricahua Indians 140, 141
Chowan Indians 12, 14, 17; *see also* Highter, King
Church of England 49, 50, 70; *see also* Anglican Church
Cincinnatus, Lucius Quinctius 97, 112
Civil War 100, 113, 114, 117–120, **119**, 133, 134, 137–139, 148, 154
Civil War Charlotte 121
Clapp's Mill, battle of 110
Clarkson, Francis 134
Clear Creek Presbyterian Church 25
Cleveland, Absalom 88, 91
Cleveland, Benjamin 81, 82, 91
Cleveland, John 88
Clinton, Sir Henry 97
Colorado 4, 177–182, **179**, **182**, 184; *see also* Tarawa, battle of
Comanche Indians 139
"Committee men" 71
Concord, battle of 68, 84; *see also* Lexington, battle of

Index

Condor 177; *see also* Tarawa, battle of
Confederate Monument, Charlotte 136–138
Congaree (*Canggaree*) Indians 12
Congress, Second Continental 66, 69, 71–78, **72**, 113
Connelly, Henry 104
Contentea Creek 18
Conventicle Act (1664) 43
"copy in an unknown hand" *see* Mecklenburg Declaration of Independence (MDI)
Cornelius, North Carolina 154
Cornwallis, Charles Earl 7, 27, 29, 35, 37, 54, 62–65, 86, 88–90, 92, 97–102, 104–107, 110, 193*ch7n*58
courthouse 90, 91, 129; *see also* Guilford Courthouse; Mecklenburg County Courthouse (original); Mecklenburg County Courthouse (West Trade Street)
Covenanters, Covenanting *see* Solemn League and Covenant (1648)
Cowan's Ford 52, 110, 121
Cozzens, Peter 140
Craighead, the Rev. Alexander 41–57, **47**, 154, 190*ch3n*13, 191*ch3n*39; *see also* Solemn League and Covenant (1648)
Craighead, Thomas (father of Alexander Craighead) 44, 45
Crawford, Emmet 140–142
"Crawford Affair" 142
Crawford Expedition 140–142
Creek Indians 88, 112
Cromwell, Oliver 43
Cromwell, Oliver (African-American solider) 84
Crotts, Allred 169
Crotts, Anderson 169
Crotts, H. Douglas 4, 167, 186, 185, 196*ch12n*1, 196*ch12n*2
Crow, Jeffrey 86, 92
Cuba 135, 138, 142–150, 152
Cumberland County, Pennsylvania 54

Daiquiri, Cuba 144
Daly, Henry 140
Dan River 73, 87
Dartmouth, William Legge, Earl of 73, 102, 107
Davidson, William Lee 35, 62, 72, 100, 110
Davidson College 154
Davidson, North Carolina 159
Davie, William R. 35–37, 58, 62, 100–105, **103**, 190*ch2n*53
Davie Copy *see* Mecklenburg Declaration of Independence
Davis, Jefferson 122
Davis Military Institute 142
Dawes, William 67
Declaration of Independence *see* National Declaration of Independence
Delaware 30, 84, 85
Dickinson, Major (Battle of Charlotte) 102

Dilworth, Charlotte 183, 185
Dilworth United Methodist Church 185
Dobbs, Arthur 10, 16, 20, 23, 27, 49
"Doctor Katherine" 159–166
Donegal, Ireland 44
Donegal Presbytery 44
Douglass, Frederick 130
Dowd YMCA, Charlotte 139
Down, County, Ireland 93
Doyle, John 109
drunkenness *see* alcohol
Dudley, Harold 196*ch*11*n*13
Dunmore, John Murray Lord 85, 86
Durant, King of the Yeopim Indians 14
Durham, I.W. 150
Durham, North Carolina 120, 137

The Earth Is Weeping 140
Estabrook, Prince 84
Eccles, H.C. 125
Eisenhower, Dwight David 66
El Poso Hill, Cuba, battle of 144
Elliott, William 142
Elmwood Cemetery 136, 167
England 26, 31, 41–43, 49, 54, 76, 109, 155, 158; *see also* Anglican Church
Eniwetok 184
Episcopal Church *see* Anglican Church
Esaw Indians 12
Evans, John 13, 14

Fagan, Chas 3, 5, **23**, **30**, **72**, 188*ch*1*n*3
Farrell, Eugenia (Mrs. Crotts) 184
Ferguson, Andrew 90
Ferguson, Patrick 62, 63, 89, 90, 110; *see also* Kings Mountain, battle of
First Ohio Cavalry 143
First Presbyterian Church 163
First Tuscarora War 18; *see also* Tuscarora
First U.S. Corps Medium Tank Battalion 173–183
Five Mile Act (1665) 43
Five Nations 19; *see also* Six Nations
Florence Crittendon Home 161
Florida 142, 143, 159
Foote, William 44, 48, 49
Ford, Gerald 66
Fort Assiniboine, Montana 142
Fort Christanna, Virginia 10
Fort Duquesne, Pennsylvania 48, 87
Fort Independence, South Carolina 88
Fort Mill, South Carolina 14, 26, 29, 38, **39**
Fourth (4th) Regiment, North Carolina Continentals 60, 96
Freedmen's Bureau 122
Friday, Ernest 134
Frohock, John 56

Garibaldi and Bruns Jewelry Company 124
Garinger High School 185

Index

Garrison, William Lloyd 118
Gates, Horatio 61–63, 81, 82, 88, 89, 97–100, 107; *see also* Camden, battle of; Gates' Defeat
Gates' Defeat 35, 82, 88, 89, 98, 107; *see also* Camden, battle of
George I, King of England 46
George II, King of England 10, 46
George III, King of England 36, 45, 46, 94
German settlers in Piedmont 20, 29
Germantown, battle of 60
Geronimo 3, 138, 140
Gettysburg, battle of 136, 176
Gilbert, Oscar 4, 196*ch*12*n*2
Gilbert Islands 170–172, 183
Glen, James 9–12, 14
Grace A.M.E. Zion Church 130
Graham, Charles (son of James Graham) 93
Graham, Elizabeth (daughter of James Graham) 93
Graham, George (son of James Graham) 93
Graham, Henry (son of James Graham) 93
Graham, James (father of Joseph Graham) 93
Graham, John (son of James Graham) 93
Graham, Joseph 3, 7, 57, 62, 68, 89, 93–113; account of MDI 57, 68, 94, 95; battle of Charlotte 97–107; *see also* Charlotte, battle of; Mecklenburg Declaration of Independence (MDI)
Graham, Mary (wife of James Graham) 93
Grant, Ulysses S. 120, 136
Great Britain 10, 66, 68, 76, 82, 88, 107, 114; *see also* England
Great Cane Break, battle of 60
Great Charter (1663) 26
Great Depression 129, 133, 169
Great Wagon (Philadelphia) Road 30, 52, 72, 73, 93
"The Greatest Generation" 167, 169
Greene, Nathanael 61, 64, 65, 81, 90
Greenwood, Janette 123, 130
Griffith, Tom 134
Grover, South Carolina 4, 92
Grubb Preservation Foundation 118
Guantanamo Bay, Cuba 143
Guilford County, North Carolina 104
Guilford Courthouse, battle of 3, 82, 90, 104
Gulledge, Earl 4, 167, 196*ch*12*n*1

Hagler *see* King Haigler
Haiglar *see* King Haigler
Hall, Moses 109
Hall, Robert 128
Hanger, George 28, 29, 35, 40, 102–108, 193*ch*7*n*58
Harding, Harry P. 185
Hardy, Michael 121
Harris, Peter 11, 26, 37–40
Harris, Wade Hampton 128

Harrison, William 140
Harry P. Harding High School 4, 167, 168, 185
Harvey B. Gantt Center for African-American Arts+Culture 8, 192
Havana, Cuba 142, 150
Hawaii 184
Hawkins, William 112
Hawthorne, Nathaniel 80
Hayes, Lemuel 84
Hayes, Webb 143–147
Henderson County, North Carolina 138
Henley, Chief Justice Peter 22
Higgins boats 173, 174, **178**
Highter, King of Chowan Indians 14
Hillsboro, North Carolina 17, 111
The History of Mecklenburg County from 1740 to 1900 113, 114, 116, 154
Holston River 90, 91
Hooper, William 71, 74–78
Hopewell Presbyterian Church 25, 109
Horn, Tom 140, 141
"hornet's nest" 7; *see also* McIntyre Farm
Houston, Margaret 170
Houston, Texas 70
Hughes (Hewes), Joseph 71, 74–78, 85
Hunter, Cyrus L. 66, 75, 76
hunting 11–14, 18, 19, 22, 34, 38, 107
Hutchinson, James 117

Indian traders 13–17, 24, 29, 30
Indian Wars in North Carolina 18
Indians *see* Apache Indians; Catawba Indians; Cheraw (*Charàh*) Indians; Cherokee Indians; Chiricahua Indians; Chowan Indians; Comanche Indians; Congaree (*Canggaree*) Indians; Creek Indians; Esaw Indians; Five Nations; Geronimo; Iroquois Indians; King Haigler; Meherin Indians; Mohawk Indians; Sapona Indians; Shawnee Indians; Shuteree Indians; Sioux Indians; Six Nations; Tuscarora (Tuskerora) Indians; Ute Indians; Waxhaw Indians; Yamasee Indians
Iredell, James 85
Iredell, Margaret 139
Ireland 10, 26–29, 34, 38, 44, 69, 70, 93
Iroquois Indians 12, 19, 21
Irwin (Irvin), Robert 100
island hopping strategy (WWII) 170–171
Ivey, J.B. 127

Jack, Captain James 2, 3, 7, 56, 66–79, **72**, **77**; account of MDI 71, 72, 74; death and obituary 78–79; Hunter's *Sketches* account 75, 76; statue in Charlotte 2, 3, **77**, 79
Jack, Patrick, Jr. (father of Capt. Jack) 34, 70
Jack Plantation (Elbert Co., Georgia) 78
Jackson, Andrew 112
Jackson, Anna Morrison 137

Index

Jacksonville, Florida 158
Jacques Farm 170, 173; *see also* Camp Elliott
James, Pethel 124
James I, King of England 46
Japan 169–184
Japanese Special Landing Forces 172; *see also* Tarawa, battle of
Jefferson, Thomas 66, 69, 76, 78
Johnson, Andrew 120
Johnson, Joseph 52, 53
Johnson, Samuel 82, 85
Johnson, Dr. Sidney 133
Johnson, William 134
Johnston, Joseph E. 120, 136
Jubilee Singers 130

Kanawha River, West Virginia 33
"Kanawha" Spratt *see* Spratt, Thomas "Kanawha"
Kennon, William 72, 94
Kentucky 111, 162
Kettle Hill, Cuba, battle of 144–146
"Killing Time" 44
King Haigler 3, 4, 7, 9–24, **23**
Kings Mountain, battle of 3, 63, 65, 82, 89, 90, 110
Kinson, Maggie 120
Knox, John 46

Lafayette, Marquis de 65
Lancaster (County), Pennsylvania 44, 70, 73
land disputes (Carolinas) 9, 20, 23–25, 27, 18, 31, 32, 34, 35, 54–56; *see also* Sugar Creek War
Largey, Louis 180–182
Las Guasimas, Cuba, battle of 144
Latta, Edward Dilworth 127
Lawson, John 10, 12–16, 19
Lee, "Lighthorse" Harry 35, 36, 89, 97, 104, 105, 108, 190*ch*2*n*53
Lee, Lawrence 18
Lee, Robert E. 120, 122, 136
Lenoir-Rhyne College 184, **185**
Leona 142
Leutze, Emanuel 84, **85**
Lexington, battle of 68
Liberty Bell 54, 60, 191*ch*4*n*21
Liberty Hall 98; *see also* Queen's College
Lincoln County, North Carolina 111, 153
Lincolnton, North Carolina 153
Locke, George 105, 106
Logan, James 27
London, England 1, 9, 16, 23, 38, 50, 51, 73, 90
Londonderry *Journal* 26
long bullets (game) 34
"Long Depression" (1873–1879) 122
Longfellow, Henry Wadsworth 67, 76
Lord Dunmore's Ethiopians 86
Lord Dunmore's Proclamation 85, 86

Lord Dunmore's War 33
Lowrie, Henry 159
loyalists 27, 35, 36, 59, 60, 73, 83, 88–90, 98, 107, 109, 110; *see also* Tories
Ludington, Sybil 67

Macdonald, Charles 105
Madison, James 84, 112
magistrates **47**
USS *Maine* 142
Makin atoll 172
Malmedy, Colonel 96
Manchester, William 169, 171, 172, 176, 178, 196*ch*12*n*2
Maramuskito Indians 16
Marine Corps *see* U.S. Marine Corps; *see also* Tarawa, battle of
Marn, Johnny 180
Marriage & Vestry Acts 50
Marshall Islands 170, 171
Martin, Josiah 102, 107
Maryland 26, 30, 63, 96, 99, 158
Massachusetts 67, 68, 80, 91, 92
Maus, Marion 140, 141
May 20th Society 92
McAden, the Rev. Hugh 48
McAdoo, Lillis (Lillie) 70
McClellan 147
McCown, Ruth 158
McCoy, Albert 114, **115**
McCoy, Elizabeth ("Lizzy") 114, **115**
McCoy, Jim 114, **115**
McCoy Slave Burial Ground 114, **115**
McCulloh, Henry Eustace 54, 56; *see also* Sugar Creek War
McIntyre's Farm 109
MecDec (MeckDec) *see* Mecklenburg Declaration of Independence (MDI)
Mecklenburg Committee of Safety 74, 101
Mecklenburg County Courthouse (original) 33, 52, **57**, 67–71, 94, 95, 101–103, **103**
Mecklenburg County Courthouse (West Trade Street) 129, 135, 149, **151**
Mecklenburg County Medical Society 162
Mecklenburg Declaration of Independence (MDI) 3, 52, 54, 56–59, **57**, 66–79, **77**, 92, 95, 113, 116, 136, 137, 148; Adam's views 69, 78; "copy in an unknown hand" 58, 59, 188; Davie Copy 58; 188; destruction of MDI (fire) 57, 58, 69; first publication by Dr. Joseph Alexander 57–59, 191*ch*4*n*17; Jefferson's view 66, 69, 78; presidential visits to Charlotte 66; "rough notes" 57–59; *see also* Graham, Joseph; Jack, Captain James; Mecklenburg Resolves; Polk, Thomas; Signers of the Mecklenburg Declaration of Independence Monument
Mecklenburg Historical Association 191*ch*4*n*8
Mecklenburg Investment Company Building 129

Mecklenburg Resolves 75, 113
Medical College of South Carolina 154
Meherin Indians 16
Mesopotamia 30
Middle Octorara Presbyterian Church, Pennsylvania 44, 45
Middleton, George 84
Milk River, Montana 142
Mills, Albert Leopold 144, 145
Mint Hill, North Carolina 25
Mohawk Indians 19
Mongiello, Marti 4, 92
Mongiello, Stormy 92
Monmouth, battle of 96
Monongahela River 87
Moore, James 18
Moravians 71, 73, 74
Morganton, North Carolina 121
Morrill, Dan 33, 113–115
Morrison, Cameron 127, 131
Morrison, William 21
Morrison Training School 131
Morton, Andrew 49, 50
Moss, Bobby 90
Mount Airy, North Carolina 136
Muir, Dick 87
Muir, John 87
Myers Park High School 185

Naiche 140–142
Nance, Dan 4, 5, *57*, *103*
Nash, Francis 60
Navy Cross 168, 183
Neely, Thomas 115, 116
Neely Slave Cemetery 115, 116
Neoheroka 18
New Bern, North Carolina 18, 49, 51, 53
New Caledonia 173
New Hebrides 173
New Jersey 31, 37
"New Light" ("New Side") 47, 49
New Providence (Camp) 35, 100
New Rochelle, New York 91
New York 18, 19, 21, 61, 91, 96, 158
New York City, New York 124, 132
Nimitz, Chester 170
Nopkehee see King Haigler
North Carolina Congressional deletes to Second Continental Congress 71, 74–78; *see also* Caswell, Richard; Hooper, William; Hughes, Joseph
North Carolina General Assembly (House of Commons) 53, 56, 65, 109, 138
North Carolina State flag 66

Oakland, California 184
Octorara Church *see* Middle Octorara Presbyterian Church
Okinawa, Japan, battle of 169
Old New River (Catawba Indian Chief) 35

Orange County, North Carolina 29
Oroloswa see King Haigler

Pacific campaign (WWII) 4, 168, 170–172; *see also* Tarawa, battle of
Palma, Tomás Estrada 150
Pamlico River 17, 18
Parsons, Abraham 81
"Paul Revere's Ride" (poem) 67; *see also* Longfellow, Henry Wadsworth
Pat Jack's Tavern 70
Patterson, Daniel 34
Pearl Harbor 170, 172
Peliieu, battle of 183
Pennsylvania 26, 27, 29, 31, 44, 46–49, 54, 60, 70, 73, 78, 87, 93, 120, 121, 158
pension applications (federal, 1832 Act of Congress) 38, 39, 78, 81, 92, 187
Perth, Earl of 43
Phifer, William 122
Phifer family cemetery 25
Philadelphia 25, 30, 60, 66, 71–76, 79, 94, 156–159
Philadelphia Presbyterian Church *see* Clear Creek Presbyterian Church
Philadelphia Presbyterian Synod 46
Philadelphia Road 72; *see also* Great Wagon (Philadelphia) Road
Piedmont 25, 26, 29, 31, 33, 35, 41, 48, 70, 73, 83, 93, 114, 121
Pinckney, Thomas 61
Pitcairn, John 84
Point Pleasant, battle of 33
Polk, Charles 60
Polk, Susannah Spratt 32, *64*, 65
Polk, Thomas 32, 52–65, *57*, *64*, 83, 99, 191*ch*4*n*21; account of MDI 56–59; founding of Charlotte 52, 53; Sugar Creek War 54–56; *see also* Mecklenburg Declaration of Independence (MDI); Sugar Creek War
Polk, William 59, 60
Poplar Tent Presbyterian Church 25
Port Tampa, Florida 142, 143
Presbyterian Church 25–28, 35, 41–47, 49, 50, 56, 68, 70, 84, 94, 98, 105, 109, 113, 118, 119, 154, 161, 163; *see also* Craighead, Alexander
Presbyterian College for Women (later Queen's University), Charlotte 161
Presbyterian Hospital 161
Prescott, Samuel 67
Presidential Service Center, Grover, South Carolina 92
Princeton, battle of 84
Providence Road 35
Purple Heart (medal) 184

Quakers 70, 73, 87
Queen's College 94, 98, 161; *see also* Liberty Hall
quit rent 9, 32

Raleigh, North Carolina 84, 142
Raleigh Register 58, 59, 78, 191*ch*4*n*17
Ramsey, J.G.M. 156
Rawdon, Francis Lord 36, 37, 100, 107
RED-3 (beach), Betio 176–178; *see also* Tarawa, battle of
Reedy Creek (River) 32, 60
Regulator Rebellion 54
Republicanism 41
Revere, Paul 3, 66, 67, **72**, 76, 77
Rhode Island 84
Rhode Island Regiment 84
Richmond, Virginia 121
Riddle, Captain Bill 91
Riga, Latvia 152
Roberts, Andrew 2
Rockingham County, North Carolina 87
Rocky River Presbyterian Church 25 49
Rogers, Lucy 91
Roosevelt, Theodore 135, 144–148, 150, 152
Ross, Lawrence 87, 88
"rough notes" (John McKnitt Alexander) *see* Mecklenburg Declaration of Independence
Rowan, Matthew 29
Rowan County, North Carolina 29, 35, 50, 83, 88, 91, 99, 109
Russ, Martin 172, 196*ch*12*n*2
Rutherford, Griffith 59, 62, 96

Saberton, Ian 27, 28, 35, 65
Sadler's Wells Theater (London) 38
Saidu Maru 175; *see also* Tarawa, battle of
St. Lloyd Presbyterian Church cemetery 118, 119, 194*ch*8*n*8
St. Louis World's Fair (1904) 162
St. Mark's Episcopal Church 114
St. Peter's Episcopal Church 139
St. Peter's Hospital 161
Saipan, battle of 183, 184
Salem, Peter 84
Salisbury, North Carolina 34, 63, 70, 72, 74, 82, 98–101, 104, 110, 149
Salisbury Road 101, 104; *see also* Great Wagon (Philadelphia) Road
Salley, A.S., Jr. 58
San Diego, California 170, 184
San Juan heights *see* San Juan Hill, battle of
San Juan Hill, battle of 135, 144–147
Sanquhar Declaration 43
Santiago, Cuba 143, 146
Sapona Indians 16
Saratoga, battle of 98
Savannah, Georgia 38
Savannah River 88
Savoy, Massachusetts 91
HMS *Scorpion* 19
Scotland 26, 29, 31, 34, 42–44, 69, 50, 69
Scots-Irish 7, 9, 20, 25–32, 34, 47, 49, 50, 53, 54, 68, 69, 93, 108, 111, 113, 114, 163; "crackers" 29, 35, 40; origins of name 26; propensity for alcohol and violence 27, 28, 34; *see also* Graham, Joseph; Jack, Captain James; Spratt, Thomas "Kanawha"
Second Tuscarora War 18, 19; *see also* Tuscarora (Tuskerora) Indians
Selwyn, George Augustus 54, 56
Settlers' Cemetery, Charlotte **64**, 65
Seven Sisters (*Pleiades*) 25; *see also* Presbyterian Church
Sevier, John 90
Shawnee Indians 23, 24
Shelby, Isaac 90
Shenandoah Valley 30, 48
Shepherd, Thankful 91
Sherman, William Tecumseh 120, 136
Sherrod, Robert 173, 175, 179, 197*ch*12*n*2
Shibaski, Keiji 181; *see also* Tarawa, battle of
Shipp, Bartlett 138
Shipp, Catherine (Kate) Cameron
Shipp, Margaret Busbee 135, 142
Shipp, William Ewen 3, 135–153, **139**, **151**
Shipp, William Marcus 138
Shipp Monument 135–138, 147–153, **151**
Shuteree Indians 12
Signers of the Mecklenburg Declaration of Independence Monument 136–138, 148
Siler City, North Carolina 169, 172, 184
Singapore 172
Sioux Indians 12, 142
Sitting Bull 142
Six Nations 19, 24; *see also* Five Nations
Sketches of Western North Carolina 75
slave cemeteries 114, **115**, 118, **119**
slavery 20, 31, 44, 51, 53, 54, 80–92, 113–119, **115**, 120–122, 137, 140; *see also* Anna ["Ray" or "Roy"] (name unknown); Lord Dunmore's Proclamation; McCoy Slave Burial Ground; Neely Slave Cemetery; slave cemeteries; Titus, Ishmael
smallpox 11, 15, 16, 37
Smallwood, William 63, 64, 99
Smith, Holland "Howling Mad" 178, 183
Smith, Julian 178
Smith, William 145–147
Snow Campaign 60
Solemn League and Covenant (1643) 42, 43, 45, 48, 49
South Carolina 9, 18, 20, 23, 24, 26, 31–33, 35, 38, 59, 70, 88, 92, 97, 100, 110, 112, 121, 136, 154
Spain 142
Spangenberg, Bishop Gottlieb 20, 30–32
Spanish American War 135
Speedwell Furnace 87
Spratt, Andrew (brother of Spratt, Thomas, Sr.) 29
Spratt, James (brother of Spratt, Thomas, Sr.) 29
Spratt, Leonidas 38

Spratt, Samuel (brother of Spratt, Thomas, Sr.) 29
Spratt, Susannah (daughter of Spratt, Thomas, Sr.) 32, 54, **64**, 65
Spratt, Thomas Dryden 33
Spratt, Thomas "Kanawha," Jr. 3, 7, 25–41, **30**, **39**, 113, 189ch3n22, 189ch2n23, 190ch2n70; see also Harris, Peter; Scot's Irish; Wahab's Plantation ("Wacab," "Wauchope," or "Walkup"), battle of
Spratt, Thomas, Sr. 25, 29, 189ch2n22, 190ch2n70
Spring Hill Forge 111
Stamp Act (1765) 49
Staunton, Virginia 73
Steadman, Charles 97, 108
Steele Creek Presbyterian Church 25, 115
Stevens, Thaddeus 120
Stimson, D.G. 190ch2n55
Stono, battle of 38
Stuart, John 17
Sugar Creek 12, 14, 32, **77**, 100
Sugar Creek War 32, 54–56
Sugar (Sugaw) Creek Presbyterian Church (cemetery) 25, 105
Sugaree Indians 12
Sugaw Creek Presbyterian Church see Sugar (Sugaw) Creek Presbyterian Church
Sumter, Thomas 38, 100

Taft, William Howard 66
tanks 4, 170, 172–173, 175–184, **179**, **182**, 196ch12n2; Japanese 172; U.S. Marine Corps use and doctrine 170–171, 177, 181
Tanks in Hell: A Marine Corps Tank Company on Tarawa 4, 196ch12n2
Tarahumara Indians 141
Tarawa atoll 171, 173, **174**, 183
Tarawa, battle of 4, 167, 168, 171–186, **179**, **182**, 196ch12n2, 197ch12n5
Tarleton, Banastre 28, 88, 97, 99, 100–109
Tate, Thad, Sr. (father of Thad Tate) 120
Tate, Thaddeus Lincoln 3, 4, 8, 120–134
Taylor, Solomon Titus 92
tax, taxation 25, 26, 31, 32, 50, 68, 70, 111; in America colonies as source of unrest 31, 32, 50, 68; in Ireland as source of unrest 26, 70
Tenth U.S. Cavalry 135, **139**, 140, 142–146, 150, **151**; see also San Juan Hill, battle of
Thomas, John 149, 150
Thomas, J.P. 139
Thyatira, North Carolina 70
Titus, Harvey 81
Titus, Ishmael 3, 4, 80–92
Titus, Primus (possibly Ishmael's brother) 90
Toole, Gray 124
Tories 35, 36, 60, 62, 78, 83, 88, 89, 91, 100
Traditions and Reminiscences, Chiefly of the American Revolution in the South 52, 53

Trail of History (Charlotte) 23, 30
Treaty of Pine Tree Hill (1760) 23
Troublesome Creek 87
Troublesome Iron Works 87
Troy, New York 91
Truman, Harry S 134
Tryon, William 50, 52, 53, 56, 83
Tryon County, North Carolina 35, 50
Tryon Street, Charlotte, North Carolina 4, 52, 56, 92, 101, 102, 106, 124, 125, 137, 139, 149, 159, 161
Tuscarora (Tuskerora) Indians 14, 16–19, 21
Twelve Mile Creek 29; see also Fort Mill, South Carolina

Ulstermen see Scots-Irish
United Daughters of the Confederacy 165
U.S. Federal Courthouse, Charlotte 135
U.S. Marine Corps 169–184, **174**, **179**
University of North Carolina at Chapel Hill (UNC) 168, 185
Ute Indians 140

Valley Forge 54, 60
Vance, Zebulon 127, 133
Van Landingham, Susie 165
Vermont 91
Vesuvius Furnace 111
Virginia 10, 27, 48, 62, 73, 80, 81, 83–85, 87, 90, 120, 158

Wachovia 73; see also Moravians
Waddell, Hugh 48
Wagon Road see Great Wagon (Philadelphia) Road
Wahab's Plantation ("Wacab," "Wauchope," or "Walkup"), battle of 35–37
Walker, Judge William P. 80, 82
Walkup's Plantation see Wahab's Plantation ("Wacab," "Wauchope," or "Walkup"), battle of
Washington, George 60, 65, 70, 74, 81, 83–85, **85**, 87; view of Charlotte ("trifling place") 70
Washington, Silas 130
"Washington Crossing the Delaware" 84, **85**
Waxhaw Indians 12
Waxhaws 21, 35, 100, 107; see also Buford's Defeat
Waxhaws, battle of see Buford's Defeat
Wemyss, James 97
West Charlotte High School 131
West Point Military Academy 142, 145, 147, 148
Whigs 54, 60, 83, 88, 137
Whipple, Prince 84, **85**
White Oaks, Massachusetts 4, 80, 81
Wilder, Hillary 128
Will, George 69
Williams, Jim 189ch2n22, 191ch4n8, 191ch4n21

Williams College, Massachusetts 80
Williamstown, Massachusetts 4, 80, 91
Wilson, Harvey 159
Wilson, Woodrow 66
Winchester, Virginia 73
Winnsboro, South Carolina 135, 136, 150, 151
Woman's Medical College, Baltimore 158, 159
Women's Medical College, Philadelphia 155
Wood, Leonard 144, 145, 147
Woodmason, Charles 28, 33, 41
World War I 131, 133, 152, 163
World War II 2, 4, 133, 168, 169, 174, 175, 184; *see also* Tarawa, battle of

Yadkin ("Deep" or "Peedee") River 29, 30, 41, 72, 88, 91, 110, 189ch2n22
Yamasee Indians 10, 12, 18
Yamasee War 10, 18
Yogaki 171
York, Pennsylvania 73
Yorktown, Virginia 90
Young, Samuel 144
Young Warrior (*Yanabe Yalangway*) 11

www.ingramcontent.com/pod-product-compliance
Ingram Content Group UK Ltd.
Pitfield, Milton Keynes, MK11 3LW, UK
UKHW041958140426
5217IPUK00015B/861